THE NEW MIDDLE AGES

BONNIE WHEELER, *Series Editor*

The New Middle Ages is a series dedicated to transdisciplinary studies of medieval cultures, with particular emphasis on recuperating women's history and on feminist and gender analyses. This peer-reviewed series includes both scholarly monographs and essay collections.

PUBLISHED BY PALGRAVE:

Women in the Medieval Islamic World: Power, Patronage, and Piety
edited by Gavin R. G. Hambly

The Ethics of Nature in the Middle Ages: On Boccaccio's Poetaphysics
by Gregory B. Stone

Presenc and Presentation: Women in the Chinese Literati Tradition
by Sherry J. Mou

The Lost Love Letters of Heloise and Abelard: Perceptions of Dialogue in Twelfth-Century France
by Constant J. Mews

Understanding Scholastic Thought with Foucault
by Philipp W. Rosemann

For Her Good Estate: The Life of Elizabeth de Burgh
by Frances A. Underhill

Constructions of Widowhood and Virginity in the Middle Ages
edited by Cindy L. Carlson and Angela Jane Weisl

Motherhood and Mothering in Anglo-Saxon England
by Mary Dockray-Miller

Listening to Heloise: The Voice of a Twelfth-Century Woman
edited by Bonnie Wheeler

The Postcolonial Middle Ages
edited by Jeffrey Jerome Cohen

Chaucer's Pardoner and Gender Theory: Bodies of Discourse
by Robert S. Sturges

Crossing the Bridge: Comparative Essays on Medieval European and Heian Japanese Women Writers
edited by Barbara Stevenson and Cynthia Ho

Engaging Words: The Culture of Reading in the Later Middle Ages
by Laurel Amtower

Robes and Honor: The Medieval World of Investiture
edited by Stewart Gordon

Representing Rape in Medieval and Early Modern Literature
edited by Elizabeth Robertson and Christine M. Rose

Same Sex Love and Desire among Women in the Middle Ages
edited by Francesca Canadé Sautman and Pamela Sheingorn

Sight and Embodiment in the Middle Ages: Ocular Desires
by Suzannah Biernoff

Listen, Daughter: The Speculum Virginum and the Formation of Religious Women in the Middle Ages
edited by Constant J. Mews

Science, the Singular, and the Question of Theology
by Richard A. Lee, Jr.

Gender in Debate from the Early Middle Ages to the Renaissance
edited by Thelma S. Fenster and Clare A. Lees

Malory's Morte D'Arthur: Remaking Arthurian Tradition
by Catherine Batt

The Vernacular Spirit: Essays on Medieval Religious Literature
edited by Renate Blumenfeld-Kosinski, Duncan Robertson, and Nancy Warren

Popular Piety and Art in the Late Middle Ages: Image Worship and Idolatry in England 1350–1500
by Kathleen Kamerick

Absent Narratives, Manuscript Textuality, and Literary Structure in Late Medieval England
by Elizabeth Scala

Creating Community with Food and Drink in Merovingian Gaul
by Bonnie Effros

Representations of Early Byzantine Empresses: Image and Empire
by Anne McClanan

Encountering Medieval Textiles and Dress: Objects, Texts, Images
edited by Désirée G. Koslin and Janet Snyder

Eleanor of Aquitaine: Lord and Lady
edited by Bonnie Wheeler and John Carmi Parsons

Isabel La Católica, Queen of Castile: Critical Essays
edited by David A. Boruchoff

Homoeroticism and Chivalry: Discourses of Male Same-Sex Desire in the Fourteenth Century
by Richard E. Zeikowitz

Portraits of Medieval Women: Family, Marriage, and Politics in England 1225–1350
by Linda E. Mitchell

Eloquent Virgins: From Thecla to Joan of Arc
by Maud Burnett McInerney

The Persistence of Medievalism: Narrative Adventures in Contemporary Culture
by Angela Jane Weisl

Capetian Women
edited by Kathleen D. Nolan

Joan of Arc and Spirituality
edited by An n W. Astell and Bonnie Wheeler

The Texture of Society: Medieval Women in the Southern Low Countries
edited by Ellen E. Kittell and Mary A. Suydam

Charlemagne's Mustache: And Other Cultural Clusters of a Dark Age
by Paul Edward Dutton

Troubled Vision: Gender, Sexuality, and Sight in Medieval Text and Image
edited by Emma Campbell and Robert Mills

Queering Medieval Genres
by Tison Pugh

Sacred Place in Early Medieval Neoplatonism
by L. Michael Harrington

The Middle Ages at Work edited by Kellie Robertson and Michael Uebel Chaucer's Jobs
by David R. Carlson

Medievalism and Orientalism: Three Essays on Literature, Architecture and Cultural Identity
by John M. Ganim

Queer Love in the Middle Ages
by Anna Klosowska

Performing Women in the Middle Ages: Sex, Gender, and the Iberian Lyric
by Denise K. Filios

Necessary Conjunctions: The Social Self in Medieval England
by David Gary Shaw

Visual Culture and the German Middle Ages
edited by Kathryn Starkey and Horst Wenzel

Medieval Paradigms: Essays in Honor of Jeremy duQuesnay Adams, Volumes 1 and 2
edited by Stephanie Hayes-Healy

False Fables and Exemplary Truth in Later Middle English Literature
by Elizabeth Allen

Ecstatic Transformation: On the Uses of Alterity in the Middle Ages
by Michael Uebel

Sacred and Secular in Medieval and Early Modern Cultures: New Essays
edited by Lawrence Besserman

Tolkien's Modern Middle Ages
edited by Jane Chance and Alfred K. Siewers

Representing Righteous Heathens in Late Medieval England
by Frank Grady

Byzantine Dress: Representations of Secular Dress in Eighth-to-Twelfth Century Painting
by Jennifer L. Ball

The Laborer's Two Bodies: Labor and the "Work" of the Text in Medieval Britain, 1350–1500
by Kellie Robertson

The Dogaressa of Venice, 1250–1500: Wife and Icon
by Holly S. Hurlburt

Logic, Theology, and Poetry in Boethius, Abelard, and Alan of Lille: Words in the Absence of Things
by Eileen C. Sweeney

The Theology of Work: Peter Damian and the Medieval Religious Renewal Movement
by Patricia Ranft

On the Purification of Women: Churching in Northern France, 1100–1500
by Paula M. Rieder

Writers of the Reign of Henry II: Twelve Essays
edited by Ruth Kennedy and Simon Meecham-Jones

Lonesome Words: The Vocal Poetics of the Old English Lament and the African-American Blues Song
by M.G. McGeachy

Performing Piety: Musical Culture in Medieval English Nunneries
by Anne Bagnell Yardley

The Flight from Desire: Augustine and Ovid to Chaucer
by Robert R. Edwards

Mindful Spirit in Late Medieval Literature: Essays in Honor of Elizabeth D. Kirk
edited by Bonnie Wheeler

Medieval Fabrications: Dress, Textiles, Clothwork, and Other Cultural Imaginings
edited by E. Jane Burns

Was the Bayeux Tapestry Made in France?: The Case for St. Florent of Saumur
by George Beech

Women, Power, and Religious Patronage in the Middle Ages
by Erin L. Jordan

Hybridity, Identity, and Monstrosity in Medieval Britain: On Difficult Middles
by Jeremy Jerome Cohen

Medieval Go-betweens and Chaucer's Pandarus
by Gretchen Mieszkowski

The Surgeon in Medieval English Literature
by Jeremy J. Citrome

Temporal Circumstances: Form and History in the Canterbury Tales
by Lee Patterson

Erotic Discourse and Early English Religious Writing
by Lara Farina

Odd Bodies and Visible Ends in Medieval Literature
by Sachi Shimomura

On Farting: Language and Laughter in the Middle Ages
by Valerie Allen

Women and Medieval Epic: Gender, Genre, and the Limits of Epic Masculinity
edited by Sara S. Poor and Jana K. Schulman

Race, Class, and Gender in "Medieval" Cinema
edited by Lynn T. Ramey and Tison Pugh

Allegory and Sexual Ethics in the High Middle Ages
by Noah D. Guynn

England and Iberia in the Middle Ages, 12th-15th Century: Cultural, Literary, and Political Exchanges
edited by María Bullón-Fernández

The Medieval Chastity Belt: A Myth-Making Process
by Albrecht Classen

Claustrophilia: The Erotics of Enclosure in Medieval Literature
by Cary Howie

Cannibalism in High Medieval English Literature
by Heather Blurton

The Drama of Masculinity and Medieval English Guild Culture
by Christina M. Fitzgerald

Chaucer's Visions of Manhood
by Holly A. Crocker

The Literary Subversions of Medieval Women
by Jane Chance

Manmade Marvels in Medieval Culture and Literature
by Scott Lightsey

American Chaucers
by Candace Barrington

Representing Others in Medieval Iberian Literature
by Michelle M. Hamilton

Paradigms and Methods in Early Medieval Studies
edited by Celia Chazelle and Felice Lifshitz

King and the Whore: King Roderick and La Cava
by Elizabeth Drayson

Langland's Early Modern Identities
by Sarah A. Kelen

Cultural Studies of the Modern Middle Ages
edited by Eileen A. Joy, Myra J. Seaman, Kimberly K. Bell, and Mary K. Ramsey

Hildegard of Bingen's Unknown Language An Edition, Translation, and Discussion
by Sarah L. Higley

Medieval Romance and the Construction of Heterosexuality
by Louise M. Sylvester

Communal Discord, Child Abduction, and Rape in the Later Middle Ages
by Jeremy Goldberg

COMMUNAL DISCORD, CHILD ABDUCTION, AND RAPE IN THE LATER MIDDLE AGES

Jeremy Goldberg

palgrave
macmillan

COMMUNAL DISCORD, CHILD ABDUCTION, AND RAPE IN THE LATER MIDDLE AGES

First published in 2008 by
PALGRAVE MACMILLAN™
175 Fifth Avenue, New York, N.Y. 10010 and
Houndmills, Basingstoke, Hampshire, England RG21 6XS
Companies and representatives throughout the world.

PALGRAVE MACMILLAN is the global academic imprint of the Palgrave Macmillan division of St. Martin's Press, LLC and of Palgrave Macmillan Ltd. Macmillan® is a registered trademark in the United States, United Kingdom and other countries. Palgrave is a registered trademark in the European Union and other countries.

ISBN-13: 978–0–230–60294–6
ISBN-10: 0–230–60294–0

Library of Congress Cataloging-in-Publication Data

Goldberg, P. J. P., 1958–
Communal discord, child abduction, and rape in the later Middle Ages / Jeremy Goldberg.
p. cm.—(The new Middle Ages)
Includes bibliographical references.
ISBN 0–230–60294–0
1. Women—England—Yorkshire—History—Middle Ages, 500–1500. 2. Women—England—Yorkshire—Legal status, laws, etc. 3. England—Social conditions—1066–1485. 4. Women—England—Social conditions. I. Title.

HQ1147.G7G65 2008
305.409428′10902—dc22 2007013801

A catalogue record for this book is available from the British Library.

Design by Newgen Imaging Systems (P) Ltd., Chennai, India.

First edition: January 2008

10 9 8 7 6 5 4 3 2 1

Printed in the United States of America.

CONTENTS

ABBREVIATIONS

BI	Borthwick Institute for Archives, University of York, Heslington, York
CCR	*Calendar of Close Rolls*
CP.E.89/26	BI call number: CP = cause paper, E = fourteenth century, 89 = file number, 26 = item number
CPR	*Calendar of Patent Rolls*
Drake, *Eboracum*	F. Drake, *Eboracum: or, The History and Antiquities of the City of York, from its Original to the Present times. Together with the history of the Cathedral Church, and the lives of the Archbishops of the See ... Collected from Authentick Manuscripts, Publick Records, Ancient Chronicles, and Modern Historians* (London, 1736)
TNA	The National Archives (formerly the Public Records Office)
YML	York Minster Library
X 1.1.1	Pope Gregory IX, *Decretales*, Liber I, tit. I, Canon I. in *Corpus Iuris Canonici, Pars Secunda: Decretalium Collectiones*, ed. Emil Ludwig Richter und Emil Friedberg, 2 vols. (Leipzig: Tauchnitz, 1879–81).

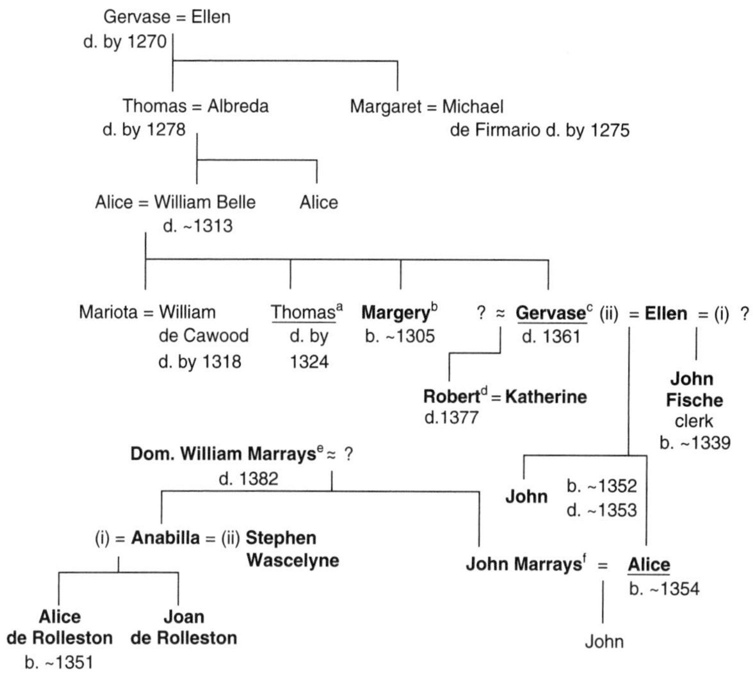

Genealogical Table 1 Genealogy of the de Rouclifs of Rawcliffe

Source: YML, Cartulary of St Mary's Abbey, XVI A.1, 2; BI, CP.E.89; F. Collins, ed., *Register of the Freemen of the City of York, 1272–1588*, Surtees Society, 96 (1896); YML, Dean and Chapter probate register 1, L2(4); BI, Prob. Reg. 1.

Notes: Names in **bold** represent deponents or persons otherwise noticed in the case.
Names underlined represent line of descent of the family property.
The symbol ≈ represents a nonmarital relationship.

a. Thomas is noted as the son and heir to William de Rouclif, aka William Belle, in 1313, but is not noticed again thereafter.
b. Margery is unlikely to be the same person as Mariota since Mariota is recorded as issuing a deed in herw own name in 1309 and thus must have been born by c. 1294.
c. Gervase is first noticed as a witness to a charter in 1311.This suggests he may havebeen born c. 1290.The first recorded deed in his name is dated 1324.
d. Robert de Rouclif, who died childless, named Master John de Rouclif, who was married to Margaret, as his heir. John had a younger brother, also called John and likewise married to a Margaret. No relationship between Robert and Master John is specified.
e. Dom. William Marrays was abbot of St Mary's between 1359 and 1382.
f. John Marrays was still living in 1395.

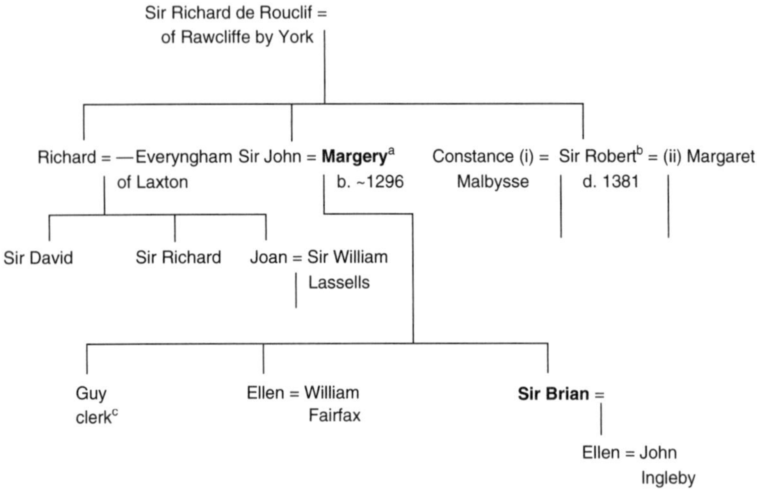

Genealogical Table 2 Genealogy of the armigerous family of de Rouclif of Rawcliffe

Source: C.B. Norcliffe, ed., *The Visitation of Yorkshire in the Years 1563 and 1564 made by William Flower, Esquire*, Harleian Society, 91 (1881), pp. 265–6; BI, CP.E.89; YML, Dean and Chapter probate register 1, L2(4); Baildon, ed., *Feet of Fines for the County of York, from 1347 to 1377*, p. 102; TNA, Prob/11/1.

Notes: Names **in bold** represent deponents or persons otherwise noticed in the case.

a. Flower does not identify John de Rouclif's wife, but she can be so identified from a land transaction: Baildon, ed., *Feet of Fines for the County of York, from 1347 to 1377*, p. 102.

b. Sir Robert was buried at Scarborough: YML, Dean and Chapter probate register 1, L2(4), fol. 73. It appears that the main Rawcliffe inheritance of the family passed from ir Richard to Sir John and so to Sir Brian.

c. Guy de Rouclif was a clerk in the Privy Seal Office and Thomas Hoccleve's superior at the beginning of Hoccleve's own clerical career. In addition to his late parents and brother, his will mentions two of his Fairfax kin by marriage, viz. his sister-in-law Elizabeth and his nephew Thomas: TNA, Prob/11/1.

Map 1 York and its environs

Map 2 South and East Yorkshire

PART I

ALICE'S EVIDENCE

DRAMATIS PERSONAE

The story that follows is peopled by a large cast. To aid the reader to follow their way through the intricacies of the discussion that follows, a list of characters was thought helpful.

Agnes the Ald. Living in Clifton at the time of the case, Agnes had previously been resident in Rawcliffe. She had given birth to a son there shortly before Alice's birth, about which she testified on behalf of Sir Brian de Rouclif, though it was specifically recorded that she was not his tenant.

John de Alne. A young man of eighteen years, John's role was to undermine the credibility of various of the witnesses for Alice de Rouclif (in effect Sir Brian de Rouclif) who he claimed to have known for the past six years. He pointed out that her witnesses were tenants of Sir Brian and that Alice Shap (presumably Sharpe) was a servant in his garden. He claimed Maud de Herthill had perjured herself by denying having committed adultery with Gervase de Rouclif (and was thus doubly damned, both for sexual immorality and for perjury). He claimed to have heard that Ellen Taliour had committed adultery with a Skelton man. Many of Alice's witnesses were poor (and hence liable to bribery).

John Barbour. A character witness for John Marrays, he spoke up for John's witnesses, but claimed not to know Alice's witnesses.

John called **Bawines.** A butcher of York, John spoke up for the standing of Sir Brian de Rouclif's witnesses.

Alice de Beleby. The wife of Richard de Warwyk, Alice was Alice de Rouclif's godmother. As was customary, she presumably gave Alice her name. She testified for John Marrays as to Alice's age by reference to Alice's baptism and her son's taking vows as a Carmelite friar the previous year.

Margery Bell. Married to John Gregson of Clifton, she testified regarding Alice's age on behalf of John Marrays by reference to the birth of her last child prior to Alice's birth and to the news of Alice's birth that circulated among her friends and neighbors.

Richard Bernard. The then bailiff of St Mary's Abbey, York, Richard presided over the formal contract of marriage (spousals) between John Marrays and his under-age fiancée, Alice de Rouclif. He testified for John.

Thomas Broun. A resident of Rawcliffe for the past ten years, Thomas claimed that Ellen de Rouclif had told him her daughter Alice's age (nearly eight) at the time her father, Gervase, died. He also testified for the good character of several of Sir Brian de Rouclif's witnesses.

Thomas de Bulmer. Described as a potter, by which a manufacturer of metal pots is implied, of York, Thomas primarily testified to matters he heard whilst in London, presumably in connection with his craft. He had been told that Ellen de Rouclif had complained maliciously about Sir Brian de Rouclif to the king in council and had received letters under the privy seal directed to Sir Brian. He further reported that on the very day of his deposition he had heard Ellen say when challenged by Sir Brian that she wished to support her daughter. He asserted that in fact Ellen was an active promoter of John Marrays's cause.

John Fische. Alice de Rouclif had two adult half-brothers. John, a clerk, was one of them, in his case the product of her mother's first marriage. He was 26 at the time of the case. His testimony was given in support of John Marrays. He claimed that Alice had been eight when her father died. He was a witness to Alice's spousals and alleged Alice was a willing party. He was also a visitor to Kennythorpe some months after Alice's removal there and stayed in the same room as her overnight. He used this opportunity to quiz his half-sister about her relationship with John Marrays.

Margaret de Folifayt. Margaret gave testimony about Alice's age on behalf of Sir Brian de Rouclif. She remembered Alice's birth by reference to the eventful delivery of a child of Maud de Herthill, whom she apparently names as "de Thornhill," revived by her own brother, Simon de Folifayt.

Agnes de Fritheby. A resident of Bootham, and hence within the influence of St Mary's Abbey, Agnes deposed that she had been present at the churching of Ellen de Rouclif following the birth of Alice and had herself given birth a few months later. Her testimony supported John Marray's cause.

Adam Gaynes. Adam was a resident of St Marygate and hence a tenant of St Mary's Abbey, so it is unsurprising to find that he testified on the part of John Marrays. He was a character witness; he claimed that John's witnesses were wealthier (and implicitly less likely to be bribed) than Alice's.

Agnes Gervaus Woman. A former servant, and perhaps mistress of Gervase de Rouclif, she was still living in Rawcliffe when she testified for John Marrays in respect of Alice's age. She claimed Gervase told her the girl's age two years before his death.

Ellen Grigge. Ellen is noted in the depositions of Alice Porter and Beatrix Milner as a woman present at the birth of Alice de Rouclif and one their informants about the event, but she is not found as a witness at the time of the case. It is probable that she is also the anonymous woman "now senile because of old age" that Ellen Taliour described as present with her at the birth; this would explain her failure to testify although apparently still living.

Maud de Herthill. The servant of Master Robert de Slaykston and at the time of the case living in "Slaykston," but described as "of Rawcliffe," Maud specifically acknowledged that she had been asked to testify by Sir Brian de Rouclif. Maud was Ellen de Rouclif's servant at the time of her marriage to Gervase and worked for her again from just before John de Rouclif was born. She claimed to have been present and to have assisted at the birth. She herself gave birth to a daughter nearly a year later. Just before the following Easter Alice de Rouclif was born and was seen by Maud in her cradle.

John de Hornyngton. A York resident and sherman, John gave testimony as a character witness in support of several of Sir Brian de Rouclif's witnesses, "persons of good standing and worthy of trust."

John de Killom. Described as "of Clifton," John deposed as a character witness for several of Sir Brian de Rouclif's witnesses, stating that they were persons of sufficient wealth.

Isold de Kirkeby. The wife of William de Kirkeby, Isold was a resident in Bootham, a suburb of York within the sphere of influence of St Mary's Abbey. She testified for John Marrays regarding the birth of her own child a few months before that of Alice de Rouclif and her participation in Alice's baptism. It was she who bought the ewer and towels to the church of St Olave that the godparents used to cleanse their hands.

William de Kirkeby. The husband of Isold and termed "breuster" or brewer, William also testified for John Marrays. He claimed that John's witnesses carried greater weight than those for Alice (i.e., Sir Brian de Rouclif) and that he had "never heard any good" of several of Alice's witnesses.

William de Lynton. William's sole function was to testify to the effect that Ellen de Rouclif was a promoter of John de Marray's cause against her own daughter.

John Marrays. Although the relationship is never acknowledged, the likelihood is that John was the illegitimate son of William Marrays, subsequently abbot of St Mary's, York. His career is obscure, though he appears to have spent time in London and may have traded as a draper.

Latterly he appears to have been a member of the abbot's household at Overton. His marriage to Alice de Rouclif would have provided him with the security of land and the status and income that derived from this. It would also have helped consolidate the abbey's interests in Rawcliffe.

William Marrays. Although, like most monks, of obscure birth, since 1359, and by the time of the case, Dom. William was the mitred abbot of St Mary's, York, the wealthiest monastery in the North of England. He was probably the father of John Marrays and his sister Anabilla Wascelyne, but unsurprisingly did nothing to acknowledge that relationship throughout the case. He gave crucial testimony regarding the consummation of John and Alice's contract of a few weeks earlier at Kennythorpe, the home of Anabilla and her husband. His evidence purported to report a conversation with Joan de Rolleston, implicitly the abbot's granddaughter, who had been present in the room when the consummation was enacted. Joan herself was too young to testify in person, so the abbot effectively lent authority to evidence, which would otherwise have been inadmissible. Dom. William died in 1382.

John de Melsay. John, married to Lettice, represented a cadet branch of the armigerous Melsa or Meaux family who were landholders in the East Riding of Yorkshire. John was the principal godparent in respect of John de Rouclif and it was he who gave the infant his name at baptism. He was able to locate this event in time by reference to his moving from Shipton, where he lived at the time of John's birth, to his present home at Houghton, which he inherited by right of his wife on the death of her father, William, some two years later. Like his fellow godparent, Lady Margery de Rouclif, he testified for Sir Brian de Rouclif. He appears to have died in 1369.

Lettice de Melsay. The wife of John de Melsay, Lettice's testimony corroborates that of her husband in interesting and telling ways. She remembered John's birth because she was very ill at the time of Ellen de Rouclif's churching. She remembered moving to Hutton from Shipton some two years later because she had given birth to her son only six weeks earlier. She was further able to locate this in time by the fact that her father died when she was so heavily pregnant that she was unable to attend his funeral. Her deposition was made in support of Sir Brian de Rouclif.

Beatrix Milner. At the time of the case, Beatrix was married to John Milner in Clifton, but had lived in Rawcliffe until shortly after Alice de Rouclif's birth about which she testified on behalf of Sir Brian de Rouclif. She remembered Alice's birth in relation to her removal, but also knew Alice's age from her Rawcliffe neighbors, from Ellen Grigge, and from Henry Vaux.

Beatrix de Morland. The widow of John de Midford, Beatrix managed a Bootham hostelry patronized by the de Rouclif family. Her husband had been killed at Corpus Christi time following Alice de Rouclif's birth. She also recalled the birth of her own (deceased) daughter prior to Alice's birth. She thus testified as to Alice's age, but also (on the basis of hearsay evidence) to Alice's willingness to be married to John Marrays, whose witness she was.

Emmot Norice [the Nurse]. Formerly Alice's wetnurse, but resident in Huby at the time of the case, she gave evidence regarding Alice's age on behalf of John Marrays. She had a son of a few months who died only the day before Alice's birth and consequently she was engaged as Alice's wetnurse for the next three years (save for a brief period that presumably coincided with Ellen Taliour's initial appointment).

Robert de Normanby. Robert, who may have lived in the vicinity of Kennythorpe, testified on behalf of John Marrays that Alice de Rouclif lodged at Kennythorpe at John's sole expense and that John was free to visit her there as a husband his wife.

Agnes del Polles. Agnes was married to Ralph de Hesyngwald (Easingwold) and was said to be 26 years at the time of her testimony. Like her fellow witness, Agnes de Richmond, she saw Ellen de Rouclif before and after her churching in respect of John de Rouclif as she was then living in St Marygate. The following Christmas she entered into service with Robert de Rouclif for four years (and so presumably worked alongside Agnes de Richmond for a while). She located Alice's birth in the Lent following John's death two weeks from Easter only a few months after his birth. She claimed to have no possessions save a (spinning) wheel, a pair of cards and a boy [*sic*]. She testified on behalf of John Marrays.

Adam Porter. As his name suggests, Adam was the gatekeeper of St Mary's Abbey, York. He would have admitted Alice de Rouclif and her mother to the abbey gatehouse and Richard Bernard's chamber prior to her spousals. Afterward, at the behest of John Marrays, he helped William Pottell to convey Alice to her new home at Kennythorpe. Adam's testimony was in support of John.

Alice Porter. A tenant of Sir Brian de Rouclif, Alice held lands and had her home in Clifton, but was married to Adam Porter, the gatekeeper of St Mary's Abbey. Alice and her husband thus had conflicting loyalties in this case, although she claimed to have been asked by one Thomas de Midelton to testify rather than by Sir Brian. At the time of Alice's birth she had been living in Skelton and heard of the birth from her Rawcliffe neighbors, from one Ellen Grigge, "who was present at Alice's birth," from the wife of William de Tange, and from Henry Vaux.

William Pottell. Employed by John Marrays, for whom he testified, as his factotum, William watched, but was unable to overhear, the spousals between his master and Alice de Rouclif. He subsequently helped to convey Alice to Kennythorpe and regularly brought her presents there from his employer. He also made up the bed when John Marrays allegedly spent the night with Alice there and subsequently teased Alice about her relationship with John. He claimed to have been told Alice's age by her mother and two of her godparents.

Anabilla Pynder. A resident of Rawcliffe and living with her mother, Anabilla saw John de Rouclif in his cradle and gave birth herself shortly after on the Tuesday following Martinmas, which like Lady Margery de Rouclif, she recalled fell on a Sunday that year (i.e., 1352). She recalled that on the following Monday, Ellen de Rouclif sent her "some writing which was said to be good for pregnant women She also remembered seeing Alice de Rouclif in her cradle when she was born rather more than a year later (i.e., 1354). Like Ellen Taliour, as a young nursing mother, she was asked to be wetnurse to Ellen de Rouclif's new baby, but likewise declined on the grounds that her own infant was too young. She testified in support of Sir Brian de Rouclif.

Agnes Quysteler. A resident of Rawcliffe for the past ten years and the wife of Robert Quysteler, she gave hearsay evidence only about Alice's age on behalf of Sir Brian de Rouclif.

Agnes de Richmond. Aged 29 years and married to Robert de Richmond at the time of the case, Agnes had been in service with Robert de Rouclif at the time of John de Rouclif's birth and had witnessed Ellen de Rouclif arrive for and leave after her churching. Agnes is described as of St Marygate and so by implication was a tenant of St Mary's Abbey. She testified on behalf of John Marrays.

Alice de Rolleston. The daughter of Anabilla Wascelyne, presumably by an earlier marriage, she was only fourteen when she testified. She had a younger sister, Joan, who was implicitly under twelve and so unable to testify in person. Her testimony closely echoed that of her mother.

Joan de Rolleston. The younger daughter of Anabilla Wascelyne and so, unlike her sister Alice, too young (i.e., below twelve) to testify in person in the case. During Alice de Rouclif's stay at Joan's parents' home in Kennythorpe, the two girls shared a bed. (Such an observation could suggest that Alice was nearer in age to Joan than her older sister.) It was from this bed that Joan was alleged displaced by John Marrays and so witnessed the couple having sex one night a little before Christmas 1364. Joan subsequently narrated what she had seen and heard to Dom. William Marrays, who was probably her grandfather.

Alice de Rouclif. The daughter and heiress of Gervase de Rouclif, a minor landowner from the village or hamlet of Rawcliffe just west of York (and now a suburb of the city), it was her marriage to John Marrays that is at the center of this case.

Sir Brian de Rouclif. Sir Brian was the senior representative of the armigerous de Rouclif family at the time of the case and was the de facto defendant of the action started in the church court by John Marrays for restitution of conjugal rights. It would appear that Sir Brian claimed wardship—and hence control of her marriage—over the orphaned Alice de Rouclif by right of his lordship over her lands in Rawcliffe, where he was a significant landowner. Sir Brian is historically obscure beyond this case. His brother, Guy de Rouclif, was a senior clerk in the Privy Seal office.

Ellen de Rouclif. The widow of Gervase de Rouclif and Alice's mother, Ellen had apparently been married once before and probably lost her first husband in the Black Death. She married Gervase de Rouclif in Alne in the aftermath of the Black Death. She testified to the dates of the births of both her two children by Gervase. Ellen appears to have been instrumental in arranging her daughter's marriage to John Marrays and was a key witness for John giving evidence for Alice's age, her spousals (including the words used) and subsequent consummation and of her affection for her "husband." She also described some of the presents Alice received from John whilst resident at Kennythorpe. She claimed that Alice was eight at the time of her husband's death.

Ellen de Rouclif. Ellen was the widow of Elias de Rouclif, and hence the mother-in-law of Eufemia, the wife of John, son of Elias, who testified for Alice. She herself testified for John Marrays in respect of Alice's age, which she remembered by reference to the birth of her own daughter.

Eufemia, the wife of John, son of Elias de Rouclif. Eufemia was almost certainly the daughter-in-law of Ellen, widow of Elias de Rouclif, her fellow witness, but she testified nominally for Alice de Rouclif, in practice for Sir Brian de Rouclif, presumably because she and her husband held their land of Alice. She proffered only hearsay evidence—"the relation of women"—for Alice's birth and hence age.

Gervase de Rouclif (deceased at the time of the case). Gervase was a minor landholder in the village or hamlet of Rawcliffe. He married Ellen shortly after the Black Death and had two children by her. John, the older, died as an infant, leaving the young Alice as his sole heiress on his death.

Isabel de Rouclif. The wife of John de Grandesby of Tollerton, Isabel was also the niece of Gervase de Rouclif and was engaged to serve him and his wife immediately following Alice's birth. She further recalled Alice's age at the time of her own marriage nine years previous. She gave evidence in support of John Marrays.

John de Rouclif (deceased at the time of the case). The first child of Gervase and Ellen de Rouclif, John died in infancy. His importance in the case is that the timing of his birth helped to locate in time that of his younger sister, Alice de Rouclif, and hence the age of Alice at the time of the consummation of her contract to John Marrays.

Katherine de Rouclif. The wife of Robert de Rouclif, Katherine lived in Bootham, a short walk from the gatehouse of St Mary's Abbey, where Alice de Rouclif's spousals were contracted. She looked after Alice in her home what was probably the following morning immediately prior to her first being taken to Kennythorpe. Her testimony was designed to show that Alice was favorably disposed toward John Marrays. Katherine also gave evidence about Alice's age, claiming to have been pregnant at the same time as Ellen de Rouclif. Her evidence was given in support of John Marrays.

Margery [or Margaret] de Rouclif. Aged sixty or more at the time of the case, Margery was Alice's paternal aunt. She gave evidence on behalf of John Marrays in respect of the births of both Alice and her deceased older brother John, and hence for Alice's age. She was present in the de Rouclif family home when John was born and also attended the churching. She came to visit and saw Alice in her cradle on the day she was born. She also remembered that Alice was nine at the time of her brother's death.

Lady Margery de Rouclif. Lady Margery, the widow of Sir John de Rouclif, is perhaps the most impressive of all the deponents in the case, though as the mother of Sir Brian de Rouclif she cannot be considered impartial. Aged seventy years at the time of the case, her testimony is full of telling details. Following John de Rouclif's birth before Martinmas thirteen years earlier, Lady Margery, as the child's godmother was present at his baptism in St Mary's Abbey. She remembered the names of her fellow godparents and that Martinmas that year (i.e., 1352) fell on a Sunday. Her memory was further aided by recollecting the birth of her daughter's son, John, whose life was initially sufficiently uncertain as to require immediate baptism, by the fact that she leased out some of her lands that year and the associated indentures were so dated, and by reference to the births of other village children to women who were then Lady Margery's neighbors since she was then living in Rawcliffe. She also testified she had heard it said that Ellen de Rouclif had acknowledged before "Lord de Percy" and "many knights and esquires" that her daughter Alice was then not yet twelve.

Robert de Rouclif. Robert is described as Alice de Rouclif's blood brother, which must make him an illegitimate son of her father prior to his marriage to Ellen. He was married to Katherine and lived in Bootham. He was a witness to Alice's spousals and claimed to know Alice's age from her mother and the wetnurse. He testified on behalf of John Marrays. He died in 1377.

William Sampson. A goldsmith of York, he corroborated Thomas de Bulmer's account of Ellen de Rouclif petitioning the king and his council, stating that Ellen "took away royal letters to the parties to have justice." He reported further that Ellen had also taken proceedings before Lord de Percy for the return of her daughter and that she had provided deponents for the action within the Church court. William's testimony offers no explanation of how he came by this information. He likewise corroborated Thomas de Bulmer's account of the verbal exchange between Ellen and Sir Brian de Rouclif, which he claimed to have witnessed. William further claimed that Margaret de Rouclif, Cecily de Shupton, and especially Ellen de Rouclif were promoters of John Marray's cause.

Alice Sharpe. A widow and resident of Rawcliffe, she gave testimony about Alice's age nominally on behalf of Alice and in effect for Sir Brian de Rouclif, whose tenant she was. She recalled Alice's birth by reference to the birth of Maud de Herthill's daughter, who was memorably revived by the intervention of Simon de Folifayt.

Cecily de Shupton. Cecily appears to have been a family friend of the de Rouclifs—William Sampson specifically described her as Ellen de Rouclif's friend—and came to their home around the time that Ellen gave birth to her two children by Gervase. She was present at Ellen's churching in respect of John. As such she was able to testify on behalf of John Marrays to both births, and hence Alice's age, and also to Alice's abduction.

Isabel de Strensall. Isabel lived in Bootham for two years around the time of John de Rouclif's birth and remembered being pregnant at the time she attended Ellen de Rouclif's churching—presumably at St Olave's—in respect of this delivery. She subsequently moved to York and was resident in Jubbergate at the time of the case. She testified for John Marrays.

Joan Symkyn Woman. Joan is described as "of Rawcliffe" and presumably was or had been closely associated with one Simon. Her testimony on behalf of Sir Brian de Rouclif, whose tenant she was, reinforced that given by her fellow witness Maud de Herthill since she was present at the birth of Maud's daughter some twelve years earlier. She is described as possessing only her clothes, a bed, and a small brass pot.

Ellen Taliour. The wife of Thomas Taliour of Skelton at the time of the case, her importance is as a key witness for Sir Brian de Rouclif in respect of Alice de Rouclif's age. Ellen had been in service with Gervase de Rouclif's friend William de Huntyngton, and had had an illegitimate baby boy. Because she was a nursing mother, her former mistress Emma de Huntyngton tried to get her to agree to act as wetnurse for Gervase and Ellen de Rouclif's first child, John. On that occasion she declined, but accepted when subsequently asked again in respect of their next child, Alice, since by then Ellen felt her son old enough to wean. Ellen claimed to have been hired against the birth and was present, together with an older (and subsequently senile) woman. Immediately following the birth, she took the infant Alice into York to be baptized. She suckled Alice for only three weeks until illness prevented her, but remained with the family for a full year in accordance with her contract.

Alice de Tange. The wife of William de Tange and a resident of Rawcliffe, she was a tenant of Sir Brian de Rouclif and testified in his favor regarding Alice's birth and age. She recalled giving birth to a son shortly before Alice was born.

William de Tange. Like his wife, William is described as resident in Rawcliffe and a tenant of Sir Brian, for whom he gave evidence. He deposed that Gervase de Rouclif, Alice's father, was his near neighbor and was godfather to his son who was born shortly before Alice's own birth.

Margery Thewed. Margery was married to Robert and, like her husband, was described as a tenant of Sir Brian de Rouclif, in whose garden she had formerly been employed. She testified in support of Sir Brian regarding Alice's age. She recalled that William de Tange, who worked with her in Sir Brian's garden, had a son a little before Alice was born and that Gervase de Rouclif acted as the child's godfather. (Margery's testimony implied that William's son—and hence Alice—was then not yet eleven, whereas William himself said he was not yet twelve.)

Robert Thewed. A tenant of Sir Brian de Rouclif, for whom he testified, he was a resident in Rawcliffe. Robert claimed a degree of friendship with Gervase de Rouclif, the father of Alice, and consequently was invited to the feast to celebrate Ellen de Rouclif's churching in respect of Alice. He also recalled the birth of his son born about a year later. In this way he gave evidence respecting Alice's age.

Master Adam de Thornton. A clerk and notary public by apostolic authority, Master Adam was a witness to Alice de Rouclif's spousals within the precinct of St Mary's Abbey. It may be surmised that he took responsibility for drawing up the marriage terms. Like all those present at the spousals, he testified for John Marrays.

Henry Vaux. A resident of Rawcliffe from birth, Henry was a tenant of Sir Brian de Rouclif and had been a servant of Gervase de Rouclif, Alice's father, a few months before Alice was born. Immediately before he entered service with Sir Brian, he had been on pilgrimage to St James (implicitly Santiago de Compostella). He was able to testify to Ellen de Rouclif's pregnancy, and hence to Alice's age, on behalf of Sir Brian.

Anabilla Wascelyne. The sister of John Marrays and, in all probability, daughter of Dom. William Marrays, the abbot of St Mary's, York, she was married to Stephen and lived with him and her two daughters at

Kennythorpe. She was a key witness for John, testifying that Alice wanted the marriage, had admitted to having had sex with John on Saturday before Christmas 1365, and was already an adolescent who looked to be about fourteen. She further recalled some of the presents Alice received from John whilst staying at Kennythorpe. Her testimony is lent added authority and liveliness by several pieces of reported speech allegedly recording Alice's intimate thoughts and concerns.

Stephen Wascelyne. The husband of Anabilla, he likewise appeared for John Marrays. He described Alice de Rouclif as boarding at his house according to an arrangement made by John. He also referred to Alice's abduction and reported Alice's alleged desire to have her contract with John properly solemnized.

PREFACE

The vivid light that trial, inquisition, or the like records can shed on past societies has long been appreciated by scholars of the premodern era, not least because they offer the promise of illuminating the lives of ordinary people. Emmanuel Le Roy Ladurie's *Montaillou* "the world famous portrait of life in a medieval village," published in 1978 and swiftly translated into English, perhaps first caught the popular Anglo-Saxon imagination, followed (at least in translation) in 1980 by Carlo Ginzburg's *The Cheese and the Worms*.[1] We may also notice Natalie Zemon Davis's gripping *The Return of Martin Guerre* (1983) (subsequently made into a film and even a musical), Gene Brucker's *Giovanni and Lusanna* (1986), Richard Wunderli's *Peasant Fires* (1992), and most recently Robert Bartlett's elegant *The Hanged Man* (2004).[2] These works make rather different uses of the underlying evidence. Neither Davis nor Wunderli have direct access to court material and hence cannot explore any actual witness testimonies. Brucker does have actual depositions, but he is more concerned to ascertain what actually happened and what light this throws on Florentine society of the mid-fifteenth century. None of these works is primarily interested in the form in which witnesses gave their testimony or (with the exception of Ginzburg) their choice of language or imagery.

Interest in the possibilities of court material for the reconstruction of the past has stimulated a growing appreciation of the difficulties inherent in using such source material fostered not least by Davis's brilliant *Fiction in the Archives*, such that the question of why the evidence takes the form it does, why do witnesses testify as they do, has begun to displace a primary concern with "what the evidence tells us."[3] Two other more recent works deserve mention here, namely John Arnold's path-breaking analysis of Inquisition records—the very sources used by Ladurie—and Noël Menuge's imaginative exploration of the relationship between romance and legal narratives.[4] This primary focus on narrative and on the way testimony is constructed is central to this present study.

Between 1 November 1365 and 28 February 1366, testimony was taken in the diocesan Court of York from a large number of witnesses respecting the marriage of the gentry heiress Alice de Rouclif of Rawcliffe, then a hamlet of perhaps less than a hundred souls, now a populous suburb of York, to one John Marrays, a man of uncertain status, but likely a kinsman (and probably the son) of the then abbot of St Mary's Abbey, York.[5] Because of the unusual volume of material surviving, not least in the form of depositions, this is one of the causes célèbres of the Court of York and one of the treasures of the Borthwick Institute, which has recently celebrated its fiftieth anniversary. It is also the subject of this present book.[6]

The case of Marrays c. de Rouclif has attracted a modest level of attention hitherto, but primarily from scholars interested in the operation of the canon law in the medieval church courts. The case is thus noted a number of times in Richard Helmholz's lucid monograph on marriage litigation in the English courts. The legal framework of the case, initiated as an action for the restitution of conjugal rights, but defended on the grounds of Alice's non-age, is succinctly explained.[7] It is discussed briefly in a paper by Dorothy Owen and at greater length by Frederick Pedersen.[8] The most original and imaginative reading of the case, however, is that offered by Noël Menuge. Her concern is with wardship and the fate of Alice as a ward, an heiress who, as a legal minor, is subject to the legal authority of a guardian who has control over marriage within (and even beyond) the constraints of canon law. Her reading offers illuminating parallels with contemporary romance literature, in this instance the person of Florence in the romance of *William of Palerne*. Romances, she argues, offer an alternative window onto the emotional world of the ward, but there is also a remarkable reflexive relationship between legal and romance narratives.[9]

Our own purpose in writing about the case is twofold. On the one hand I wish specifically to take up the challenge laid down by Dorothy Owen in 1978. She argued that the York cause papers cannot be used "to draw any 'total' picture of fourteenth century female life, and hopes that they might provide material for a miniature study emulating *Montaillou* have vanished."[10] The case, with its many voices, in fact offers us something of a microcosm of English society in the generation after the Black Death. For women's lives too it is especially rich. On the other hand, the many witness statements—depositions—contained within the case cry out for closer scrutiny. Whose voices, we may ask, are we hearing? What are they saying and why? Can we trust them?

Not everybody associated with the case in fact speaks. Notably silent is Alice. Though her marriage is central to the case, Alice herself occupies a marginal, or more precisely, liminal position. Alice's liminality is reflected in her age: she is observed on the cusp between childhood and adulthood, between girlhood and womanhood. Her status is likewise liminal. She is both an heiress, but also a legal minor since in feudal law girls only came of age in their own right once fifteen. She is of aristocratic birth, a Rouclif of Rawcliffe, but her patrimony comprised but one part of a hamlet. She was what modern scholars have tended to term "parish gentry."[11] More important landholders locally were another family of Rouclifs of which Sir Brian de Rouclif was evidently the family head. It is not clear whether they represent different branches of the same family, but Sir Brian implicitly understood himself to have rights over Alice either as the head of the family or as her superior lord.[12] Her minor gentry status is such that her rank is hardly greater than some substantial peasants or franklins as they are dubbed in contemporary sources.[13] Even her marital status is liminal. She is contracted to be married, but until the court determined the case, no one could say for sure whether she was married or single. Her location is liminal: the village or hamlet of Rawcliffe was but a short journey from York and fell within the suburban parish of St Olave, standing in the shadow of the great Benedictine abbey of St Mary. On the very day she was born she was carried down the Clifton road by her nurse to be baptized in the parish church.[14] Her deceased older brother had been baptized within St Mary's Abbey itself. Her family were clearly regular visitors within the city. Finally, her household status can be seen as liminal. As a young girl she grew up in her parents' home in Rawcliffe and continued to live there with her mother after her father's death when she was about eight. After her betrothal to John Marrays, however, she went to live with her prospective sister-in-law Anabilla Wascelyne at her home up on the Wolds at Kennythorpe.[15] The intention was that she would remain there until the marriage to John had been solemnized, but instead she was abducted by Sir Brian's men. Her position at Kennythorpe was thus neither that of daughter, servant, nor mistress of the household, but rather as foster child, visitor and lodger.

The study that follows is drawn almost entirely from an analysis of Marrays c. de Rouclif as it is preserved in the Borthwick Institute. I have been able to make only limited use of additional sources, though a small number of contemporary wills that are pertinent to the case survive from both the Dean and Chapter's probate jurisdiction and that of the diocesan Exchequer Court. The estate and manorial records associated with St Mary's Abbey were largely destroyed during the Civil War when the tower in which they were housed at the corner of Marygate and Bootham was blown up during the siege of the city. Fortunately the abbey's cartulary has survived.[16] Although a fairly complete set of nominative poll tax listings survive for the West Riding in 1379, Rawcliffe and neighboring settlements on the eastern bank of the River Ouse all fall within the North Riding. Almost no medieval court records survive from the Liberty of St Peter.[17] The records of the Privy Seal office, which would otherwise have provided information on the petition made by Ellen de Rouclif, Alice's mother, to Edward III about Sir Brian's actions, have likewise been lost in a fire. Even the records of the case itself, together with the larger archive of cause papers, were twice nearly destroyed when York Minster was on fire in 1829 and again in 1840.[18] John Marrays is scarcely documented beyond the case. So far as I have been able to ascertain, save for a single deed recorded in the St Mary's cartulary, Alice de Rouclif, along with a number of other persons noted in the action, has made no other mark on the historical record.

The purpose of the book that follows is twofold. First I want to use the evidence from the case to illuminate the society and culture of the English later Middle Ages. The depositions can readily be used to illuminate social and gender relations, the dynamics of local power structures, even something of the local economy. This alone, however, is insufficient to justify this study. The main purpose of this book is to explore the relationship between the written depositions generated by the case as legal records of oral testimony and the people whose testimony is ostensibly so recorded. Is the testimony simply a product of the questions posed? Is what is said so much a product of the essentially adversarial legal process that the motives and perspectives of individual witnesses are ultimately hidden? Is it possible to know anything about individual witnesses as people? Most difficult of all, can anything be retrieved of the young heiress who is the essentially mute focus of the entire case? In attempting these questions I am entering epistemologically problematic territory and not all will be sympathetic to my approach. If I only provoke some of my readers to take issue, I will nevertheless have helped further the scholarly endeavor.

It is with Alice's history, largely as reconstructed from the case itself, that this book begins and she will remain very much the focus of our book. Chapter 2 will explore the vexed question of the nature of the depositions and the degree to which they are shaped by the articles or questions that lie behind the recorded testimony. The four following chapters will explore individual witnesses and their depositions from a number of different perspectives. Central to the analysis is a concern to understand why witnesses provided testimony in the specific form suggested by the resultant depositions. Chapter 3 focuses on memory and how history is recalled in a largely oral and visual culture. Chapter 4 is concerned with the social networks that bound people together or, conversely, in opposition to one another. Chapter 5 continues this analysis by considering the networks of kinship that are shared between various deponents. So many of the depositions in the case relates to events that were public or semi-public—baptisms, celebrations of churchings, spousals—but others relate to more intimate events—childbirth, private conversation. Chapter 6, however, explores events that are hidden and witnessed only accidentally. It also moves from an exploration of the depositions as documents of social and cultural history to a consideration of their contemporary reception and use within the court itself. Finally, chapter 7 attempts to read behind partisan testimony to rediscover a voice for Alice. Part two of the book (chapters 8 and 9) will explore some parallel cases from the Court of York and these will help inform the Conclusion, but Alice will again be an integral part of our discussion.

This book is a product of an interest in Marrays c. de Rouclif that dates back to my first reading the case in 1983. I returned to it nearly a decade later when I transcribed and translated the case for teaching purposes and subsequent publication. Since then I have used it with a range of final-year undergraduates and master's students. Their contributions to discussion over the years have been invaluable. I am most grateful to Prof. Mark Ormrod, my current head of department, for helping me find the opportunity to put my thoughts to paper and for specific advice about the Privy Seal office. I wish to thank Dr. Philippa Hoskin of the Borthwick Institute for Archives for her support and advice. I am grateful to my colleagues and graduate students for helping to make the Centre for Medieval Studies such a stimulating environment in which to teach and engage in research. I owe my greatest debt to my wife Patricia and my daughter Helena.

CHAPTER 1

ALICE DE ROUCLIF: AN EVENTFUL CHILDHOOD

The feast of the Apostles Peter and Paul fell on a Sunday in 1365. Medieval folk were adept at combining worship and recreation. Such a major festival would have been a day of rest and of devotion throughout the realm, but especially within the diocese of York, whose cathedral church was dedicated to St Peter. For the residents of the Yorkshire Wolds' hamlet of Kennythorpe, the day must have been focused around parish mass at the neighboring village church of Langton, a mile or so across the fields.[19] It was high summer, a time when the daylight extended from early morning until late in the evening. We do not know at what time of day Sir Brian Rouclif's men made their own way across the fields to the home of Stephen Wascelyne, but the likelihood is that they took advantage of the light to approach either soon after dawn or in the late evening before or after the household was up and about.[20] The men were no doubt armed, but the house would have at best been lightly defended and the household staff would be more used to making beds or tending livestock than fighting. Their objective would have been quickly achieved. Whether the young girl they carried away from the Wascelyne house and its orchard that had been her home for only a matter of months cried out or resisted her abductors or what she may have said to them or they to her, we do not know. It is even possible that she welcomed their coming. What we can be sure of is that they would have used as little violence toward her and caused her as little upset as the circumstances would allow. The girl was too precious a commodity. She was Sir Brian's kinswoman, an heiress and an orphan.

The last Sunday in June was another eventful day in the life of Alice de Rouclif. She had grown up in the village of Rawcliffe, then called Rouclif after which she took her name, just outside York. The semi-moated house in which she may well have been born and grown up, a moderately substantial timber-framed structure comprising service and domestic ranges attached to an earlier hall, befitted her social rank.[21] She was a child of her mother's second marriage; Ellen de Rouclif may well have lost her first husband in the Black Death leaving her with a son, John Fische, then aged about nine. Ellen had married Alice's father in the parish church of Alne, some ten miles northwest of York, around Michaelmas 1350 (or perhaps 1351). Two years later she gave birth to a son John, but he was not to survive infancy; Alice never knew her older brother. Alice herself was born on Saturday 29 March 1354 (or perhaps the day before) in a basement room in the family home in Rawcliffe. Alternatively, Alice was born on Saturday 9 March 1353. Ellen Taliour, who was to be Alice's wetnurse, helped at the delivery as did another woman who had since become senile, perhaps one Ellen Grigge.[22] But Ellen Taliour seems not to have remembered the presence of Cecily de Shupton who also claimed to have been present as she had been previously at John's birth. That Alice was born on the Saturday before the first Sunday in Passiontide is agreed (and regularly repeated with formulaic certainty). On the precise year, much of what follows depends.

Alice was baptized with customary haste, lest her infant soul be denied salvation in the event of an untimely death, being carried to the parish church (or perhaps strictly chapel) of St Olave in York by her newly hired nurse. Her godparents were Thomas Smyth of Clifton, the village lying between York and Rawcliffe, Alice de Beleby, the wife of Richard de Warwyk, who presumably chose her name, and another woman.[23] The infant's inferior status as a girl baby is signaled by the fact that she was baptized in the parish church, whereas her older brother had been baptized in the adjacent abbey church to which the parish church belonged. The church of St Olave, the local corruption of St Olaf, a relic of Danish rule in an earlier era, stands by the main entrance gate into the abbey and effectively formed part of the fortified precinct wall.[24] John de Rouclif's privileged place of baptism signals the family's close ties with the abbey. In time these ties would also come to bind Alice.

Gervase de Rouclif, Alice's father, appears not to have had any further children by his wife. Alice would thus have grown up with an older half-brother, but no full siblings of her own.[25] Gervase seems, however, to have fathered a son, Robert, who is described as her blood brother. Whether Robert de Rouclif was the child of one of Gervase's liaisons with his female employees, we do not know. Perhaps he was the son of Maud de Herthill, originally Ellen's servant, who had been employed at various times in the Rouclif household and who had allegedly admitted adultery with Gervase. He may well have been the father of the daughter

Maud, conceived a month or so immediately following the birth of John de Rouclif.[26] Maud was a servant in the household at least until John's birth, but may in any case have been invited to the Christmas festivities.

Alice was perhaps a little too young to be aware of her father's matrimonial infidelities, which were in any case perhaps not so unusual for a man of his (albeit minor) aristocratic rank.[27] It may be unwise to speculate as to how far such infidelities were symptomatic of an unhappy marriage that, subsequent to Alice's birth, produced no more children. It may well have been an arranged marriage, just as Alice's was to be, but again this need not have made it a loveless marriage. We simply do not know. What we do know is that at Michaelmas 1361 Gervase de Rouclif died, possibly a victim of the second pestilence, sometimes knows as the Grey Death, which struck the region around that time.[28] Alice succeeded in name to her father's lands, but as a girl of seven or eight she was not yet of age to inherit as such. This would have to wait either until she was fifteen, the conventional age for women to come of age in feudal law, or until she married.[29] But according to canon law she could not marry before she had reached her canonical majority at twelve years. In the meantime, Alice would be a ward. Her guardian would manage her lands and would have quasi-paternal powers to arrange her marriage so long as she remained a minor. This is precisely what happened.

So far as we can tell, Alice continued to live with her mother. Such an arrangement for wards was entirely normal since the mother was thought to be most well suited to the care and nurture of a young child and perhaps particularly of a daughter.[30] Ellen appears also to have exercised de facto guardianship of Alice.[31] Mothers could be made guardians of their own children, but such was not the usual arrangement. Normally guardianship would have been claimed by the senior male representative of the wider family. We may assume this to have been no less that the Sir Brian de Rouclif, by whose authority she was abducted in the summer of 1365. The abduction can thus be seen as an assertion of Sir Brian's rights of guardianship over his young ward, which would have included control of her marriage, but his action was provoked by the events of the immediately preceding months. As Scott Waugh has observed, "men intent on personal gain preyed on the vulnerability of women and pushed aside the rules of lord, Church, and social decency to get what they wanted." Abductions of marriageable women may have been uncommon, but they were an established strategy within aristocratic culture; Sir Brian's actions were the logical response of a lord who considered that his rights had been usurped.[32]

Of Alice's life during the three years following her father's death we know next to nothing. The family had been wont to visit York periodically in Gervase's lifetime for they stabled their horses at Beatrix de Morland hostelry on Bootham, the main street into the city from Rawcliffe and the north. It is likely that these visits would have continued. Certainly Beatrix had knowledge of the family up to the time of the case in the Church court of York upon which this history depends. A few weeks before Christmas 1364, however, Alice came to York with her mother and her half-brothers, John Fische and Robert de Rouclif. It was already growing dark—it was said to be twilight before supper time—the days being short in the winter months, but especially so in mid-December. If they had stabled their horses in the Bootham hostelry, they would then have walked the short distance down Marygate, known then by its earlier name of St Marygate.[33] They would have been met at the main gatehouse of the abbey by Adam Porter, the eponymous gatekeeper, and no doubt directed by him to the chamber of Richard Bernard, the abbey's steward, within the abbey precinct and quite probably within the gatehouse itself.[34] There in the presence of the notary public, Adam de Thornton, Alice was made to enter into a verbal contract to marry one John Marrays, who was also present in the room. John's man, William Pottell, looked on from the doorway.[35]

John Marrays, we may assume, was a kinsman of William Marrays, the then abbot of St Mary's, York, the largest and wealthiest Benedictine monastery in the north of England. This probably explains why the formal contract took place at St Mary's even though the abbot was not present on this occasion. The use of the steward's chamber as a sort of registry office for the contracting of marriages may have been open more generally, however, perhaps to more important tenants or members of the Liberty of St Mary.[36] The contract itself was clearly the initiative of Alice's mother, although other unnamed members of the Rouclif family were also said to have been involved. It anticipated that the couple would in time be formally married at which moment a dowry would be paid in respect of Alice to John. The value of this dowry was stated to be either £100 or 100 marks (£66 13s. 4d.), an indication of Alice's comparative standing as an heiress of gentle birth. Barbara Harris found that a century or more later the median dowry payment in respect of a knight's daughter was double this, but Alice was not a knight's daughter.[37]

At the time of this contract or, to use contemporary terminology, spousals, Alice was in the eyes of the Church still too young to marry then being only ten or eleven years of age. Canon law, however, allowed children to enter into spousals from as young as seven, so there was nothing illicit or improper about this arrangement. It was not a marriage, but rather a formal legal agreement intimating intention to be married at such time as both parties were of sufficient age.[38] In this instance, since John Marrays was almost certainly already adult, this would be in only a year or two once Alice had reached twelve. At that point Alice could either repudiate the intended marriage, because in canon law there was no marriage without consent, or she could affirm it. In practice there was precious little scope for twelve-year-old girls to repudiate marriages their parents or guardians had arranged for them and, even had she so wanted, Alice had little opportunity to repudiate hers prior to her abduction. We should also note that, by analogy with a number of marriages relating to girls and young women of much higher social rank than Alice, that the lay aristocracy may have interpreted the ruling that a girl must be twelve years of age for a lawful marriage to occur to mean her twelfth year.[39] It follows that from the point of view of the local aristocracy, the spousals were perhaps understood to constitute a de facto marriage.

What was contentious here was not so much the earlier contract or spousals but rather whether she affirmed it. This could have been done either by a simple verbal affirmation before witnesses or, as seems to have been both the norm and expected, by allowing the relationship to be physically consummated. But Alice was not yet twelve. She was too young to cohabit with her husband-to-be, too young to affirm the intended marriage, too young to be the mistress of a household, indeed well nigh too young to leave her mother and her childhood home in Rawcliffe.

It is not clear where Alice spent the night following her spousals, whether in a guest chamber at the abbey or, more likely, at the family's usual hostelry. Early the following morning until midday, however, she was at her half-brother's house in Bootham.[40] Katherine, her half-brother's wife, asked her about her husband-to-be and how she felt about leaving her mother and going to live at Kennythorpe. Alice reportedly replied that she was happy if John willed it so, an answer that, even if true, better reflects Alice's sense of familial duty than youthful enthusiasm. That afternoon Alice was brought to Kennythorpe, some dozen miles northeast of York, by Adam Porter, the gatekeeper, and William Pottell, her husband-to-be's factotum. Kennythorpe was, as we have seen, the home to Stephen Wascelyne and his wife Anabilla. Anabilla was John Marrays's sister, so this was the home of Alice's prospective brother- and sister-in-law.[41] Here Alice could learn how to manage a household from Anabilla, who became her substitute mother, until such time as she was of age formally to solemnize her marriage and set up home with John. For Alice the strangeness of being uprooted from her mother, her most immediate kin, her childhood home, her natal village and of being made to live among strangers would have been compensated for, at least to a degree, by having two girls near to her own age as companions. Alice de Rolleston and her younger sister Joan were Anabilla's daughters. Like Alice, they were almost certainly what contemporaries would have understood as orphans since it is probable that this was also Anabilla's second marriage. During her stay in the Wascelyne household, Alice shared a room and a bed with Joan, presumably the girl considered closest in age to her. On one level this was symbolic of Alice's status within the household, being placed on an equal footing with the householders' own children, but it probably also made Alice's stay much more bearable.

Alice arrived at Kennythorpe about three weeks before Christmas 1364.[42] A little over a fortnight later, on Saturday, 21 December, the feast of St Thomas the Apostle, John Marrays came to Kennythorpe.[43] That night he displaced (so we are told) Joan de Rolleston from the bed she shared with Alice, which John's man, William Pottell had made up. Joan lay down in another part of the same room. During the course of the night John forced himself on Alice. Joan, from across the room heard what was going on and remembered Alice crying out "silently." Whether Alice regarded this as consensual sex is a moot point, but she apparently readily acknowledged that it had taken place. Alice's concern was not, as we would see it today, that her husband-to-be had effectively raped her, but rather that he had had sexual relations with her prior to the solemnization of their marriage. Her lament was that she was willing to be his wife, but not his mistress. She complained to Anabilla, urging that the marriage take place as soon as possible and made her case in person before John, who ordered her to be quiet and wait patiently. In the meantime John, who was in London at some point at least, continued to send her various gifts as he had done since even before their spousals. These gifts, carried by Thomas Pottell, had included variously a blue cloth to make matching tunic, coat, and hood, a furred robe, three tunics, two kerchiefs, and a knife.[44] Alice was disappointed, however, that no wedding veil was sent.

Winter passed. Spring passed. Summer arrived, but no veil was ever sent. The next visitors to come for Alice were uninvited. They were Sir Brian's men, with whom this account began. Alice now disappears from view, becoming in effect a chattel of Sir Brian, who would, as the case that subsequently followed implies, have every reason to persuade Alice to repudiate her contract of marriage made to John Marrays whilst she was still a minor.[45] At some point after that, Sir Brian appears to have gone overseas, presumably to serve in John of Gaunt's Iberian expedition.[46] But the story does not end here. Ellen de Rouclif, Alice's mother made courageous efforts to regain custody of her daughter, and hence to release her from Sir Brian, even taking her cause before the king in council. On the basis of her appeal, letters were issued under the privy seal addressed to Sir Brian. Before Christmas 1365 she also involved Lord de

Percy, presumably Henry Percy, third lord of Alnwick, hoping that his intervention would help secure the return of her daughter. These attempts appear not to have secured the desired result. It is against this background that in the months after the abduction John Marrays also initiated legal proceedings in the ecclesiastical Court of York for restitution of conjugal rights. His case was simple. He had lawfully married Alice as his wife. Now, and some time after the couple married, Sir Brian had unlawfully snatched her away.

Actions for restitution of conjugal rights are pretty unusual.[47] The Church courts dealt with a range of business from litigation about tithes or parochial rights to disputed wills and defamation. Cases concerning the validity of marriages were a significant part of that business. Because marriage was a sacrament of the Church, such cases fell exclusively within the jurisdiction of the Church courts and the canon law. Most matrimonial litigation comprised actions either to enforce marriages or to annul them. John Marray's case and its defence display elements of both. Marrays's plea was parallel to a simple action to enforce a contract in so far as to convince the court that his wife should be restored to him, John had to show that she really was his wife and that the marriage had been consummated.[48] Canon law recognized two forms of binding contract. The first was an exchange of consent using words of present consent—"I take you to be my husband/wife." Such de presenti contracts constituted immediately binding marriages so long as both parties were free to marry. Consummation was not of itself necessary for Mary and Joseph were truly wed, though they lived a celibate marriage. Future or de futuro contracts—"I will marry you when...," "it is my intention to marry you," and so on—did not constitute marriages and could be displaced by a subsequent de presenti contract. A future contract could, however, be translated into an immediately binding marriage if the couple were to consummate the relationship subsequent to the contract; this act would be deemed as a nonverbal expression of a desire to make immediate what had previously been a future intent.

The case that John Marrays initiated in order to secure the return of Alice de Rouclif essentially asserted that a de futuro contract entered into by the two of them had subsequently been consummated—the sixth of John's initial articles states that "they lay together naked in the one bed," more or less a euphemism for sex.[49] It follows that evidence for consummation served two important functions. It demonstrated that this was an established marriage—a necessary part of the restitution action. More crucially, it also satisfied the need to show that a future contact had been ratified and made immediately binding by reason of consummation. The case was complicated, however, in that Alice had been under age when she had made the initial contract. John therefore needed to show also that at the time of the alleged consummation, Alice had already achieved her canonical majority, or, to add to the complexity of this particular case, had come sufficiently close to achieving her majority that a canonical exception around the issue of puberty came into play. Whereas John's libel simply asserts that Alice had reached puberty, the critical sixth article allowed for ambiguity—"Alice had reached puberty or had at least nearly reached puberty [pubes facta seu saltem proxima pubitati]" (BI, CP.E.89/26). John's action was nominally against Alice. To be more precise, it was actually against the court appointed guardian who could answer for her since, if Alice truly were under age, then canon law would debar her from speaking in her own right. To allow Alice to "defend" the case in person would be in effect to prejudice the outcome.

John's case revolved around four necessary elements: there had been a verbal contract or spousals; subsequent to this Alice had achieved her canonical majority or at least satisfied the exception allowed by canon law; Alice was at the time of the spousals and subsequently desirous of the marriage; this wish had been made immediately binding by the couple's consummation of the contract. Simple suits to enforce a contract of marriage have been likened to engagement disputes.[50] They do not concern established marriages. John Marrays's action was different. His was allegedly an established marriage that had been unlawfully interrupted by the forceful abduction of his wife. Here John had an advantage. The Church courts were much more wary of ruling against the validity of an established marriage than they were in respect of marriages that had never really begun.[51] Those seeking to deny John's claims had, therefore, to make a very strong case to show that any one or more of the four elements just described was untrue.

Although the "defence" of John's action was nominally by the court-appointed Master Edward of Cornwall (de Cornubia), in practice it was stage-managed by Sir Brian de Rouclif, supposedly in the name of Alice, his de facto ward and hostage.[52] The case that Sir Brian organized homed in on the most vulnerable element in John's libel. In canon law it was consent, not sex, that made a marriage, but only those who had attained a certain intellectual maturity consequent upon age could reasonably exercise that consent. If it could be shown that Alice had not reached her canonical majority prior to the abduction then there would be no marriage, regardless of the earlier spousals and regardless of the alleged consummation that followed so soon after. This is essentially the case that was made, although it was also alleged that Alice was forced into the spousals against her will.[53] These are classic elements in a number of actions for nullity, especially those associated with families of some social standing.[54]

Whatever Alice's own views prior to the abduction, Alice would now be opposed to the marriage. Sir Brian would require her to be.

The case that followed is extraordinary. It is extraordinary for the number of witnesses brought by the contesting parties to try to prove their version of events or to undermine the case for the opposing side. And it is extraordinary for the number of female witnesses brought.[55] Fifty-seven different witnesses were examined, a few more than once. This compares with a mean of little more than six witnesses per case from twelve other extant marriage cases relating to rural society in the period 1350–99. Even if the depositions made by the witnesses in respect for some of these other cases have not survived in their entirety, and hence the true mean should be rather higher, the difference in numbers still represents a quantum leap. This same sample produces a total of sixty-four male witnesses to only nine female (a ratio of 7.11 males to every female witness). This compares with a total of twenty-four male, but thirty-three female witnesses (a ratio of 0.73 males to every female) within this present case. Many of the witnesses lived in Rawcliffe or had done so previously. Indeed the thirteen specifically identified as resident in Rawcliffe at the time of the case perhaps constituted a significant minority—perhaps a third—of the adult population of the vill and represent a majority—perhaps some two-thirds—of all households.[56] Several had been employed by Alice's parents. Another overlapping group were tenants of Sir Brian. It will be to their voices, mere whispers after the passage of some 640 years that this book will repeatedly return.

The first witnesses were examined on 1 November 1365, the last on 28 February 1366.[57] Delays were caused by the court's customary vacations at Christmas and Easter.[58] The initial exchange involved twenty-four of John's witnesses testifying to show that a valid marriage existed on the basis of spousals willingly ratified by a pubescent Alice countered by another seventeen witnesses to the effect that Alice was too young to have lawfully consented.[59] On the 8 January both parties rejoined the action by formally challenging the credibility of the witnesses for the other side, a tactic regularly found in Church court litigation. Alice's exception went on to introduce the argument that the timing of the birth of Alice's deceased older brother John meant that she could not possibly have been born as early as 1353. Six witnesses testified to that effect.[60] John responded toward the end of the same month by arguing that John de Rouclif had in fact been born a year earlier than was alleged. He likewise mustered six witnesses to this effect.[61] The final group of four witnesses testified in support of the reputation of Alice's witnesses, though an exception on behalf of Alice dated 18 March, presumably just before the court's Easter recess, again asserted that John's witnesses were untrustworthy. If this exception was subsequently followed up by the presentation of witnesses, neither the associated schedule of questions nor any depositions survive.[62] The likelihood is that it was not allowed to be pursued.

Up until 12 April 1366 the case proceeded under the direction of the Official, one Thomas de Buckton. Although cases were regularly heard by the Official by virtue of his office (from which the title derives), we may strongly suspect that Buckton was not entirely impartial: he was clearly on good terms with St Mary's Abbey since he was to bequeath the house half his books. It was, however, not to be his judgment that prevailed. Events intervened. Thomas was called away on a diplomatic mission to the pope at Avignon and was thus obliged to hand the case over against the reconvening of the court after the Easter break to Adam of York, who had recently been appointed precentor of the cathedral church of York. It was thus Adam of York who on 11 July 1366 issued judgment.[63] Presumably Thomas briefed Adam on the case before his departure. Perhaps he indicated his sympathies for the St Mary's Abbey and hence John Marrays's petition. There is, however, reason to suspect that Adam may already have shared these sympathies. The clue is provided by the will of Master John de Rouclif, senior, a married clerk and likely kinsman of Robert de Rouclif, a supporter of the Marrays's cause and a firm friend of the abbey. He left provision for the marriage of one Katherine Wascelyne, who may well have been a child born to Stephen and Anabilla. He also left money to provide for his soul and those of two other named persons; Adam of York was one of these.[64] Whether or not he was partisan, we do know that Adam's judgment was that John Marrays had proved his case sufficiently. Alice was to be restored to him and the marriage was to be formally solemnized.

Despite (or rather because of) its formulaic structure, the judgment is very bald. It offers no legal summing up, commentary or explanation why one account is to be preferred over the other. What we can observe, however, is that John, started with the advantage of claiming an established marriage. In cases of conflicting testimony, moreover, the canon law clearly stated that the standing and numbers of witnesses should be weighed.[65] John was able produce a greater number of witnesses, although it is less clear that their overall standing was greater than that of Alice's; John's star witness was the abbot of St Mary's, but those testifying for Alice included, alongside some conspicuously poor peasant women, John de Melsay and his wife and Lady Margery de Rouclif, all three of gentry rank. Lady Margery's testimony was especially powerful: if her testimony to the precise date of birth of Alice's dead older brother had been believed, it would have entirely undermined the value of Dom. William Marrays's evidence. Canonical convention, however, tended to place weight on the volume of consistent testimonies that was in the particular credibility of any one deposition, so it may be unwise to see this as clear evidence that in this instance the presiding officer was biased. Lady Margery was, moreover, no less likely to be partisan than Ellen de Rouclif or Dom. William Marrays: her son was none other than Sir Brian de Rouclif.

Whereas John was able to support every aspect of his case, "Alice"—in effect Sir Brian—was unable to show that she had opposed the marriage. Another factor is John's use of the canonical exception that allowed for a legally binding marriage in cases where the man had intercourse with his underage fiancée so long as she was already near, but had not achieved her canonical majority.[66] The wording of the law makes it clear that this was seen to constitute an indissoluble union and hence that those opposed to the marriage would have to work that much harder to have the union annulled. The exception also served to undercut the argument that Alice could not lawfully have consented since she had not yet reached her twelfth birthday, though, as the law specifies, the exception would apply only if she were already eleven; if Alice had been born in 1354, as some witnesses attempted to show, she would only have been ten at the time.

In the summer of 1366, therefore, a whole year after her abduction, Alice should have been returned to the care of John Marrays either at Kennythorpe or actually in a shared home. And so this narrative should end. In fact the verdict was almost immediately appealed, but what, if anything, became of that appeal is not known.[67] As we shall see, such slight evidence as we have would suggest that Alice was in fact fairly swiftly restored to John. Certainly by late September 1370 the couple acted as husband and wife to lend their names to a deed quitclaiming property rights that Alice stood to inherit from her mother.[68] The validity of the couple's marriage was now beyond dispute; the record of the action in the Court of York ceased to be a working document, becoming instead yet another addition to a growing, but ultimately neglected archive.

CHAPTER 2

WILLIAM POTTELL: STORIES AND STORYTELLERS

The narrative of Alice de Rouclif's childhood culminating in her betrothal, her subsequent forced abduction, and lastly the court action that was provoked by her abduction is known to us almost entirely from the surviving court records. These records comprise a variety of documents, but it is the records of the testimony of witnesses that are far and away the most illuminating in trying to recover the experiences and perspectives of those touched by the case or even of the principal parties who by canonical convention did not testify in person. Oral testimony was recorded as written depositions. They record a variety of voices, each with its own story to tell. This chapter is concerned to explore this surprisingly complex process of story telling.

Depositions were produced not so much as an aide memoire of what was said in court, but as an essential element in the judicial process. The oral testimony was merely a necessary stage in the production of depositions rather than, as in a modern court of law, the very fabric of the case. Once all the examinations had been completed, the resulting depositions were collected together and placed in the hands of the presiding officer of the court known as the Official. (We have already seen that in this present case, the presiding officer actually changed prior to this final stage because the then Official of the Court of York was sent to Avignon on diplomatic business.) He then reached his judgment on the basis of a careful reading of the testimony. In so doing, he would pay attention to two particular criteria. The first was the validity of the cases argued by the contesting parties according to the yardstick of canon law. The second was how credible the respective cases were. Consistency between witnesses was one of the factors considered here. The integrity of the witnesses was another. Where there was little to choose between the merits of conflicting testimonies, then simple weight of numbers became a telling factor.[1]

It is this careful reading of the recorded depositions originally undertaken by the Official that we may vicariously reenact. Indeed this is precisely the exercise a number of historians of canon law have undertaken to determine the degree to which the courts abided by the canon law and the reasons for the verdicts that were reached.[2] This last is a necessary question. Although a judgment was invariably made by the Official (or, as here, some other president) at the conclusion of the case and this sometimes, as in this case, survives, there is no equivalent to the modern judge's summing up. The judgment is bald. Of itself it offers no clue as to how and why it may have been reached. The temptation to think ourselves into the position of the Official, to test our own knowledge of medieval canon law, and to weigh up the testimony is thus considerable. This is reinforced by the very nature of the depositions. The present case is no exception.

The depositions relating to Marrays c. de Rouclif appear alluringly immediate, intimate and authentic. Annabilla Wascelyne's recollection of Alice de Rouclif's childish plea—"Dame, I have a secret to tell you if you will hear it"——resonates with our own knowledge of how children seek to communicate their anxieties and concerns. Ellen Taliour's testimony, recalling the occasion the young single mother was asked to work as a wetnurse, that "she loved her son just as much as Ellen [de Rouclif] loved hers and consequently she did not want to allow her own son to die on account of Ellen's son and so she refused to be John's nurse" (BI, CP.E.89/4), speaks to our own cultural assumptions about the strength of the maternal bond. We want to believe it. Similarly we cannot help but be struck by the poignancy of Isabel de Strensall's testimony that she had given birth to a child, but could not remember "whether with a boy or a girl." This is treacherous ground.

Robert Bartlett has recently described reading depositions as providing "as good an idea as we are likely to get of the spoken words of the past in the time before the tape recorder."[3] Although he later notes the way in which testimony was shaped by the questions asked, this seems a remarkably upbeat, even polemical stance.[4] An earlier, more nuanced, but still upbeat view has been voiced by Elizabeth Cohen from her work with Roman depositions of the early modern era.[5] Against this we may set John Arnold's contrasting view that stresses the way in which depositions can be seen as products of the inquisitorial process.[6] By reading depositions as texts, he challenges the "a priori assumption of individual voices and speaking subjects who communicate through the records."[7] To no small extent, these rather different positions follow from the particular kinds of depositions used by Bartlett and Arnold respectively. Bartlett draws upon testimony given in the process of canonization; in this instance, an alleged miracle of Thomas Cantilupe, bishop of Hereford, was investigated by questioning a large body of witnesses including the man whom the saint had supposedly revived after he had been hanged.[8] Arnold, however, is using essentially very different Inquisition material, reflective of a process where kin and neighbor were pitted against one another to testify about their knowledge of heresy and heretics. Witnesses were quizzed in a climate of fear, ignorant of just how much information their interrogators had already garnered from informants and prior testimony. A battle of wits is thus played out as the inquisitor attempts to delineate heretic and orthodox by his skilful questioning of deponents who in fact occupy a much more ambiguous and heterodox world. Bartlett's witnesses might at worst find that the authenticity of the miracle to which they testified was found unproven, but Arnold's might see their neighbors, their loved ones, even their own selves burn as condemned heretics. On balance, the depositions within the Court of York are more akin to Bartlett's than those of Arnold. There is, however, one key difference that renders these even more unlike Arnold's Inquisitorial depositions. Whereas the deponents facing the Inquisitorial process faced questions devised by the inquisitor, of which they could have had no advance notice, the witnesses in this present case faced only questions, referred to as articles, drawn up by the legal counsel acting for whichever party the witness was appearing. As shall shortly be seen, witnesses probably knew and were able to prepare for (or be prepared for) the questions posed to them.

There are a number of reasons why we need to hesitate before accepting this testimony contained in the depositions as an essentially trustworthy record of the deponent's actual words, let alone a form of life writing. The process resulting in the recording of a deposition is a convoluted one. We need to follow it through its different stages. Each witness was examined separately and individually, normally in York but outside the actual court, two exceptions being John de Melsay and his wife, who were examined in their own home.[9] The witnesses responded to questions that had been drawn up in advance and were not, in any modern sense, cross-examined. The questions would have been put to them in the vernacular, though they are recorded only in Latin. Their answers likewise would have been made in the vernacular, but for the purposes of drawing up the depositions, these were also translated into Latin. There is thus a necessary distance between the words spoken and the resultant text. (This distance is only increased by the present writer's attempts to render the Latin of the depositions into a modern English translation.)

This process of converting verbal responses into written depositions begs a number of questions. How far does the clerk attempt a verbatim transcript that is then reworked as a Latin text? By the fifteenth century, reported speech at least is recorded in English with increasing frequency. The presentation of the depositions also changes. They become messier, with text crossed through and the quality of the hand tending to deteriorate. There is thus more sense that we may have contemporaneous notes, but this can hardly be true of most earlier depositions including those in this case. Here we have a Latin text written with some care, albeit with numerous standard abbreviations, and in a hand that is largely indistinguishable from other material preserved as a record of the case. This hardly suggests a simultaneous translation and transcription, though the apparent neatness and uniformity of the text may simply suggest that what has been preserved is a copy of the materials produced for the court, not the originals. This view is reinforced by the observation that several groups of depositions have been enrolled together, though depositions made on different days may follow one another on the same membrane.[10] Alternatively it may suggest that the deposition was worked up from some kind of contemporaneous transcript or notes. There are other reasons for thinking this.

Although the Latin conceals the actual language used by the witnesses, the tone is formal. We might expect witnesses appearing within the probably unfamiliar and perhaps intimidating context of the consistory court to adopt a more formal register than they would use in everyday speech, but this does not seem sufficient explanation. Anabilla Wascelyne's deposition begins, "on the first and second articles she says that they contain the truth [continent veritatem] and this she knows by confession of the parties in dispute [inter quos agitur] and by the account of others and common report [communem famam] circulating about them"[11] (BI, CP.E.89/27). The three phrases represented in the original, though expanded, Latin represent common usages, part of a quasi-legal discourse, and thus probably not precise translations of the perhaps wordier account of the original witness. On the other hand the Latinity of the clerks is not particularly sophisticated. There is no attempt at literary elegance and the vocabulary used is comparatively restricted; in this sense the translation feels more like a fairly literal translation.

Much the same point can be made in respect of the dates provided by witnesses. Thus Henry Vaux refers to "a fortnight before the feast of the nativity of St John the Baptist twelve years ago" and several witnesses tie Alice de Rouclif's birth to "the Saturday before the first Sunday in Passiontide." The location of past events by reference to saints' days probably reflects common usage in a society where the normal rhythms of working life and the passage of the seasons were punctuated by major festivals.[12] The recording of time by reference to calendar months was probably a clerical convention and a feature of literary rather than oral culture. The use exclusively of saints' days can, however, only have been reinforced by this ecclesiastical context. The dating of Alice's birth, nevertheless, sounds formulaic. Vaux's dating is tied to the point at which he entered employment as a servant, that is, at the feast of St John itself, but it is questionable how far so important a feast, popularly associated with midsummer (St John's eve) and thus a time of celebration, would have needed so precise a definition. The argument here is that the dates provided by witnesses have been tidied up and standardized according to the conventions of the court, but there is no reason to doubt that they represent the dates signaled by the witnesses.

The role of the clerk writing the deposition thus far seems fairly benign, but another possibility is suggested from a reading of the depositions, namely that the process of tidying may also have included a degree of pruning. The answers that witnesses give to the questions asked of them—the "articles" as they are regularly described in the depositions—are consistently to the point. Rarely, if ever, does the witness appear to stray from the subject. Would witnesses be so disciplined? Or is the apparent discipline a product of tacit editing by the clerk? The latter is perhaps more likely. Agnes Quysteler knew of Alice's birth from "her neighbors" and Eufemia de Rouclif "from the relation of women." The importance of their testimony is thus marginal; they do little more than swell the ranks of witnesses.[13] The women themselves may not have realized this. It is scarcely likely that this knowledge constrained them to say as few words as possible. Indeed these witnesses may have attempted to offer lists of names and anecdotal detail about who said what, where, and when. Yet their recorded depositions are very brief. It is the contention here that they have been firmly pruned.

Despite, indeed perhaps because of, this evidence of editorial intervention, the depositions themselves try to project a sense of immediacy, the fiction that they really are accurate renditions of oral testimony. Thus the depositions are peppered with "dicit" and "ut dicit"—"he says," "so she says," and so on. The more the depositions reiterate their origin in speech, the more they in fact draw attention to their fictive nature as texts. Their fictive nature is not, however, solely the product of the clerk. Rather it is shaped by a number of different agents. The clerk is not the most important, merely the most recent. We need to retrace the process by which a deposition came to be created.

As has already been noted, witnesses gave their testimony in response to predetermined questions. In the case of questions to witnesses for the plaintiff, these are known as articles, but in the case of questions to the defendant's witnesses drawn up in response to or as a counter to the plaintiff's case, the equivalent term is interrogatories.[14] The articles themselves derived ultimately from the original libel drawn up on behalf of the plaintiff that summarized their case. In theory, the libel was used to generate a series of statements or positions to which the defendant responded. Only those statements that were challenged by the defendant needed to be demonstrated by reference to witnesses. In practice, in this case, as was increasingly the norm, the articles incorporate the positions.[15] The purpose of the articles was thus to facilitate answers that would help substantiate the plaintiff's case. The value of the answers given therefore, lay in the degree to which they upheld and lent credence to the points raised by the questions. The deposition of William Pottell can be used illustrate this point.

Pottell testified, along with a number of other witnesses, to a series of six articles put to him in November or, more likely, December 1365.[16] The first article set out to show that spousals had been exchanged between Alice and John by mutual consent. The second asserted that Alice's mother and kin [parentes] were present at the spousals and that they had consented to them. Pottell replied to these first two articles that they were true; he knew this because he was standing in the doorway of the room where the spousals took place, though he acknowledged he was unable to hear the words exchanged. The third article asserted that Alice was twelve at Easter. Pottell replied that her mother and two of her godparents had told him that this was indeed her age. The fourth article claimed that Alice had, and was known to have, reached puberty when she ratified the contract. Pottell's response is frankly oblique. He remembered that on a number of occasions he took gifts from John to Alice at Kennythorpe, that he had asked her why her husband spent so much time away from her, and that Alice had used him to convey to John "her greetings as her master."

The fifth article built upon the fourth by asserting that Alice had, once she reached puberty, acknowledged her contract "freely, knowingly and frequently [sponte, scienter et pluries]" in the presence of John and of others. Pottell's response was simply that Alice had never denied it. The sixth article, perhaps the most crucial, amplifies the fourth article asserting that both parties had reached puberty "or had at least nearly reached puberty [pubes facta seu saltem proxima pubitati]" at the point at which they lay in bed together naked and embraced "as man and wife," and that afterward Alice received gifts from John. This time Pottell's reply is more obviously pertinent. He made the bed in which the couple lay "alone and naked together." (The clerk here uses the formulaic construction "solus cum sola et nudus cum nuda.") When he asked Alice if "she was happy with John as her master," she replied, "she was well satisfied to have him for a husband." This prompted him to assert the wish that she "grow up sufficiently that he is able to do with you as is fitting," to which Alice retorted significantly, "I am adequate to be his wife, but not his whore." The final article claimed conventionally that the points asserted were matters of public knowledge in Rawcliffe, Kennythorpe, and neighboring places.[17]

Pottell's testimony is almost entirely shaped by the articles put to him. His testimony is valuable—at least from the perspective of the party for whom he appears—only so far as his answers confirm the veracity of the points asserted in the articles. His constant repetition of the statement "it contains the truth" is what is expected of him and his explanations of why the articles were true are what the articles are specifically designed to elicit. Indeed, we could turn the observation around. The articles are generated in order to elicit these responses. It is not so much the questions that construct the answers as the desired answers that construct the questions.

It would doubtless be possible to find examples that better satisfy this artificially neat model. Pottell's deposition is noteworthy precisely because it falls short; his responses to the fourth and sixth articles are not exemplary responses. Article four is predicated on the canonical rules regarding the minimum age at which matrimony might legally be contracted. A girl had to be of sufficient age lawfully to contract marriage. This age was specified as twelve, hence the third article. But canon law qualified this by allowing some modest variation whereby the minimum age might actually be a little younger than twelve in such cases as the somewhat early onset of puberty.[18] Pottell could simply have said that "he knows not to depose"—this was an acceptable answer given that the same set of articles was regularly used with several witnesses, although in fact some witnesses knew of only some of the matters raised, others of different matters. Failure to offer specific information on some of the articles presented need not detract from a witness's credibility. In fact Pottell tries to demonstrate the truth of the article's statement: he took gifts from John to Alice and he took back Alice's greetings to him!

In response to the sixth article that demands testimony that the couple had reached or nearly reached puberty, had slept together, and that John had subsequently sent Alice gifts, Pottell's response seems more focused.[19] He made the bed in which they lay together alone and naked. He insinuated that Alice was not yet old enough to have a sexual relationship, but she responded in a way that implied that she was already having such a relationship and was indeed of age so to do. These are useful answers. A sharp eye would realize that Pottell never claimed actually to have seen the couple in bed together, merely that he had made the bed ready for them. Alice's reported response does not explicitly say she had had sexual intercourse with John, but that is its implication. Her words would, however, serve to demonstrate her desire to be married; the testimony is designed to show that for Alice at least the marriage was consensual, precisely the point that article five intended to demonstrate. What then of the issue of gifts given by John to Alice after the alleged consummation? Pottell is apparently silent when prompted by article six, but paradoxically eloquent on the matter when prompted by article four on puberty. It may be that Pottell said something of the same again, but the clerk suppressed it as repetitious, but why suppress the information at the point that it becomes relevant? Or maybe the clerk has scrambled the deposition through a certain carelessness in translating his contemporaneous notes into fair copy. Both explanations are possible, but neither seems entirely plausible.

A third explanation is superficially more straightforward. It is not the record that has been compromised; rather it is Pottell's capacity to answer the question. The depositions are substantially accurate. Pottell answered the questions as he thought appropriate, but, as a humble menial employed to run errands, he was fazed by the procedure of the court and was stressed by the sense that if he performed badly his job might be on the line, so ended up saying some of the right things in the wrong places. But there were right things to say, so why did Pottell get confused? The clue is in the initial similarity of the fourth and the sixth articles. Four is designed to establish that Alice had achieved puberty when she ratified the contract. Six is designed first to establish that Alice (and John) had achieved puberty (or nearly so) when they slept together—the alleged act of ratification. The two thus have similarities and could easily be confused by an agitated witness, but only if that witness had been expecting them. Why should a witness anticipate a particular question? There are two possibilities. One, the witness logically assumes that certain questions are likely and so prepares answers that are then rehearsed when like questions actually materialize. This does not explain, however, Pottell's seemingly inappropriate response to article four. Two, the witness knows what questions to expect and has been briefed accordingly. In this case, Pottell expected the sixth article and thought he heard it when the fourth article was read to him, hence his apparently irrelevant account of the gifts he took to Alice. When subsequently confronted with the anticipated article, Pottell offers material that could just as well have been used in respect of article four, but includes his remembrance of making the bed no doubt prompted by the "they lay together naked in the one bed" of the article.

Pottell it seems gave the right answers to the wrong questions. It may even be that Pottell's unhelpful response to article five had really been intended for article four. Pottell's fault is that he has learned his part, but has muffed his cues. If there are parts, then there must be playwrights. The one person who would have been best placed to brief the witnesses in advance of their giving testimony would be the proctor or advocate acting on behalf the plaintiff since it would be he who would have drawn up the initial libel from which the articles were derived. He would have been unusually well placed to see that the questions posed and the answers given allowed the evidence to be communicated in a way that best addressed the canon-legal hurdles presented by the action and would carry the most weight with the court. In this case, John Marrays's action was for restitution of conjugal rights. To prove the case in law, Marrays would have to show that he was indeed lawfully married to Alice prior to her being taken away. To do this, he had to show that there was a valid, witnessed contract made whilst Alice was below the age of consent and that Alice had subsequently ratified this on achieving, or at least approaching, her majority, ratification here being through consummation. Pottell had a useful role to play here. He had witnessed, but not heard, the original contract. He had been told Alice's age by her mother and two of her godparents. He had privileged access to Alice at Kennythorpe in his apparent capacity as John's factotum. (Pottell's deposition fails to identify him as a servant of John Marrays, but he patently performs a variety of menial tasks at his behest.) He had direct knowledge of the gifts that John had given and Alice received. He had made the bed in which the couple had allegedly consummated their relationship. He had conversed with Alice and Alice's replies conveyed that she wanted to be married to John and that she had slept with him.

We can conclude that Pottell's recorded responses are determined by a number of factors. They are not solely constructed by the questions put to him, nor are they determined by the canon lawyer who helped frame them because aspects of Pottell's testimony are unique and personal to Pottell. They are not solely the product of the way the clerk has recorded and edited the responses; he has clearly intervened and imposed some standard phraseology, but he has not attempted to "correct" Pottell's garbling of his responses. These responses are not, however, Pottell's unmediated testimony. The following schematic diagram attempts to represent graphically something of the network of agents and factors that explain how the witness's "experience," that is, his or her particular involvement in the events at the heart of the litigation, come to be represented as the recorded deposition. Indeed, we might talk in terms akin to Natalie Davis's account of a process of negotiation between a number of different agents.[20]

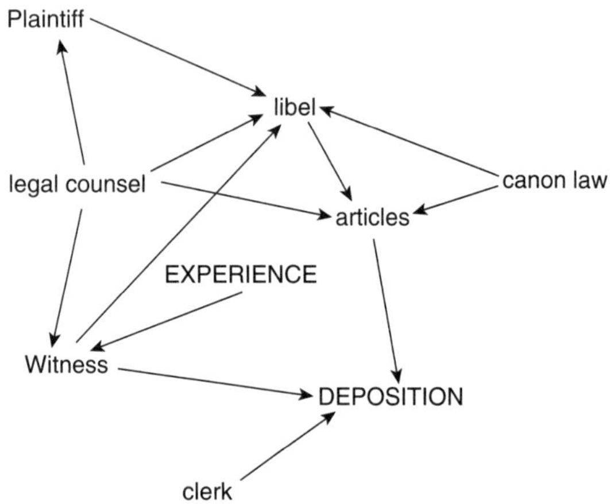

It is not possible to tease out any one agent or factor as being of overriding importance in this process culminating in the recording of the deposition. All have a part to play. Any given agent or factor operates only in tandem with one or more other factors or agents. The articles upon which the witness is examined, for example, are drawn up on the basis of the libel in order to highlight key elements of the narrative that would satisfy the canon-legal basis of the action. The libel itself, however, is negotiated between the plaintiff, whose unresolved grievance is the basis for litigation, and the legal counsel engaged by the plaintiff. In helping frame the libel, the legal counsel is necessarily mindful of these same canon-legal requirements, but presumably also of what likely witnesses themselves knew of the circumstances and what elements within the narrative they could vouch for. Because the procedure of the court was that evidence was admitted almost exclusively in the form of depositions from witnesses, the parties themselves were effectively mute beyond their initial libel or replication.[21] The case presented in the libel rested entirely on the degree to which the various elements of the narrative could be substantiated by witnesses. It follows that the knowledge of prospective witnesses must have formed part of the basis of the libel. A degree of circularity is introduced here: the knowledge of the witness informs the libel and hence the articles; the witness is questioned on the articles with a view to substantiating the libel. This circularity is entirely logical: the ability of one or other party to prove their case depended on their ability to call upon witnesses who could verify the substance of their libel.

We have already discussed the complexities of the relationship between the witness as respondent, the clerk as recorder and compiler of the depositions that are generated from these verbal responses, the articles as providing the framework for the witness's responses, and the legal counsel in advising or even coaching the witness in how best to respond to each article in turn. This is a complex, dynamic interaction. Although we may offer differing evaluations of the various power relationships involved that would in any case change according to the gender, age, and social status of the witness concerned, we can only begin to make sense of the final deposition if we allow that all these interdependent elements carry weight. The corollary of this is that the experience of the witness and the person of the witness are real and constituent elements that we dismiss at our peril.

An analogy for the larger process whereby the depositions are realized in court would be a play developed by a process of improvisation derived from the experiences of the various actors. There is a predetermined convention that shapes the order in which the actors (deponents) appear and there is likewise an authorial voice (legal counsel) that helps give an overall shape and direction to the narrative. That narrative is, however, voiced by a range of different actors, each of whom is drawing from their own experience and knowledge and each of whom has the advantage of playing themselves. Some actors, as we shall see, are more skilful than others. A few play their roles with a particular authority and conviction that ultimately derives from the fact that they play their own roles. These parts have come down to us as written texts that only imperfectly represent the live performance. In so much as the court action was like a drama, however, the ability of individual actors to remember their lines or to perform as intended could not ultimately be controlled.

William Pottell's deposition may once again be used to explore these points. Pottell's "experience" is intrinsic to his position as a lackey of John Marrays. He accompanies his master to the occasion of the formal contract in St Mary's Abbey, but must look on from a doorway at sufficient distance that he was unable to hear the words exchanged. He runs errands, taking "clothes, kerchiefs, and other necessaries" to Alice when instructed to do so by John. He makes the bed up for the couple when John himself comes to Kennythorpe. Pottell's access to Alice follows from the errands he runs and is probably sanctioned only because Pottell is John Marrays's man and Alice still a child. Conventional fears of impropriety that would normally disallow such unsupervised interaction between a man and an unmarried woman of gentle rank are dispelled. Pottell is Alice's social inferior, the employee of her husband-to-be, and so in a sense, bound also to her; he could hardly be thought so bold and so foolhardy as to try and take advantage of Alice's innocence. Alice herself is also a child, too young (and perhaps too well brought up) to behave inappropriately herself. His access, however, does permit him to converse with Alice other than in a way that reinforces the distance in age, social status, and gender that separate them. He teases her by repeatedly [sepius] asking why her master stays away from her. His wish—"May you grow up sufficiently that he is able to do with you as is fitting"—adopts the bantering style that adults sometimes adopt when addressing children. It also uses a construction used by social inferiors to flatter their superiors. This, however, is no innocent joke; the sexual innuendo is very much that of the male addressing the female, but it also here the adult male addressing a girl who might be thought too young properly to grasp or understand the innuendo.

We actually know one further piece of information about Pottell. According to his fellow witness, Adam Porter, a gatekeeper at St Mary's Abbey, the two were charged with conveying Alice to Kennythorpe immediately following the contract. It is interesting that Pottell himself does not provide this information, which would at least have served to strengthen Adam Porter's testimony. The reason is simple enough. Unlike Pottell, Adam Porter is only able to offer hearsay evidence; he knew things because people told them to him, not because he had witnessed them. His accompanying Alice to Kennythorpe is the only moment when he directly participates in the drama, so it becomes integral to his testimony. For Pottell, however, it is of less importance and from the perspective of making the case according to the exacting criteria of the canon law, it becomes redundant. We see here then something of the way in which Pottell's own "story" was edited in negotiation with legal counsel to create the most effective responses to the articles. We will see it again in other testimonies.

CHAPTER 3

ELLEN TALIOUR: GENDER AND THE REMEMBRANCE OF TIMES PAST

> *That same Martinmas this witness left William's service and then Emma de Huntyngton, William's wife, wished to hire this witness that she should be John's nurse and this witness responded that she loved her son just as much as Ellen loved hers and consequently she did not want her son to die on account of Ellen's son and so she refused to be John's nurse.*
>
> (BI, CP.E.89/4)

So testified Ellen Taliour in late January 1366 in one of the most emotionally charged and moving passages to be found within the medieval records of the Court of York. Ellen was the wife of a Thomas Taliour and resident at the time of the case in the adjacent village of Skelton. This was the second time she had been called as a witness. The first time she had given evidence in respect of the birth of Alice de Rouclif. This time she was questioned about the birth of Alice's older brother, who died in infancy before Alice was born. Her task was to help demonstrate that Alice, whose brother John had been born about sixteen or seventeen months previous to her some thirteen years before, had not yet reached her twelfth birthday at the time ofher testimony. Remembrance of Alice's birth and, as here, that of her deceased older brother, were thus crucial benchmarks in a case that rested on whether Alice had or had not achieved her canonical majority. As a witness appearing (in effect) for Sir Brian de Rouclif, Ellen Taliour was of the latter camp.

Ellen's testimony is colored by the fact that she has a particular case to make. In so doing, Ellen was going against Alice's mother, her former employer. We cannot always know why individual witnesses supported one party or the other. Those who were tenants of Sir Brian presumably took his side out of a simple concern for their own livelihood. In other instances familial ties readily account for allegiance. Thus the support given by the Wascelynes or Dom. William Marrays and similarly John Fische and Robert de Rouclif for John Marrays is self-evident. Ellen's support for Sir Brian runs at first sight contrary to expectation and so raises the possibility that her motives may have been personal.[1] Perhaps her time in the employ of Gervase and Ellen de Rouclif had been difficult. There is some reason to think this because Ellen Taliour was hired at the time of Alice's birth to be her wetnurse. For exactly three weeks Alice was fed by Ellen, but a fever then obliged Ellen to stop suckling her charge. In accordance with custom and the contemporary labor legislation, however, Ellen had been contracted to serve a full year.[2] Because her inability to continue her duties as a wetnurse were a consequence of illness rather than neglect on Ellen's part, her employers were obliged to continue her employment. Finding work for a supernumerary servant who had been employed in the first instance because she was a nursing mother with milk to sell and not because of her qualities and capacity as a household servant may well have been the cause of friction. It is highly unlikely that such employers would otherwise have hired a single mother with a young child to support, who may have had to be accommodated in the family home. These, however, are speculative observations. Ellen's importance is not that she may have had a grudge, but that Sir Brian thought to use her as witness.

This last observation begs a number of questions. Ellen Taliour was, at the time of the case, a married woman. She was not, however, at least in terms of her past, a model of female respectability such as might otherwise have lent a certain authority to her testimony. Her own testimony shows that she was a servant—hence implicitly a single woman—who whilst in the employment of William de Huntyngton gave birth to an illegitimate baby boy. As was common in this region, her contract ran from Martinmas to Martinmas (11 November) and her child was born 24 July. She must therefore have conceived her child soon after her contract had begun. One is tempted to suspect that William de Huntyngton was the father. On leaving William's service, and as a nursing mother, she was then asked by her former mistress if she would take a position as wetnurse in respect of the newly born John de Rouclif, the subject of the quotation with which we began. On this occasion she declined the position, but accepted when Alice de Rouclif was subsequently born since her own son was by then old enough no longer to be dependent on his mother's milk. How Ellen had managed in the intervening period, we do not know. Nor do we know anything of her subsequent to her leaving the de Rouclif household at Pentecost 1354 or 1355 save that another witness, John de Alne, claimed to have heard that Ellen had committed adultery with a Skelton man. The accusation of adultery probably means that Ellen was by this stage already married, though it could apply if her alleged partner was married. We cannot know if this claim, made with a view to destroy the credibility of Ellen as a witness and hence her testimony, had any justification, but it was presumably a credible claim.[3] Ellen Taliour was no model of feminine virtue. She was the very opposite of what would otherwise appear the "ideal" witness: mature, male, well-to-do, and of irreproachable moral standing.

Ellen's testimony needs to be placed within a larger context. Taking matrimonial cases from the York *curia* for the period 1350–99, but excluding this present case, male witnesses outnumbered female by nearly three to one. As we noticed in the previous chapter, if only cases associated with rural society are considered, this disparity increases markedly, the equivalent ratio being over seven men to every one woman witness. It is very hard not to conclude that, whatever the perception of the court itself, litigants were prejudiced against the use of female witnesses and that these prejudices were more deeply entrenched in rural society than urban. Ellen Taliour's appearance as a witness cannot be divorced from this context. Three conclusions are possible. It could be that Ellen and a number of other female witnesses in this case were called because impoverished village women were comparatively easy to bribe or cow into giving false testimony. It could be that their deployment represents a strategy of last resort: in the absence of male witnesses to the key events in dispute, the parties were obliged to turn to women. Both these possibilities beg the question why the same pattern or patterns appear not so obviously to have applied in respect of other near contemporary marriage cases. The third possibility, superficially the least likely, but in fact the one preferred here, is that in relation to the particular evidential needs of this case, the testimony of women was actually preferred.[4] We need not, however, regard these three possibilities as mutually exclusive. For example, pressure and financial incentives may have been used to secure women witnesses precisely because these witnesses were in demand.

Ellen Taliour's appearance as a witness can be accounted for with reference to any one of these explanations. Unlike some other deponents, we know nothing directly of her economic standing. Her background hardly suggests affluence. Her husband may well have been a tailor, but again we would not expect a small village tailor to be a man of any substance. She is not described as being a tenant of Sir Brian, but a major local landowner who is prepared to use force to break into other people's houses and abduct minors is hardly to be resisted with impunity. She could have been bribed. She could have been cowed. Turning to the second explanation, Ellen offered crucial testimony regarding the date of Alice's birth as someone present at the birth. Indeed, according to Ellen's first deposition, only one other person, a local woman who had become senile by the time of the case, was in attendance at the birth. The paucity of helpers at the birth may be surprising, even suspicious, but that only other women were present to assist the mother at the time of her delivery was absolutely normal. Only women could testify to the actual birth because the culture barred the presence of men save in the most exceptional circumstances.[5] Ellen also provided the telling detail that the birth was located in a basement room, an observation that tallies with what is known of premodern birthing practice, where a womb-like birthing chamber was kept warm, dark, and enclosed. It accords well with a description of childbed located in "a downstairs parlor [in bassam parluram]" found in another case a century later.[6]

Ellen Taliour's alleged eyewitness account of the time of Alice's birth is undoubtedly valuable testimony that could not have been given by a male witness, but in fact she was but one of a considerable number of witnesses who gave evidence relating to the time of Alice's birth. None, however, claimed to have been present at the birth. It follows that Ellen's deployment as a witness cannot be explained primarily in terms of a paucity of alternative male witnesses. Indeed we have only to turn to the depositions respecting proofs of age made under feudal law to find the testimonies of men respecting the time of birth, and hence age, of heirs and heiresses. The feudal jurisdiction demanded the testimony of males. The canon-legal jurisdiction, based on an understanding of the fundamental equality of male and female in the eyes of God, did not. Despite the prejudices that still militated against the use of female witnesses, it is striking that in this case the majority of witnesses testifying to the births of Alice and her deceased older brother were female. Set against the evidence of the feudal courts, it is hard not to conclude that the testimony of women was actually preferred. (It should be noted here that an even larger group of women were originally lined up to testify. It is not uncommon to find the names of witnesses listed on the back of the articles or interrogatories and this is true here. Twenty-four names are listed on the verso of John Marrays's initial articles (CP.E.89/26), but of these names, ten, of whom nine are female, are not matched by depositions.)[7]

This observation can been located within the larger context of matrimonial litigation from the Court of York during the whole of the fourteenth and fifteenth centuries. Only a handful of other cases, from a sample of nearly 150, show any significant grouping of female deponents. These cases are all impotence cases where an action is brought to secure an annulment on the grounds of the husband's permanent physical incapacity.[8] In such cases the court adopted the procedure of requiring that the man's alleged impotence be tested by a jury of seven women. These women subsequently testify to the court. In one sense this pattern follows the second of our "explanations," that women testify in the absence of suitable male witnesses. Given that the procedure was that the women attempt sexually to arouse the man by cracking lewd jokes whilst baring their breasts and genitals, this explanation fits well enough. But the issue is not so much that the man's virility (or lack thereof) could be tested by a woman in a way that would not be possible by a man, but that there were women who were willing and able to provide this service to the court.[9] It appears, perhaps unsurprisingly, that these women were not the matrons noted in the canon-legal treatises, but sex workers. It is thus not reputable married women and widows who testify, but women at the very bottom of the moral hierarchy—women who would otherwise be challenged as untrustworthy witnesses because morally tainted. Their testimony is not just allowed, it is required; the women employed in impotence cases are thus described not as "meretrix" (whore), but rather as "bona fama" (of good repute).[10]

The present case does not pertain to impotence. Some of the witnesses, including Ellen Taliour, may be poor women. Their moral standing may be open to challenge, as was Ellen's, but they were peasants, not urban sex workers. A more pertinent parallel would be other cases where one or other party attempts to disprove the validity of an alleged marriage by claiming that the marriage was contracted below canonical age. Such actions are in fact very unusual: only three other such cases have been noticed for the period before 1500. In the earliest of these, Draycote c. Crane, four male deponents made statements respecting the ages of a couple at marriage, but their knowledge of their births is entirely hearsay. The issue here in fact was the unwillingness of William Crane to be married.[11] The extant depositions in the next case that is almost contemporary with the Rouclif case, are badly damaged, but all those that can be identified were made by men.[12] Enough survives to show that the case made here was similarly not whether William Aunger was underage, but whether he had ratified a contract made when underage. This is a subtle, but significant variation on the Rouclif case. The witnesses in the third such case are likewise exclusively male. Once again, ages are asserted, but little is done to substantiate them. Despite the limitations of the extant evidence, it appears once more that the issue in this case was less Cecily Thweng's youth as the unwillingness of her betrothed to ratify the marriage.[13]

Marriage cases where one or both parties contracting were underage are clearly very unusual. This present case is unique in that the central question was not so much Alice's willingness to ratify her spousals, though this was still an issue, as whether she was legally of sufficient age for such ratification to have any validity. What had to be demonstrated before the court, therefore, was not whether the contract had been made whilst one or both parties were underage such that subsequent ratification was a prerequisite of a valid union, but specifically that Alice de Rouclif had or had not achieved her majority by the time of the alleged ratification or abduction. Very precise testimony thus needed to be brought respecting her age and hence of when she was born. In the absence both of birth certificates and baptismal registers, and in accord with the canon-legal convention of proof by deposition rather than by documentary evidence, the resort to the kind of proof of age procedure normal in a feudal context is perhaps to be expected. Such a procedure may well have been familiar to various members of the Rouclif family, stemming as they did from the lower echelons of the aristocracy.[14]

We return to the earlier question. Evidence regarding Alice's birth was pivotal in this case, but why were female witnesses apparently preferred when men could, and in other legal contexts did, testify? It is now clearer that the second of the "explanations" outlined previously is inadequate. The first, that poor female witnesses were more easily bribed or coerced into giving testimony can likewise be shown to be less than conclusive. Bribery and coercion assume that the witness will not speak willingly or, more specifically, will not willingly offer the testimony desired by the party responsible unless by reason of such monetary incentive or constraint. This makes sense where the required testimony departs from the witness's own knowledge or experience. Where these two coincide, it is very hard to see why threats or incentives would be necessary, unless, of course, the witness is intimidated by the opposing party, a possibility that must be acknowledged.

All who testified agreed that Alice's birthday fell on the Saturday before the first Sunday in Easter. What was disputed was whether the year of her birth was 1353 or 1354, though the dispute is always couched in terms of how long previous to the case Alice had been born and never by reference to calendar or regnal years.[15] In "remembering" or asserting one of these dates over the other, witnesses were either telling the truth, telling (mistakenly) what they believed to be the truth, or knowingly lying. It is neither credible nor possible that most of the witnesses for the rival parties were knowingly lying. It is possible that all were telling the truth or at least believed that they were telling the truth. On balance the first "explanation" looks flawed, but we have not yet discounted the possibility of corruption and intimidation. This last is hard to discount, but it may well be unwise to assume that female witnesses would have been any more susceptible to intimidation than male in this case or any other. The threat of intimidation may have been real, but it hardly explains the deployment of female witnesses.

The possibility of bribery was something the court was undoubtedly sensitive to. A number of witnesses were evidently asked about their material worth because information relating to this is recorded alongside the initial personal details of a number of witnesses. Thus we find "Alice Sharpe of Rawcliffe, widow, a tenant of Sir Brian de Rouclif, having goods to the value of forty shillings," and "Margery, the wife of John Gregson of Clifton otherwise called Bell, having in goods, allowing for monies owing, scarcely five shillings." Agnes Quystler had "little in goods," Alice, wife of William de Tange, "goods to the value of one mark." It is not just female deponents that are asked: William de Tange admitted to being of the same worth as his wife—probably this represented their shared assets for Isabel de Rouclif, wife of John de Grandesby, is described as "having goods in common" worth in excess of ten marks; Henry Vaux possessed goods to the value of five marks. Female witnesses are, however, very much in the majority. A couple of female witnesses, moreover, were desperately poor: Joan Symkyn Woman admitted to only the clothes on her body, her bed and a small brass pot; Agnes del Polles, a married woman, said she had nothing save a spinning wheel, a pair of cards, and a boy.[16]

The court clearly took interest in the material worth of some comparatively poor female witnesses, but a much smaller number of equivalent male witnesses. It is possible that the court acted on the suspicion that women were particularly vulnerable to bribery qua women, but it is at least as likely that the court's suspicions were roused by the simple fact of poverty. The two cannot, however, be divorced.[17] More women were asked because a rather higher proportion of the female witnesses appeared to be poor. That the court asked questions does not mean that witnesses had anything to hide. It seems hardly likely that either party should have thought it a sensible strategy to save money by bribing supposedly less credible, because female, witnesses rather than male witnesses. The very numbers of witnesses appearing in this case shows that both parties were willing to incur significant costs in pursuing the case. And what was the point of bribing very poor women if their poverty would immediately undermine the credibility of their testimony. Corruption, on closer inspection, seems a feeble explanation.

We are left, therefore, with our third "explanation," that female witnesses were actually preferred. The example of the female sex workers used as deponents in impotence cases is worth returning to here. Known sex workers, whose testimonies were tantamount to confessions of extreme moral laxity and incitement to commit adultery, were presented in court as witnesses of good standing. The validity of a marriage, one of the sacraments of the Church, rested entirely on their depositions. At first sight this appears a topsy-turvy world in which the usual benchmarks of probity are entirely set aside. In fact there are good pragmatic reasons to treat the women's testimony with such gravity. The impotence trial demanded rigorous investigation of the man's capacity to have sex. Given that even after two years of marriage his (presumably) virgin bride had been unable to arouse him, the logic was that only the services of professional sex workers, used to catering for the sexual needs of a range of male clients, would provide a sufficient test. We may in retrospect doubt the psychology of the procedure, but the point remains. These women were credible witnesses, and could indeed be described as "of good standing," because theirs was expert testimony.

A like argument can be made in respect of a number of the women who made depositions regarding Alice's or John's births. Thirty-five witnesses gave testimony in respect of the births of either or both of Alice and John de Rouclif. Of these, all but four were female, a ratio of only 0.13 males to every female. The four male witnesses may be briefly described. John de Melsay was one of John de Rouclif's two godfathers, being the one who lent his name to the infant and hence the more important. Henry Vaux was in service in the household of Gervase de Rouclif from early June, that is, about the time Alice would have been conceived, to the following Martinmas, by which time Ellen de Rouclif's pregnancy would have become obvious. Like Ellen Taliour's, his testimony conflicts with the case supported by his former mistress, but by the time of the case, Vaux was a tenant of Sir Brian. This last is true also of the remaining two male witnesses, William de Tange and Robert Thewed. Both were the husbands of women who also testified. In a sense they reinforce their wives' testimonies, though in fact Robert Thewed and his wife Margery gave rather different, but not conflicting accounts. Robert, like William de Tange and his wife Alice, remembered Alice's birth by reference to the birth of his own child. Margery Thewed, however, who then worked as a servant in Sir Brian's garden alongside William de Tange, remembered the birth of William's son, but failed to mention her own baby. Perhaps she forgot. Perhaps she overlooked the obvious.

As we have just seen, some of the thirty-one female witnesses were married, but only the two just noticed had their testimony supported by their husbands. The implications are twofold. First, the testimony of the women was normally considered sufficient in its own right. Second, in the two cases where husbands were also called, the husbands were at least as likely to be reinforcing their wives' testimonies as the other way around. This tends to add weight to the view that the testimony of women was sought not in the absence of men, but rather because it was actually preferred. Only two women who testified in the case as a whole did not give evidence respecting the birth of one or other of the Rouclif children. These were Anabilla Wascelyne and her daughter Alice de Rolleston, who were key witnesses to Alice's time at Kennythorpe, her attitude toward John Marrays and the alleged consummation. The fact that thirty-one other women testified as witnesses to the children's births indicates that this was their key function. It is the argument here that it was also their expert function.

At first sight some of the evidence presented would seem pretty slight in comparison with that of Ellen Taliour. Eufemia, wife of John son of Elias de Rouclif, who was described as a tenant of Alice, but who gave testimony in support of Sir Brian, knew of Alice's birth only "from the relation of women." Rather more authoritative is the testimony of Lady Margery de Rouclif. Lady Margery was able to locate in time John de Rouclif's birth date by reference variously to the birth of a grandchild, to "the dates of writings and indentures by which she demised certain of her lands at farm," and lastly "by the births of other children at Rawcliffe." We may also note how a couple of women tied their recollection to the visual mnemonic of having seen the infant Alice in her cradle.[18] Maud de Herthill, who claimed to have been present at John's birth, was in Rawcliffe "at the time of Alice's birth and saw her in her cradle." Anabilla Pynder, also of Rawcliffe, remembered seeing John in his cradle and subsequently saw Alice "in her cradle and knew her from that time up until the present day." Margery Gregson, alias Bell, recalled that "when Alice was born it was discussed among her friends [i.e., family] and neighbors that Gervase's wife had given birth to a daughter that was Alice." Agnes Quysteler, who had only moved to Rawcliffe a couple of years after Alice's birth, knew the date of Alice's birth only from her neighbors at Rawcliffe. Beatrix Milner, who moved from Rawcliffe to Clifton soon after Alice's birth, remembered her birth by reason of her moving, but also "by the telling of Ellen Grigge who was present at Alice's birth, Henry Vaux [one of the few male witnesses] who served Alice's father at the time her mother was pregnant with her, and other neighbors of Rawcliffe." Alice Porter, then living in neighboring Skelton, learned of Alice's birth in precisely the same way.

A number of observations follow. The witnesses demonstrate, and the court implicitly believed, that childbirth was a subject women were interested in and knowledgeable about by reason of their gender. Eufemia's account of Alice's birth "from the relation of women" no longer appears to be the rather slight circumstantial evidence we might anachronistically understand it to be. Whereas in other contexts the conversation of women might be disparaged, here it represented the exchange of information that was very particularly their province.[19] Information about the births of village children was readily exchanged between female neighbors. Lady Margery knew of the births of numbers of her Rawcliffe neighbors' children such that she was able to use them as a way of locating in time John de Rouclif's birth. The birth of a child to the inhabitants of the big house was a particular point of conversation: "it was discussed among her friends and neighbors that Gervase's wife had given birth to a daughter." If Agnes Quysteler is to be believed, they were still talking about it some two years later. A number of village women even got to see the infant lying in the cradle, presumably within the family home and hence presumably by invitation, an indication of their having some ties of intimacy. Alice's aunt, Margery de Rouclif, came to see her new niece "lying in her cradle" the very day after she was born. Maud de Herthill had been a servant of Ellen de Rouclif at the time of her marriage and was present at the birth of her first child. Ellen de Rouclif was sufficiently friendly with Anabilla Pynder that she sent her a text "said to be good for pregnant women" the day before she was delivered of a son.[20] Some sixteen months later she asked Anabilla to be a wetnurse for Alice, but Anabilla declined. Interestingly despite, or perhaps because of, these former ties, both Maud and Anabilla gave testimony in support of Sir Brian. Maud acknowledged that she had been asked to appear as a witness by Sir Brian, but claimed she "was not instructed." Ellen Taliour, herself a prospective wetnurse, had likewise seen John in his cradle when she had first moved to Rawcliffe. John would then have been about four months.

Another way in which village women remembered the time around the births of the two Rouclif children was by reference to the observation of Ellen de Rouclif's pregnancies and subsequent churchings. Ellen, widow of Elias de Rouclif, recalled seeing a heavily pregnant Ellen de Rouclif shortly before she gave birth to Alice. Margery Gregson likewise had noticed Ellen pregnant with Alice. The ceremony of churching, the ritual reincorporation of the mother into the community following the pollution associated with childbirth, took place in the mother's parish church a month after delivery. In the case of Ellen de Rouclif, churching necessarily took her into the York suburb of Bootham to the parochial chapel of St Olave. Agnes del Polles saw Ellen come and go in respect of her churching following the delivery of John from her home in St Marygate, the road down which the church was located. Agnes, subsequently wife of Robert de Richmond, but then a servant in the household of Robert de Rouclif in Bootham, likewise observed her. The passage to and fro of a party of well-to-do women in their best dresses was doubtless a matter of interested comment. Alice's aunt, Margery de Rouclif, was personally present on that same occasion as were Cecily de Shupton, who stated that she attended Ellen at both her deliveries, Agnes de Fritheby, and Isabel de Strensall.

Unlike childbirth, the churching ritual was not one that was exclusively attended by women. Robert Thewed claimed to have been present at Ellen's churching in respect of Alice, though he was the only male witness so to do. Clearly there was likewise nothing to prevent men from witnessing the women going to or coming away from the service in just the same way as Agnes del Polles and Agnes de Richmond. Men were similarly in a position to observe the physical manifestation of pregnancy, as did Henry Vaux who remembered that Ellen de Rouclif was pregnant with Alice at Martinmas, the point that he left service in the Rouclif household. Ellen would then have been five months pregnant. Again the issue is not that women testified because men were not available to testify, but that women's testimony seems actually to have been preferred. Women's supposed interest in and knowledge of childbirth is here extended to matters connected to childbirth, in this instance pregnancy and the ritual of churching. In feudal proofs of age depositions, men testified as much to the party that followed as the churching itself, the implication being that this event was thought to be of more interest to, and hence more memorable by, men. Robert Thewed stated that he had been invited to the feast that followed the churching because of his friendship with Gervase de Rouclif, but he had also been to the churching itself.[21]

As we have just seen, knowledge of the births of John and of Alice de Rouclif may have been conveyed by a variety of means. At least as important—indeed, given the need to establish a precise chronology for Alice's birth and hence age, more important—was the mechanism whereby witnesses located this knowledge in time. Again we can draw on the concept of expertise. Many of the women witnesses correlated the times of one or other of Ellen de Rouclif's deliveries with the births of their own children. Thus Agnes the Ald testified that "exactly fortnight before the day of Alice's birth this witness gave birth to a son at Rawcliffe, now dead." Likewise Agnes de Fritheby recalled how she "gave birth to a daughter, still living, on the eve of St Lawrence following Alice's birth who is now twelve years of age." Lettice de Melsay referred to both the conception and the birth of her son, but this did not form part of her husband's testimony. For women the experience of childbirth was sufficiently memorable in itself. For mothers who may well have experienced a number of pregnancies and deliveries, it further provided a frame of reference by which they could locate specific births.[22]

This last is not specifically stated in any of the depositions, but is implicit. It is the rationale for asking about the relationship between the timing of Alice's birth and that of her deceased older brother that is a crucial part of the conduct of this case. It is hinted at in the rather sad testimony proffered by Isabel de Strensall. Isabel remembered John de

Rouclif's birth from her attendance at his mother's churching and the subsequent feast, but she located this in time by the fact she was then pregnant and by the fact that she moved to Bootham after the churching. Here pregnancy rather than childbirth as such helps fix past events, but Isabel's deposition elaborates on this pregnancy: "she does not know whether with a boy or a girl, nor at what time of year she gave birth to the child."[23] Isabel's mental lapse is presumably a reflection on the experience of many medieval mothers who endured repeated pregnancies, miscarriages, deliveries, and deaths of children whilst still in infancy, but it also indicates that the births of children could be located chronologically by reference to a process of mental mapping around gender and birth order. Margery Bell's testimony is a little more explicit: "this witness gave birth to her most recent child on the morrow of St Luke before Alice's birth which, if he were alive now, would be twelve years and approaching thirteen years of age."

Excluding Ellen de Rouclif's own deposition, the experience of giving birth forms part of the testimony of twelve of the witnesses. A further five women remembered the births of other people's children to locate the births of the two Rouclif infants. William de Tange's recollection of becoming a father is in this context unique. Once again the argument could be made that men were no less capable of remembering and locating in time past events by reference to the births of the children they had fathered. The choice of women as witnesses thus again appears deliberate. So why was women's testimony preferred? On one level the experience of childbirth, marked out by the process of confinement and subsequent reincorporation through the ceremony of purification, was much more significant in the lives of women as mothers. Childbirth itself was memorable because painful. This was Eve's punishment for the Fall.[24] But the experience of pain was also a way of helping to imprint information on the memory or simply of remembering a particular event. Corporal punishment was readily inflicted on children that they might learn correct behavior. Small boys might also be struck when taken on a tour of the parish bounds in order to help them recall the route when they were grown up.[25] On another level, women were deemed the custodians of knowledge about the birth of children because, as we have already seen, these were matters women were held to be interested in and because the care and rearing of children fell so much within their realm.

One particular birth is noticed several times because it was intrinsically memorable. On 25 August prior to Alice's birth, Maud de Herthill gave birth to a daughter, still living at the time of the case. Although it is not mentioned in Maud's own depositions, the delivery had evidently been problematic since the child only survived as a consequence of the intervention of Simon de Folifayt.[26] This was recalled by the widow, Alice Sharpe and by Margaret de Folifayt, Simon's sister. Joan Symkyn Woman also attended the birth, but failed to describe Simon's role. It is noteworthy that though Margaret de Folifayt was called to testify, Simon was not. The value of Margaret's testimony was that she was able to relate the birth of the de Herthill baby to that of Alice. The former was memorable because of her own brother's life-saving intervention, but its importance was only as a chronological reference against which Alice's birth could be set. So long as Simon would be seen as a less credible witness for the actual time of Alice's birth, since, as a male, he would be thought less likely to have taken an interest in the matter, his testimony would carry little weight. Simon's absence reinforces the point that in matters relating to childbirth, women were the experts. Males played at most brief walk-on roles.

Ellen Taliour's testimony shares common ground with others just discussed, in that, she uses her own experience of maternity to locate in time the births of John and Alice. It also introduces us to three other mnemonic elements, that is servanthood, with its fixed terms of contract, migration, and the gender-specific element of wetnursing. In fact these three elements are here interrelated and to no small extent consequent upon Ellen becoming a mother. Each element will initially be considered separately in respect of all the witnesses in the case before returning to Ellen.

The later medieval practice, reinforced by the contemporary labor legislation, of hiring servants on long contracts, frequently of a year's duration and based around customary hiring dates is well documented and fully reflected in this case.[27] Besides Ellen, seven deponents made reference to their having worked as servants. All bar one happen to be female, although near contemporary poll tax evidence would suggest that in the countryside male servants tended to outnumber female.[28] Their involvement in the case is only in part determined by their position as servants or former servants: in several instances their service brought them into close contact with the de Rouclif family; most were also mothers. There is no reason to think that female servants were as such specifically favored as witnesses.[29]

The length of service with an individual employer suggested by these witnesses in fact frequently runs well beyond a year. Ellen Taliour herself, as remarked earlier, served only a year with the de Rouclifs, but it is likely that she would have been hired considerably longer had she been able to fulfill her original role as a wetnurse. Emmot Norice, who was employed as Alice's wetnurse in succession to Ellen, served the de Rouclifs for three years. Agnes Gervaus Woman recalled that she served Gervase de Rouclif for two years. Agnes del Polles stated that she was in service to Robert de

Rouclif for four years.[30] Maud de Herthill was currently a servant at the time of her deposition. She had been Ellen de Rouclif's servant for six months from the time of Ellen's marriage, though the deposition renders it ambiguous as to whether she had also served her prior to her marriage. She returned to work for Ellen again after an absence of eighteen months, serving for at least a further year, but perhaps longer; Maud had a child in later August, some nine months into what would have been her second year of service, but her testimony leaves it unclear as to whether she was still employed by Ellen at that point.

The commencement of service in the case of Ellen Taliour and Emmot Norice, taken on as wetnurses, was necessarily dictated by the needs of a baby and the accident of its nativity, not the pattern of customary hiring dates. Of the other servants we may note that Agnes del Polles commenced her service at Christmas and Maud de Herthill at Martinmas. Henry Vaux, who served Gervase de Rouclif, commenced his employment on the feast of the nativity of St John the Baptist (10 June), but left again the following Martinmas. We have already seen that Ellen Taliour's earlier employment as William de Huntyngton's servant ran from Martinmas to Martinmas. Other cases from the York court confirm that Martinmas was easily the most common and hence most important hiring date north of the Trent. This limited evidence also demonstrates that other hiring dates operated and that contracts lasting only about half a year were possible.[31] It is these hiring dates that in the instances just cited serve as chronological benchmarks against which other events might be set.

Migration served much the same function, punctuating people's lives in ways that were readily memorable or, more importantly, credibly memorable, hence their use by a number of deponents. Several witnesses specifically use the moments they moved from living in one place to another to help anchor past events. Thus John de Melsay, who was John de Rouclif's godfather, and his wife Lettice both locate John's birth with reference to their moving from Shipton to Houghton about two years later. Isabel de Strensall retraced her migration history to locate in time the birth of her own child and the birth of John de Rouclif some months earlier: after her own churching she had moved to Bootham; two years later she had moved into York itself, her home for twelve years—she is described as living in Jubbergate at the commencement of her deposition. Henry Vaux, still resident in his native Rawcliffe at the time of his deposition, was not actually a migrant, but his pilgrimage to St James, presumably at Compostella, served as a like benchmark. He recalled returning "from St James a fortnight before the feast of the nativity of St John the Baptist twelve years ago."

Ellen Taliour also used aspects of her migration history to map out events surrounding the births of John and Alice de Rouclif. Her story begins with her year in service with William de Huntyngton, a prosperous apothecary living in York's Petergate, but who also possessed lands in Bootham and Huntington.[32] Her contract ended at Martinmas and the following Lent she moved to Rawcliffe where she lived for the next three years. It was during that three-year sojourn that Ellen spent a year working in the de Rouclif household. These removals thus help provide a chronological framework for the births of John de Rouclif, shortly before her term of service with William de Huntyngton finished, and of Alice, about a year after her arrival in Rawcliffe. Ellen's remembrance of service and of migration do not really explain her importance as a witness. Her particular value lay in her position, albeit fleetingly, as Alice's nurse and in her earlier refusal to act as nurse to the newborn John de Rouclif.

Two other women testified in relation to nursing Alice de Rouclif. Anabilla Pynder had given birth to a son who had been born at Martinmas. It is almost certain that her baby was born out of wedlock. At the time of her deposition, Anabilla appears to have been unmarried and was living with her mother. Since Alice was born in the March of the year but one following, Anabilla's child would have been some sixteen months old when Ellen de Rouclif approached her to be Alice's wetnurse. Anabilla refused for "it seemed to her that her son was too young to be taken off milk." Ellen Taliour, as our initial quotation demonstrates, had reacted in like fashion when asked to suckle John de Rouclif when her own infant would have been less than four months: "this witness responded that she loved her son just as much as Ellen loved hers and consequently she did not want her son to die on account of Ellen's son." Ellen's robust and emotionally charged response rings out across more than six centuries. No doubt they were designed to ring out within the Court of York—so far as verbal testimony reduced to written deposition can be said to ring out. Ellen subsequently agreed to be nurse to Alice de Rouclif, by which time her son would have been just over eighteen months.

Ellen Taliour was Alice's nurse only briefly. She went down with a fever after three weeks and had to stop feeding her charge. Her position was immediately taken by the aptly named Emmot Norice (Nurse), whose own infant had died the day before Alice's birth. She fed Alice for three years at which point Alice was presumably fully weaned, but since she was still known as "Norice," even though she had subsequently moved to Huby, her career as a wetnurse must have ran on.[33] The ostensible value of Ellen's testimony, as that of the other two women, is that their employment or the request for their employment coincided with the births of the de Rouclif children and thus helped locate them in time. But other considerations are also pertinent. The ability to suckle an infant is again quintessentially an area of women's expertise; it is specific to women as mothers. As mothers both Anabilla Pynder and Ellen Taliour expressed the deepest of maternal emotions when asked to act as wetnurses at a time they considered their own babies too young to be weaned. The depositions deliberately give full voice to these emotions. Anabilla talks in terms of the bond of dependence between mother and baby. Ellen takes this further: "she loved her son just as much as Ellen loved hers and consequently she did not want her son to die."

Ellen presents the bond between mother and baby as natural: just as Ellen de Rouclif loves her newborn infant, so she loves her own baby. Ellen de Rouclif's love, though unknown to Ellen, is taken for granted. The effect of Ellen's words are also to create a degree of equality between herself and her would-be employer that belies their actual social differences, the one an unemployed single mother of peasant stock, the other a lady of gentle birth. The effect is to neutralize, or at least to attempt to neutralize, any tendency to devalue Ellen's testimony on the grounds of her low social and moral standing. Indeed, by stressing her love for her baby, a love that obliged her to place the welfare of her child over her own material welfare, Ellen presents herself as a good mother. One is reminded again of Paul's words that "she shall be saved in childbearing."[34] The message is simple: in matters relating to maternity and the care of infants, a mother's testimony is expert testimony; as a good mother, Ellen is a trustworthy witness.

Thus far our analysis of the ways in which testimonies represent the past and the ways in which certain sorts of memory are seen as especially useful or trustworthy has tended to focus on women witnesses. Although the present case is atypical in preferring female over male deponents, the testimony of men still plays an important part in the case. The evidence presented by male witnesses tends to serve different purposes and reflect rather different spheres of expertise. We may note in particular two categories of male witnesses: one, comprising two groups, testifies for and against the moral standing and credibility of some of the key witnesses; a second (smaller) category provide testimony concerning various kinds of legal business and events in London and the wider locality. The few remaining male witnesses, who fall into neither of these two main categories, will be considered first.

Six male witnesses testify in respect of Alice's time at Kennythorpe, her attitude toward John Marrays, and the supposed consummation of her spousals. Stephen Wascelyne testifies in his capacity as head of household, but his testimony is less informed than that of his wife. John Fische, Alice's half-brother, was a witness to the spousals and hence falls into our second category, but he was also a visitor at Kennythorpe and had an intimate discussion with his little sister. Robert de Normanby seems only to testify in order to make up numbers since his knowledge is confined to what others told him, though he states that Alice was maintained at Kennythorpe at John's expense. The value of Adam Porter's testimony is little greater. He helped convey Alice to Kennythorpe after the spousals. William Pottell we have already met. Like John Fische, he enjoyed privileged access to Alice and intimate conversation with her whilst she was resident at Kennythorpe. Dom. William Marrays, presumably a close kinsman of John Marrays, though no relationship is stated in his deposition, likewise had privileged access to the house at Kennythorpe. We will return to his testimony at length in chapter 6.

There is little here to suggest that any of these men testified because they were deemed to possess particular expertise by virtue of their gender. The factor that binds most of them is their contact with Alice de Rouclif. Stephen Wascelyne, John Fische, and William Marrays derive this from their relationship to her or her fiancé, to borrow a slightly anachronistic usage. In this respect their position is little different from that of Anabilla Wascelyne and Alice de Rolleston. Pottell is John Marrays's man, part of his *familia*, though no relative. Adam Porter's association with Alice is both brief and slight, but he does help establish the plaintiff's narrative that takes Alice from her spousals in St Mary's Abbey to her new home in Kennythorpe. Robert de Normanby provides the next plank by asserting that Alice's stay at Kennythorpe was provided for by John de Marrays. Such matters of resources and governance fall within the male sphere, but there is also a sense that Robert's testimony is so slight and otherwise so dependent on the report of others that its authority, exiguous though it is, derives from his being male.

The group of male witnesses who testified to matters of a legal nature include witnesses to the spousals at St Mary's abbey, essentially a legal rather than a religious ceremony, and to Ellen de Rouclif's petitioning of the king and Lord de Percy, presumably in relation to rights of wardship under feudal law. Once again, interest in and knowledge of the law or of matters relating to the law may be seen as falling within the male sphere. The point is not that women were ignorant of such matters; Ellen de Rouclif's actions clearly refute such a suggestion. Rather it is that these were matters that men, at least of a certain standing, were expected to be interested in and hence to be likely to remember. They were in effect expert witnesses.

Of the witnesses to the spousals in St Mary's, Master Adam de Thornton, described as clerk and notary public by apostolic authority, was clearly an expert witness in a narrower, technical sense. Richard Bernard, the abbey steward, in whose chamber in the abbey they were conducted, can be seen in a similar light for the words proffered by the couple were at his direction.[35] Alice's half-brothers Robert de Rouclif and John Fische also testified to the spousals. William Pottell, as we saw earlier, merely observed from a distance—this is not the most significant or authoritative part of his testimony. That the only other witness, beside the couple themselves, was Alice's mother tends to reinforce the perspective that the spousals, as an essentially legal rather than a religious or social occasion, were understood as a matter primarily of male interest or concern.

Two further male witnesses offered detailed testimony relating to Ellen de Rouclif's attempts to regain control over Alice following the abduction. Thomas de Bulmer, a York "potter" or metal founder, recalled how the word on the street in London was that Ellen had petitioned the king in council against Sir Brian de Rouclif and had been issued with royal letters under the privy seal directed to Sir Brian.[36] William Sampson, a York goldsmith, likewise testified as to how Ellen de Rouclif "just lately pursued the present business in the presence of the lord king in his council and took away royal letters to the parties to have justice and also proceeded before Lord de Percy before Christmas last in order to have his help to gain restitution of his daughter Alice." Thomas de Bulmer's knowledge came from his visiting the capital, implicitly in relation to his craft. He thus presents himself as a craftsman of some substance whose trade network extended far beyond York. William Sampson's statement appears as little more than an assertion predicated on his authority as a goldsmith and hence member of York's privileged mercantile elite.

These two last overlap with a larger group of (exclusively male) deponents whose function is to discredit witnesses for the opposing party, in this case Ellen de Rouclif among others. William de Lynton, who was examined at much the same time as the potter and the goldsmith, spoke only against Ellen and solely on the basis of report. A further group of four men testified in support of some of the witnesses appearing for Sir Brian. Of these, two were York men, that is, the butcher John called Bawines and John de Hornyngton, who can be identified as a sherman and, from his preferred place of burial—the Minster cemetery—presumably lived within the parish of St Michael le Belfrey.[37] The other two were John de Killom of Clifton, who had testified earlier about Alice's birth on the basis of what Ellen de Rouclif had told him at the time of her husband's death, and Thomas Broun of Rawcliffe itself. Since the witnesses in question were all of peasant stock and hailed from Rawcliffe, the implication is that local Rawcliffe peasant males were not considered to carry sufficient weight to speak about the credibility of witnesses, but that York citizens did.

One further group of witnesses gave testimony primarily designed to discredit witnesses for the opposing party, namely Sir Brian de Rouclif, though John Barbour testified only to the worth of John Marrays's witnesses, claiming not to know any of those for the other side. The three other deponents cannot be described as particularly impressive. Adam Gaynes, who was described as living in St Marygate, was only able to assert that John de Rouclif's witnesses were wealthier than "Alice's" who were all poor. William de Kirkeby claimed of Alice de Rouclif, Robert Thewed, Alice Porter, Beatrix Milner, William de Tange and Henry Vaux that he had "never heard any good of them." John de Alne was a little more specific, but his authority to speak must be questioned. De Alne was one of only six deponents whose ages are recorded for reasons that are not immediately obvious, but at eighteen he was the youngest of these.[38] In a society marked by hierarchies of rank, gender, household status, and age, de Alne does not obviously score highly. The clue may lie in the testimony he gives.

The more substantial citizen witnesses discussed previously were required to provide testimony either to uphold the standing, and hence credibility, of other witnesses of lesser rank or were asked to provide details of legal business and the actions of a lady of some social rank. The nature of their testimony demanded that they were able to present themselves as credible witnesses, men of some substance following honorable and trustworthy trades. The most substantive part of the testimony that John de Alne provides is very different. Here he targets two of Sir Brian's key witnesses. Of Maud de Herthill he says she "is of ill repute and low standing and perjured in that she swore on the book that Gervase de Rouclif did not know her carnally in adultery and she swore falsely as subsequently she confessed that she had committed adultery with Gervase." This statement cleverly blends two different charges: that Maud is an adulteress and hence a woman entirely lacking in honor; and that she is a liar who has perjured herself in the past (and within an ecclesiastical forum) and hence is entirely untrustworthy.

His second target is Ellen Taliour. He deposed that "he had heard it said that Ellen, the wife of Thomas Taliour committed adultery with John [name uncertain] of Skelton." Whereas the charge against Maud was verifiable, since it presumably related to actions within the Church courts, that against Ellen was purely hearsay.[39] The charges in both instances were entirely typical of the tactic that was commonly resorted to in the Church courts, as in wider society, to undermine women's honor, invariably understood in terms of sexual conduct, and hence by extension their credibility as witnesses.[40] Indeed in canonical terms, a witness so tainted by sin was not an admissible witness.[41] In the case of Ellen Taliour the attack is designed to undermine her trustworthiness by taking away from her authority as a mother and reminding the court of her supposed promiscuity and lax morals. This is perhaps not the sort of hearsay mudslinging that would look well from the mouth of a man of rather greater maturity and rank than appears to be true of de Alne. It is, however, part of the currency of adolescent males who seem often to have acted as the de facto arbiters of female reputation as we find for example in respect of charivari.[42] Once again we can credit a witness with a kind of expertise: John de Alne was an expert in respect of women's "honor" where the currency was not objective fact, but hearsay and the word on the street.

It is tempting to conclude that all witnesses were in their own way expert witnesses. What is perhaps more difficult to determine is how this came about. It could be that each was carefully chosen by one or other of the parties because their particular expertise was recognized. On the other hand, we could understand this expertise as a product of careful grooming by their legal counsels and the skilful honing of questions, and hence answers, to make the most effective use of each witness's knowledge. The transformation of Ellen Taliour from unmarried mother and poor peasant woman to key witness presenting testimony as crucial to Sir Brian's action as was that of Dom. William Marrays, mitred abbot of one of the greatest religious houses in the country, to John Marrays's petition is remarkable. Also, it is hardly possible to ignore the simple fact that the party that put the most weight on the testimony of women was also the party that was unsuccessful.

CHAPTER 4

ROBERT THEWED: THE TIES OF TENURE AND LOCALITY

The previous chapter, in exploring the relationship between gender and memory, grouped witnesses by the nature of the testimony proffered. Gender, however, constitutes but one of a number of identities by which we may explore medieval people. One of the distinctive aspects of the case of Marrays c. de Rouclif is the social diversity of the parties and witnesses. They range in rank from poor peasant to lesser aristocracy, but also include members of the urban franchise and a mitred abbot. This social diversity is contained within one small region, a narrow strip of land stretching from Rawcliffe along the Clifton Road, Bootham, past St Mary's Abbey, and into Petergate within the city walls and in the shadow of the Minster. In moving along even this modest stretch of road travelers would pass from the Forest of Galtres to the city of York. They would pass through the Liberties of St Peter and of St Mary, from the parish of St Olave to that of St Michael le Belfrey, and through land held variously by lay and ecclesiastical lords. This present chapter proposes to explore the ways in which witnesses may be understood and related to one another in respect of social rank, neighborhood, and jurisdiction. Our starting point will be the testimony of one particular peasant.

Robert Thewed's deposition is neither one of the most detailed nor one of the most strategically important of the case, but it is one of the more interesting. Both Robert and his wife Margery testified, albeit on separate days.[1] Both were described as tenants of Sir Brian de Rouclif. Both were "of Rawcliffe." Margery recalled that at the time of Alice's birth she was "a servant working in Sir Brian's garden at Rawcliffe." Robert's own testimony described how his son had been born the Lent following Alice's birth, in other words a whole year later. It is thus possible, but not certain, that he married Margery at some point after Alice's birth and after she ceased to be employed as Sir Brian's servant.[2] Though we can only be somewhat tentative about his marital status at the time of the events described, we can be a little more confident of his social status. A tenant, a resident of Rawcliffe, and the husband of a woman once employed as a servant in Sir Brian's garden—these clues tend to suggest that he was of peasant stock and thus of comparatively modest social rank. This makes his reported engagement with Gervase de Rouclif especially remarkable. Giving testimony about the time of Alice's birth, Robert explained that:

> he was present at the churching of Alice's mother and was friend enough of Alice's father that he knew about almost all his doings and he told him at Alice's birth when she was born and of the time of his wife's churching, and even invited him to his feast on the occasion of the aforesaid churching. (BI, CP.E.89/16)

Robert Thewed was no doubt talking up the degree of intimacy between himself and Gervase de Rouclif. His pride in being on such good terms that "he knew about almost all his doings" and that he "even invited him to his feast" cannot be entirely contrived, however helpful it was to his testimony to imply a greater familiarity than may in fact have existed. Besides, Robert's testimony had to be credible. If the intimacy were largely a fiction designed to strengthen the authority of the evidence, then it would have been immediately undercut by its inherent implausibility. What we have here then is two men occupying rather different social positions, or, to take a Marxist perspective, different classes: Robert is the peasant, Gervase the aristocrat. Robert's account implicitly reinforces the point that there was at least a social distance between the two.[3] The invitation to the feast is narrated as an honor bestowed by a superior, whose own status is reflected in his capacity to bestow favors.[4]

It would be easy to dismiss this passage within the testimony of one deponent among many, as little more than a historical footnote that can have little to say about social relations within the period more generally. There are, however, further passages that collectively serve to provide a wider context. Together they suggest an ambiguous picture that should warn against simplistic and dogmatic readings in favor or against the notion that the relationship between lords and peasants was essentially antagonistic and exploitative. They may also suggest that analysis along status or class lines is too restrictive and that there are a variety of other components influencing the social dynamic.

Margery Thewed remembered Alice's birth because William de Tange, whom she worked alongside in Sir Brian's garden, became a father shortly before. She recalled further that "Gervase de Rouclif, Alice's father, raised from the holy font" the newborn baby boy. Because the boy's name is not recorded, we cannot know if Gervase as principal godparent, the implication of his raising the baby from the font, gave the child his own name, though that would have been the expectation.[5] More significantly, this is again an example of a man of higher status, a petty landowner, conferring a favor on an inferior, a manual laborer. At least in theory, the honor bound the two families by ties of spiritual kinship. William de Tange's own deposition hints at another bond, that of neighborhood and neighborliness. "This witness," the deposition asserts, "was then and still is a neighbor near the house in which Alice was born." Again, de Tange's purpose is in part to enhance the authority of his testimony—a near neighbor would be better placed to learn what was going on in the house across the way than someone more remote. Juxtaposed with the observation that Gervase "was his son's godfather," the effect is again to undercut the sense of social distance we would otherwise expect in this hierarchical society.[6]

Perhaps we should not make too much of the actual significance of spiritual kinship. Sir Geoffrey Luttrell a generation earlier had been godfather to children of servants employed within his household, yet there is every reason to believe that Sir Geoffrey possessed a very clear sense of hierarchy and of his own position at the apex. On the other hand, the imagined society of the Luttrell Psalter was also a utopian society where harmonious relations prevailed precisely because all knew their place within a divinely ordained system. By laboring under Sir Geoffrey's good lordship, the peasants ensured a good harvest.[7] By acting as a godparent to his peasant neighbor's child, Gervase de Rouclif may have been reinforcing social hierarchy as much as undermining it, but within a context of a social system where hierarchy went hand in hand with obligation, and not a social system intrinsically characterized by mutual distrust and conflict. Of course, this is precisely the sort of message that the deponents (or their legal counsel) would wish to relay to the court.

There are other ways in which the depositions could be read as demonstrating comparatively harmonious social relations. The way in which the births of the de Rouclif children were a matter of interest and discussion particularly among the women of the village has been noted in the previous chapter. The interest, however, was mutual. Lady Margery de Rouclif, who stated that she was seventy when she gave her testimony, remembered John de Rouclif's birth partly by reference to her recollection of the births of other children in the village of Rawcliffe where she was living at the time. Ellen de Rouclif sent Anabilla Pynder, the peasant woman she was subsequently to ask to be her daughter's wetnurse, "some writing which was said to be good for pregnant women" about the time she gave birth to a baby boy.

Further, but still more ambiguous evidence for a degree of social harmony is provided by the very depositions themselves. Large numbers of the witnesses for either side were their peasant neighbors in Rawcliffe and Clifton. Seven of the witnesses testifying for Sir Brian's cause were his own tenants. Maud de Herthill, who is not described as a tenant, noted in her deposition "that she was asked to proffer her testimony by Sir Brian de Rouclif, but was not instructed." One reading would be that these peasant witnesses agreed to testify out of a shared sense of obligation to their social superiors. Another more cynical reading would be that they testified under the implicit threat of reprisal and dispossession. It may well be that the witnesses themselves would have understood these to be two sides of the same coin. The court was evidently concerned that some of the deponents at least might have been open to bribery since, as we have remarked previously, questions were asked about the material worth of a number of witnesses. Inevitably a variety of motives may have influenced each witness.

Other evidence of interaction between the peasant populations of Rawcliffe and its neighborhood and local gentry families, and specifically the various branches of the de Rouclif family, includes service and concubinage. Both tend to reinforce differences in power relations. The latter was potentially more exploitative than the former, but we may suspect that service by young women presented opportunities for abuse by the employer. Some discussion of servants and service has already been provided in the previous chapter. We noted that servants in a rural, arable economy were most likely to be male. A predominance of male servants was also a facet of greater aristocratic identity.[8] All bar one of the life-cycle servants noticed in this case, however, were female. They were employed neither in husbandry nor by a greater aristocratic household. Two of the women servants observed, Agnes del Polles and Agnes Richmond, were employed, perhaps in succession, in Robert de Rouclif's house in suburban Bootham. The remainder were associated with the household of Gervase and Ellen de Rouclif. It is tempting to conclude that here hierarchies of gender reinforced hierarchies of age, household, and social status. Whereas a great lord could exercise authority over other men, including well-born males, persons of much lesser rank were more comfortable exercising like authority over peasant women.

Our knowledge of concubinage is largely circumstantial and relates to Gervase de Rouclif's likely affairs with peasant women. The inequality between Gervase and the women he slept with suggests that it would be inappropriate to read these as anything other than essentially exploitative relationships, although the women themselves may have anticipated or even received some material recompense for acquiescing. Gervase's affair with Maud de Herthill is known to us solely through John de Alne's testimony discussed in the previous chapter, but the reference to swearing on the book does imply that the alleged adultery came to the attention of the Church courts. We know from her own testimony that Maud gave birth to a daughter on 25 August following John de Rouclif's birth, but we can only speculate that Gervase was the father.[9] We can be reasonably sure that her child would have been conceived around or soon after the previous Martinmas, but this would have been after Ellen de Rouclif's churching and may have been after her term of service with the family had ended. If, on the other hand, Gervase had initiated the relationship during his wife's confinement, when Maud would still have been their servant, then we may speculate that it may have continued for a time after: it is more likely that Maud conceived as a consequence of an established sexual relationship than as the result of a single occasion.

Suspicion regarding Gervase's sexual escapades is also prompted by the name by which the first witness to testify in the case is identified. Agnes "called Gervaus Woman" testified that she had been Gervase's servant for two years before he died. Such a period of service is hardly remarkable. Four years, moreover, had elapsed since Gervase had died. It is consequently hard to see why Agnes should continue to be so closely identified with her former employer. The possibility arises that the very possessive form "Gervaus Woman" in fact hints that Agnes's services extended beyond purely household chores.[10] Agnes is stated to have been twenty-four at the time of her testimony, so would have been Gervase's servant between the ages of eighteen and twenty. The last years of Gervase's marriage produced no further children. Ellen de Rouclif's age is not recorded, but her son John Fische was said to be twenty-six at the time of the case. The easy implication is that Gervase preferred the attractions of the young servant woman over those of his somewhat older wife. The evidence, however, is slight.

More certain is that Gervase fathered a son implicitly out of wedlock for otherwise he and not Alice would be the heir to his lands. Robert de Rouclif is described in his deposition as Alice's "blood brother" in contradistinction to John Fische, her "uterine brother." The epithet "blood" demonstrates that Robert was fathered by Gervase, but patently he had a different mother. Who this mother was and what was her status are, however, unknown. So too is the date of Robert's birth or Gervase's then age, but Robert was a married householder by the time of the case. The likelihood is that he was born some years before Gervase's marriage to Ellen. We do not know whether Gervase would have been single at this point or whether, like his wife, he had been married previously albeit with no surviving children. It is apparent, however, that Robert was recognized as his father's son and an integral member of the family. Both he and John Fische were among the very small group of persons present at Alice's spousals and it was at his house in Bootham that Alice lodged immediately prior to her departure for Kennythorpe. It would be tempting here to suggest that Robert's recognition was a consequence of his gender and his father's (at the time) unmarried state, but this is to stretch already tenuous evidence too far.

The relationship between the de Rouclifs and their peasant neighbors, whether as tenants, employees, friends, or mistresses, represents but one facet of the society of Rawcliffe and its neighborhood. We need to consider what this case can tell us about peasant society and social relations between peasants. In conjunction with other sources, we may also be able to say more about the social world occupied by the various members of the de Rouclif family and about the larger society of the Liberty of St Peter. Our perspective is of course shaped by the particular concerns of the case. For example, the very sharp focus on the legal obligations of servile peasants to their lords that is characteristic of customary court records is here entirely lacking. We know that these tenants and others who gave testimony were of free status because serfs were normally debarred from making depositions within the Church courts, but we cannot know what proportion of the peasant population were freemen.[11] Likewise we are provided with few clues about the nature of the local economy beyond the wheel and cards noted by Agnes del Polles.

There are certain facets of peasant society that are comparatively well documented. As we have seen, infant and child mortality is illuminated as a consequence of the number of births noticed as benchmarks for the births of the de Rouclif children. There is slight evidence regarding the peasant economy. The case also throws light on the movements of people within the community and neighborhood: in several instances this is made explicit within individual depositions, but some further clues are provided by naming evidence. The depositions also offer some evidence for social interactions within the peasant community, but it should be noticed that the case itself can be seen as dividing that community.

Patterns of infant and child mortality may not immediately appear particularly useful to an understanding of peasant society, but they represent an important component in the wider demographic regime and have implications for population growth, landholding, and family strategies.[12] Of the fourteen children whose births are noticed, comprising eight boys, four girls, and two where the sex is not stated, and including the two de Rouclif children, only four were definitely still living at the time of the case. Five more are specifically stated to be dead. In the remaining five instances we are not specifically told that the child had since died, but this is implicit in the case of Isabel de Strensall's unremembered infant, and is quite likely in most if not all the other cases. In two cases—John de Rouclif and Emmot Norice's baby boy—we know that the child died in early infancy, but otherwise the record is silent.

The underlying mortality rate was clearly high, especially if we assume that most or all the children not known to have survived were in fact dead. All the children concerned were born subsequent to the Black Death itself, but some may have perished in the second pestilence of 1361. Children would have been particularly vulnerable since unlike adults they would have had no previous exposure to the disease.[13] These apparently high infant and child mortality rates compare with equivalent rates derived from some poor developing countries today. They arise despite the evidence for prolonged maternal breastfeeding that helped protect very young children from diarrhea and also provided antibodies against infection from mother to child.[14] Anabilla Pynder, it will be recalled, refused to serve as a wetnurse when her son was some sixteen months because he was still too young to be weaned, although Ellen Taliour, who had refused to so act when her son was four months, agreed when he had reached eighteen months. Emmot Norice, Alice's eventual wetnurse looked after her charge for three years. Presumably Alice was fully weaned by the time Emmot's contract ended, the implication being that, like Shakespeare's Juliet, three years was regarded as an appropriate age for a child to be weaned.[15]

Less readily documented within the case itself is the local economy, but, placed alongside other sources, there are some clues. Perhaps the most significant clue within the case itself is Sir Brian de Rouclif's garden. Despite the superficially intimate and domestic associations that the term garden, especially within an aristocratic context, may signal, it must be remembered that medieval gardens were frequently highly functional and even commercial. Sir Brian's garden employed at least two staff—Margery Thewed and William de Tange—around the time of Alice's birth and, some dozen years later, the widowed Alice Sharpe was said to be working there. That three of our handful of Rawcliffe deponents were associated at one time or another with this garden seems more than coincidence. The likelihood is that this was a comparatively significant source of employment predicated on the proximity of York and the ready demand for market garden produce.[16]

The wet, low lying nature of the land, located as it is on the north bank of the River Ouse, is manifest both from documentary reference to drainage ditches and the description of significant areas as marsh. These drainage ditches are also apparent archaeologically. It follows that although land was set aside for arable—and a small area of ridge and furrow was described when excavations took place in Rawcliffe in the earlier 1990s—most land was probably used for pasture and peat extraction. Rights to turbaries are several times noted in recorded property deeds.[17] Once again the proximity of York may have created demand for fuel extracted only a short boat journey from the city.[18]

The influence of York as a major textile-manufacturing city is also reflected in the depositions.[19] John de Hornyngton, a witness for Sir Brian, for example, can be identified as a shearman.[20] Agnes del Polles, the wife of Ralph de Hesyngwald [Easingwold], memorably described her impoverished state by describing her sole possessions as "a boy and a wheel with a pair of cards." The reference to the boy is enigmatic, but perhaps implies that the child contributed economically by assisting her in her work. Spinning was quintessentially women's work in the Middle Ages, but carding was perhaps a little less gender-marked and younger children in any case often assisted with "feminine" tasks. Though the child was implicitly her son, his description as "puer" rather than "filius" probably serves to clarify his youth. Agnes's place of residence is unrecorded; before her marriage she had worked first in St Marygate and subsequently served in Bootham for four years, so she may well have continued to reside just outside the city walls. This would fit a larger pattern of employment of spinsters in poor suburban areas by city textile producers.[21] What is particularly interesting here is that Agnes was utilizing a spinning wheel rather than the less efficient, but much more versatile distaff. The implication is that spinning represented her primary source of income rather than one of a number of work activities, itself a reflection on the scale of demand for spun yarn to meet the needs of the city's burgeoning cloth manufacture. Although married, she probably in effect supported herself.

The pull of York is seen again in terms of patterns of migration.[22] Though the number of cases observed is small, the pattern recorded directly within the depositions is predominantly local. A certain amount of movement is simply along the Clifton road. Of particular interest is Isabel de Strensall. She was probably living in Rawcliffe at the time of John de Rouclif's birth—her deposition is not explicit, but she was a guest at the churching feast held a few weeks following the birth. After the churching she moved to the Bootham suburb of York for two years before living in the city for the next twelve years prior to the case. At the time of her testimony she was said to be living in Jubbergate, in the heart of the city, probably within the parish of St Sampson.[23] Alice Porter, who at the time of the case was married to the gatekeeper of St Mary's Abbey and resident in Clifton, was living in Skelton, further out along the Clifton road, at the time of Alice's birth. Beatrix, the wife of John Milner, was likewise currently living in Clifton, but had moved from Rawcliffe about a dozen years before. Ellen Taliour's migration history likewise follows the Clifton road. We do not know where she spent her childhood, but thirteen years or so previous to the case she had spent a year as servant to William de Huntyngton, presumably in Petergate, and afterward moved to Rawcliffe. At the time of the case she was married and living in Clifton.

Such small-scale, intensely local migration is largely invisible but for this kind of deposition evidence. Unlike early modern depositions such information is not recorded systematically, but rather serendipitously for the reasons outlined in the previous chapter.[24] On the basis of this tiny sample we may notice that the direction of the movement was north to south from Rawcliffe and Skelton to Clifton, Bootham and on into the city of York. This probably represents a real trend, but it must be remembered that since most of the witnesses were focused on events taking place within Rawcliffe some twelve to fourteen years previous to the case, persons migrating the other way and arriving in Rawcliffe some years after the births of the de Rouclif children would be of little value as witnesses. Similarly the depositions will not tell us about the migration history of Rawcliffe residents prior to the key events since this will have no bearing on their testimonies. Henry Vaux alone is described as a native of Rawcliffe—"born there"—as if this experience was perhaps unusual or remarkable.[25] But we cannot even be sure of this: Vaux's deposition contains the observation that "this witness came from St James [Santiago de Compostella] a fortnight before the feast of the nativity of St John the Baptist twelve years ago" just before taking up a position as servant to Gervase de Rouclif, so it may have been considered useful to clarify that his ties to the community were in fact of longer standing.

A parallel pattern of local, but less immediately parochial, migration is true of the evidence of toponymic surnames, but this tends not to relate to witnesses with clear Rawcliffe ties.[26] William de Huntyngton, a resident of Petergate in York, for example, presumably hailed from the neighboring village of Huntington where he held land.[27] Isabel de Strensall bears the name of a village no more than five miles distant. John de Alne is associated with a village some ten miles to the north. Bielby, from whence Alice de Beleby or her immediate ancestors came, was only about fifteen miles distant. Follifoot, ancestral home of Magaret de Folifayt was a like distance, but to the west rather than the east. Normanby, associated with Robert de Normanby, is twenty-eight miles northeast of York, but in this case we have no reason to believe that he was a resident of either Rawcliffe or York: his testimony relates to Kennythorpe and he most likely lived in that neighborhood.

On one level, the pattern of migration is entirely unremarkable. The evidence of toponymics suggest that people migrated from places no more than a day's walk away.[28] The only exception is that of Robert de Richmond, whose wife, Agnes, testified. The couple were resident in St Marygate and had no connection with Rawcliffe. On another level, however, there is a discernable pattern here that cannot be ascribed to chance: a significant proportion of movement occurred between locations within the Liberty of St Peter. William de Huntington had lived within the Liberty when resident in Petergate, but his likely natal village of Huntington also lay within the Liberty.[29] Alne, Bielby, Shipton, and Strensall likewise noted among deponents' toponymics, are all located in the Liberty.[30] Alne and, more especially, Bielby were some distance from Rawcliffe or York. On the other hand a number of more accessible localities are not noticed. Thus the villages of Overton, Benningborough, and Newton on Ouse, all located immediately further up the River Ouse, but associated administratively with St Mary's Abbey and the hospital of St Leonard respectively, are conspicuously absent. Similarly we do not find toponymics associated with places on the opposite bank of the River Ouse.

The toponyms associated with the Liberty of St Peter are not randomly distributed between the deponents. They nearly all belong to the witnesses appearing for John Marrays: John de Alne, Alice de Beleby, Cecily de Shupton, and Isabel de Strensall. Isabel, whose migration history we have already described, may also have been resident within the Liberty at the time of her testimony. Alice de Beleby more certainly was, since her husband, Richard de Warwyk, held property in Petergate.[31] Another migrant, Isabel de Rouclif, had been a servant to Ellen and Gervase, her uncle, shortly following Alice's birth, but subsequently married John de Grandesby and came to live in Tollerton, also within the Liberty.[32] She too testified on behalf of John Marrays. The one possible exception is John de Killom of Clifton: part of the vill of Kilham was within the Liberty.

One or two other toponyms may be associated with the abbey's lordship and property rights. Robert de Normanby may have had connections with the abbey's manor of Normanby. Robert de Richmond, living in St Marygate and hence within the Liberty of St Mary, may likewise have been associated with the town of Richmond, the site of St Mary's daughter house of St Martin. Both Robert de Normanby and Robert de Richmond's wife, Agnes del Polles, testified—as might be expected—on behalf of John Marrays.[33] Of the other place-name surnames observed, there are several that cannot be identified, though a couple can. William de Lynton, whose place of residence is not recorded, is associated with Linton-on-Ouse, whereas Margaret de Folifayt, who may have lived in Rawcliffe, can be associated with Follifoot, a village some fifteen miles to the west. These two last testified on behalf of Sir Brian de Rouclif.

Our discussion of migration suggests three observations. The first is unremarkable: most migration was over comparatively short distances. The deposition evidence is invaluable, however, in showing up some very local migration that is invisible from conventional analyses of toponymics. This very local migration is associated with people who had been villagers in Rawcliffe. The slightly longer distance migration suggested by toponymics may more readily pertain to St Marygate or Bootham—in effect, suburbs of York—and not to Rawcliffe natives or residents. What we cannot know is how commonly villagers moved and so how typical was the experience of migration. The second observation is that the migration field is not accidental or arbitrary, but rather is influenced inter alia by administrative and property connections, here the Liberty of St Peter and the interests of St Mary's Abbey. It is likely, however, that our picture is distorted by the fact that our sample is not drawn randomly from the populations of Rawcliffe and the surrounding area. This last takes us to our third observation, though this must also be our most tentative since the samples are so small: we have a clear hint that the witnesses appearing for John Marrays were themselves connected, perhaps particularly through the Liberty of St Peter, but also through St Mary's Abbey.

Although the Liberty of St Peter may have helped foster its own internal network of personal connections, it is not the only institutional framework pertinent to the lives of the people involved in this case. We need also to consider the ancient royal Forest of Galtres. The forest comprised a large area to the north and northwest of York extending right up to the city walls and effectively encompassing the wapentake of Bulmer, though it is probable that the parts closest to York, including Rawcliffe and Clifton, were by this date but sparsely wooded.[34] Around the time of the case it was generating a modest but steady income for the crown of some £15–20 a year.[35] No forest court rolls survive for the fourteenth century.[36] An eyre record from 1528, however, suggests that the judicial administration of the forest may have rather greater relevance to this case. This records that in addition to the regular officers of the forest (foresters, verderers etc.), the court was also attended by the constable and four men from each of the vills of Alne, Clifton, Easingwold, Haxby, Huby, Newton, Stillington, Strensall, Tollerton, and Wiggington, a collection of localities that overlaps to a degree with those already noticed, but also mirrors the more important settlements within the bounds of the forest.[37]

The forest and its regular attachment courts may thus have served to reinforce networks created by the Liberty of St Peter; Gervase de Rouclif had himself been one of the regarders of the forest.[38] However, whereas the Liberty (metaphorically and sometimes, as in the case of the Huntyngton family, literally) took its subjects beyond Bootham and into the city along Petergate, the forest ended where the city began.

If the spatial ties between those testifying for John Marrays are becoming a little clearer, we need now to ask what factors link Sir Brian de Rouclif's witnesses? The answer is clearly colored by the observation already made that several of his witnesses were his own tenants, but the striking unifying factor is their residence in the village of Rawcliffe and its immediate vicinity. Eleven of Sir Brian's witnesses, of which Robert Thewed was but one, were specifically described as residents of Rawcliffe. Another four were resident in Clifton and one further resided in Skelton. Of these, eight were tenants of Sir Brian, one was a tenant of Alice, and one specifically denied being Sir Brian's tenant. In contrast to John Marrays's deponents, only Agnes Gervaus Woman and Ellen de Rouclif, Alice's mother and key ally of John Marrays, were specifically described as being resident in Rawcliffe. Margery, the wife of John Gregson otherwise Bell, was a resident of Clifton. Of John's remaining witnesses, at least three—Dom. William Marrays, the abbot, Richard Bernard, the bailiff, and the gatekeeper Adam Porter—were closely associated with St Mary's Abbey. Adam Porter's wife, Alice, lived in Clifton, but it is likely that as gatekeeper Adam was largely accommodated in the gatehouse. Significantly Adam and Alice testified on opposite sides. Two witnesses lived in St Marygate and consequently within the Liberty of St Mary. Another eight can be located in Bootham, which until 1354 had been claimed as part of the Liberty: five deponents or their spouses are so described in their depositions; a further three can be identified from extant poll tax evidence. The 1377 poll tax returns for Bootham survive as part of the otherwise fragmentary nominative returns for the city of York. These may be augmented by the somewhat more substantial returns for the 1381 tax: William Sampson, goldsmith, is listed in close proximity to Margery de Rouclif, who is herself very close to Robert de Rouclif; Beatrix de Morland is not listed, but a Thomas Moreland, who can be identified as a marshal, is.[39] Agnes del Polles, whose place of residence is not stated, was living in St Marygate at the time of Alice's birth and had subsequently been in service in Bootham with Robert de Rouclif. Robert de Rouclif's own connection with St Mary's Abbey is apparent from his will.[40] The likelihood is that he too was in some way employed by the abbey. To these we may add the members of the Wascelyne household at Kennythorpe, probably a property of St Mary's Abbey, and single witnesses from Huby, Tollerton (both within the Forest of Galtres) and, within York, Petergate and Jubbergate.[41] The location of a further five witnesses is unknown, though some may well have come from the same neighborhood.

What emerges is that there were geographical and tenurial dimensions to the social fissions caused by the marriage. Sir Brian de Rouclif's witnesses are largely drawn from the village of Rawcliffe and, to a lesser extent, its immediate environs. John Marrays's case is perhaps less geographically focused, but, besides the associations with the Liberty of St Peter and the Forest of Galtres, there is a core of witnesses drawn from St Marygate or Bootham. One particular friendship network is apparent from the case and may be further illuminated from other sources. Alice's parents were "great friends" with the Huntyngtons. This was, according to Ellen Taliour, the reason why Emma de Huntyngton asked her to become the de Rouclifs' wetnurse at the time of their first son's birth.[42] Twenty years earlier Gervase de Rouclif had supported William de Huntyngton's sister Agnes in another marriage case no less convoluted than the present.[43] Gervase and William were the first two persons named when in 1352 the treasurer of York Minster complained that his trees at Alne, Tollerton, Acomb, and Newthorpe had been unlawfully felled.[44] William de Huntyngton, although himself resident in Petergate, owned at his death the Bootham home of the married clerk, John de Rouclif, apparently a close kinsman of Richard de Rouclif, Alice's half-brother. William also owned a toft in Bootham adjacent to property "formerly" owned by Walter de Shupton, a probable kinsman of another intimate of the de Rouclifs, Cecily de Shupton.[45] Gervase de Rouclif and one Roger de Schupton had served together in 1362 as jurors for Bulmer.[46]

Underlying the geography just outlined, there are political considerations. Whereas Sir Brian's presence in Rawcliffe probably made him an immediate power within the vill, St Mary's Abbey had extensive property and administrative rights within the broader locality. As we have noted, much of Rawcliffe, Clifton, and the entirety of St Marygate fell within the Liberty of St Mary. The abbey owned numbers of properties within the same area, including Bootham.[47] Large parts of Rawcliffe, Clifton, and Bootham also fell within the parish of St Olave, which the abbey administered as if a dependent chapelry. The abbey also had rights and interests in the Forest of Galtres, which, just as was true of its liberty within Bootham prior to 1354, were to provoke violent resistance the following century.[48]

The ways in which individuals were pulled one way or another by sometimes conflicting loyalties and obligations is most graphically illustrated by Alice and Adam Porter, who, as we have seen, testified on opposite sides. Adam as an employee of St Mary's, testified alongside his employer, Dom. William Marrays, in favor of the abbot's kinsman, John Marrays. Conversely, his wife Alice, as a resident of Clifton and a tenant of Sir Brian, appeared on behalf of her landlord and hence in contradiction to her immediate "lord," her husband. Not all Sir Brian's witnesses were his tenants, however.[49] It is possible that other factors helped give the Rawcliffe deponents a shared sense of identity and common cause. William de Tange described how he "was and still is a neighbor near the house in which Alice was born." He deploys the concept of "neighbor" here to explain his knowledge of Alice's birth, but neighborliness can also be understood as performative.[50] It might involve sharing through the exchange of narratives a common understanding of village history. We are reminded here of Margery Bell's observation that Alice's birth "was discussed among her friends and neighbors." Still more significant is Agnes Quysteler's testimony that, as a new resident in Rawcliffe ten years earlier—and hence at least a year after Alice's birth, she was told of Alice's birth by her neighbors.[51] Neighborliness might also involve backing one's neighbors in court.

There may be another factor binding the Rawcliffe deponents. John Marrays's cause cannot but have been associated with the interests of the then abbot of St Mary's and hence with St Mary's Abbey more generally. This may well have been a cause of antagonism, for the intrusion of the abbey in the lives of the Rawcliffe villages was probably resented. The destruction of the abbey's estate records in the Civil War means that little can be said specifically about the abbey's direct involvement with the villagers, but some observations are still possible. Until the settlement of 1354, the Liberty of St Mary had coincided with the parish of St Olave, but even after that date and the effective removal of Bootham from the Liberty, it still encompassed substantial parts of Rawcliffe including the de Rouclif family home.[52] The remaining parts of Rawcliffe, comprising much of the housing, but not the associated lands, were contained within St Peter's Liberty. The marriage of a de Rouclif heiress to one so intimately connected to St Mary's Abbey may well have been understood as an attempt further to extend the abbey's authority.[53]

The abbey's interests in Rawcliffe were probably less substantial than those in Clifton. At the time of the Dissolution, Clifton, which constituted a manor under the abbey's lordship, yielded an annual income of nearly £55. In contrast, Rawcliffe, which was bracketed administratively with Skelton, yielded only about a tenth of that.[54] Clearly the main landholder in Rawcliffe at the time of the case was Sir Brian, though apparently more modest holdings belonged to Alice de Rouclif as heiress to Gervase de Rouclif.[55] It may be that the peasant residents preferred the more informal and flexible relationship possible with resident lay lords, and as exemplified by Robert Thewed's testimony with which we began, to the more autocratic and legalistic relations characteristic of institutional lords.[56]

One reflection of this inflexible and legalistic mindset relates to the abbey's control of the parish church of St Olave. The pre-Conquest church predated the abbey, but was given soon after the Conquest to the first monks as their abbey church. A new abbey church was constructed on an adjacent site before too long, but St Olave's remained a possession of the abbey and came to be contained within the precinct. Although the church functioned parochially, being both the place of baptism and burial for the resident population,[57] it was treated as a chapel by the abbey who controlled entry to the church through the abbey gatehouse and denied those who used the church automatic right of entry.[58] This was the basis of a dispute that simmered over a very long period and was only partially resolved in 1466.[59]

The latter years of the fourteenth century saw particular friction. In 1390 we find the abbey taking action to thwart the St Olive's congregation on learning that "the said parishioners intend to make it parochial to the prejudice of the abbey."[60] The dispute prompted a ruling of the archbishop, confirmed by papal authority, that though the church remained a chapel, the parishioners should take responsibility for the repair of the church.[61] The parishioners thus found themselves in a position marginally worse than that typical of appropriated churches. Their tithes augmented the income of the sacrist of the conspicuously wealthy abbey without benefit to the parishioners and their church lay outside their own control, accessible only through goodwill of the monastery.[62]

The rather different solidarity of the witnesses living in Bootham and St Marygate probably reflects a rather different relationship to St Mary's Abbey. We may dismiss Adam Porter, an employee, as partisan for obvious reasons. Similarly we may suspect that Agnes de Richmond and Adam Gagnes as residents of St Marygate, within what remained of the Liberty of St Mary within the suburbs of York, were tenants of the abbey. Robert de Rouclif and his wife, Katherine, although close kin of Alice, were also substantial residents in Bootham and evidently closely involved with the abbey.[63] We know little of Cecily de Shupton or Agnes de Fithby, also resident in Bootham, but William de Kirkeby, brewer, and his wife Agnes, together with the hostel-keeper Beatrix de Morland, probably represent traders whose enterprises owed much to the proximity of the abbey and the business that it generated through the constant flow of visitors, including pilgrims to the chapel of Our Lady next to St Olave's.[64] They may well have been sympathetically disposed to the abbey.

CHAPTER 5

ANABILLA WASCELYNE: THE TIES OF KINSHIP

The preceding chapter focused on the way deponents and litigants were bound by associations of neighborliness, community, or tenure. These, however, are but one set of elements in a more complex web of relationships. Ties created by birth or marriage are no less important and these are the focus of this present chapter. Interestingly these are ties that take us beyond the coresident group of the household so beloved by demographic historians.[1] There are two principal kin groups associated with the case. There are also several cases of husband and wife testifying. The most conspicuous of these two groups is that represented by Alice de Rouclif's kin, the minor gentry family of the de Rouclifs. Less conspicuous, but not necessarily so much less significant, is that represented by the kin of Alice's would-be husband, John Marrays.

A question invariably asked of witnesses appearing to testify in the Church courts was their relationship to one or other of the parties involved in the litigation. This relationship might be by reason of blood, marriage, or service. In most York cases after the last decades of the fourteenth century this is routinely spelt out at the head of the recorded deposition: witnesses were regularly stated to be "related neither by blood or marriage nor ties of service to either party." Conventions were not so firmly established in 1366; in the present case such ties are only recorded where specifically declared. If witnesses were required verbally to deny such ties in all other instances, it is not recorded. Thus, whereas John Fische is precisely, almost clinically described as "uterine brother of the Alice in question" and Robert de Rouclif more simply, but in fact no less precisely, as "blood brother of the Alice in question," Dom. William Marrays's deposition does not pause between the description of his title and his response to the first two articles. He conspicuously does not notice any connection to John Marrays in his deposition, nor is stated at the beginning. The form of the record leaves it ambiguous whether the abbot was able to duck the crucial question by not being specifically asked to deny any relationship or whether he was simply economical with the truth.[2]

So what was the truth? This is always a difficult question to ask, especially in respect of such slippery source material as we are presented with here, but that the two were kin is almost beyond question. There are good grounds for stating this. The name Marrays, or Marreys as it is more frequently recorded outside this case, is not found with any frequency. Although the abbot's name can be found recorded as a toponymic (de Marreys), with one possible exception, it does not correspond to any readily identifiable locality.[3] It may instead derive from the Middle English "mareis" or marsh.[4] Almost nothing seems to be known of Dom. William beyond the extent of his abbacy (1359–82).[5] It may be that he came from a family of clerics. In a case from 1382–83, for example, we find him named as an arbitrator in a dispute between the rector of Huggate and one Master Robert Marrays, the former rector.[6] On balance, the likelihood of two unrelated persons with the same, unusual surname being involved in the same case does not seem great. It is, however, the nature of the involvement that is more striking.

The appearance of so senior an ecclesiastic, let alone a religious, as a witness is unusual and possibly unique. Broadly speaking, the greater aristocracy seem not to have used the Church courts, preferring to petition their diocesan directly.[7] The ecclesiastical aristocracy may have shared this prejudice. Lesser clergy, however, appear with comparative frequency as witnesses, partly because they were seen as well informed about members of their communities and partly because they were regarded as especially trustworthy, hence authoritative witnesses.[8] We need not be so surprised to find a member of a religious order as a witness. A couple of monks, for example, appear as witnesses in a case of a disputed inheritance dating to 1370–71.[9] Here, as in our own case a few years before, the religious who made depositions were monks from St Mary's Abbey in York. The implication is that, for this wealthy Benedictine house, the appearance of monks out of cloister was not so unusual, a view that gives credence to the adverse comments of some diocesans when conducting visitation.[10]

Dom. William's testimony will be explored at length in the next chapter. For the moment, it suffices to say that the abbot was intimately connected with the household of Stephen Wascelyne at Kennythorpe. He is allowed to ride out with Joan de Rolleston, who was probably Stephen's step-daughter, "in the fields of Grimston." She in turn confides in him her knowledge of the alleged consummation of the spousals between Alice de Rouclif and John Marrays that she witnessed by reason of sleeping in the same room.[11] Dom. William may have been seen by the child as a confessor figure, but that neither explains his presence in the Wascelyne household, nor the otherwise (to modern eyes at least) inappropriateness of his contact with Joan.[12] What then can we know of the connection between Dom. William and the Wascelyne household?

Two observations are possible. First, St Mary's Abbey held property at Kennythorpe and also at North Grimston.[13] In one sense this is an unremarkable observation since the abbey was a major property owner in the region, but since Kennythorpe was little more than a hamlet, the connection begins to look more significant. The ownership of property is, however, hardly reason to explain an abbot's visit to the people who lived there, let alone his intimate conversation with their young daughter. Second, the mistress of the Wascelyne household was John Marray's married sister. Anabilla Wascelyne was, moreover, the mother of Alice and Joan de Rolleston presumably by a previous marriage.[14] If Dom. William were close kin to Anabilla, this would readily explain his contact both with her and with her daughters. Whatever kin tie he shared with Anabilla, he must have shared the same with John.

At this point we move from the probable to the purely speculative. Were the connections innocent, the failure of Dom. William to declare his relationship with John Marrays is puzzling. If we suppose that Dom. William were in fact the father of John and Anabilla, his involvement in the case would become immediately apparent, but his failure to declare the relationship in court would likewise make sense.[15] For the abbot openly to declare that he had had an illicit affair and fathered two children would hardly reflect well on his position as a senior religious and would tend to detract from the credibility of his testimony. If, however, he was tactfully not asked to declare a relationship, then the embarrassment of the relationship could be avoided. It could be something that everyone knew, but no one had the temerity to mention. Dom. William's intimate access to the Wascelyne household and to his little granddaughters would make sense as would the possibility that he had provided for his daughter and orphaned granddaughters by using abbey property to provide for them.

If Dom. William Marrays, despite his success in being elected abbot of one of the wealthiest religious houses in the country, is otherwise obscure, John Marrays's only claim to fame is his association with this case. There is a John de Marrays, franklin, listed with his unnamed wife in the 1379 poll tax returns for Burton Salmon.[16] It would be tempting to identify him with the John Marrays of the case. Unfortunately there is little to connect the two save that the description "franklin," a term apparently used to describe persons occupying a position between the upper echelons of the peasantry and persons of the rank of esquire, would fit rather well and the chronology is compatible.[17] However, even if the two were the same man, it probably does nothing to help explain his origins. It is somewhat more likely that he can be identified with the John Marreys recorded in the York franchise register as father to John Marreys, mercer, who was made free in 1387, a remarkably exact twenty-one years after the Court of York ruled that conjugal rights be restored to John Marrays.[18] If this identification is correct, and if John senior were also a mercer, this would help explain John's time in London and something of the nature of the gifts of cloth he supplied his child bride. He was still living in 1395 for in that year he was bequeathed a "spangled hat [spanged hate]" by William Malbys, who was probably an employee of St Mary's Abbey and perhaps of the abbot at his principal manor house at Overton. Malbys's will can in fact be read to imply that John was himself then a member of the abbot's household.[19] Since it was at Overton that in 1370 John Marrays, together with Alice, by this date specifically designated his wife, sealed the one deed recorded in his name, it is tempting to conclude that John was indeed employed in the abbot's household, perhaps supplying its requirements for cloth, household utensils, and the like.[20]

Unlike nuns, most monks in fact originated from comparatively humble, nonaristocratic backgrounds.[21] They may even have been the sons of tenants on the abbey's estates; St Mary's in fact owned extensive lands in Marshland, an area of low-lying land near the confluence of the Ouse and the Trent.[22] The likelihood, therefore, is that the family origins of Dom. William and of John Marrays—assuming him for the moment to have been a kinsman, but not a natural son—were obscure. It follows that John Marrays's only real importance would have been his relationship to the abbot of St Mary's. Such a connection would have had to have been pretty close for it to have made him a suitable spouse for an (albeit minor) gentlewoman and heiress. Again, it is easier to make sense of this if we suppose John to have been the abbot's son.

The marriage arranged by Ellen de Rouclif for her daughter now begins to make sense. For Ellen and those other members of the de Rouclif family who chose to support John Marrays in court, the alliance with John Marrays was tantamount to an alliance with St Mary's Abbey, at least for the extent of Dom. William's abbacy. As the principal landholder within the locality, St Mary's would have been a powerful ally and patron and a useful bulwark against rival interests, even one might suppose against Sir Brian de Rouclif. Ellen, as a widow, might especially have found such a powerful protector attractive. If, moreover, Dom. William was able to look after his illegitimate son and daughter, then he might also be able to look out for his daughter-in-law and her immediate kin. Scott Waugh's observation of the greater aristocracy that "marriages were arranged to consolidate relations among landholders who shared the administration and power in a county or region" needs only modest qualification to be equally apposite in the present case.[23]

The attraction of such a marriage alliance for Dom. William and for John Marrays follows similar lines. St Mary's Abbey held extensive property rights all around York, not least, as we have seen, along the north bank of the Ouse extending through Clifton, Rawcliffe, Skelton, Shipton, and Benningborough, including the abbot's principal residence at Overton.[24] The marriage would have served to reinforce the abbey's influence within the locality, particularly following the curtailment of the Liberty only five years before Dom. William was elected to office. Somewhat speculatively, it is tempting to suppose that the abbey would have had an interest in countering the influence of Sir Brian de Rouclif as the principal lay lord within Rawcliffe. The polarization of the dispute between, on the one hand, Sir Brian de Rouclif and the residents of Rawcliffe and, on the other, supporters of the abbey and of Ellen de Rouclif and her family, now begins to appear more inevitable.

Because Anabilla de Wascelyne was John Marrays's sister, and very likely close kin to Dom. William, we should add the Wascelyne household to their kinship network. Stephen Wascelyne, though the head of the Wascelyne household by virtue of his gender and marital status, was related only by marriage and is thus most peripheral in kinship terms. This is mirrored in his comparatively small role as a witness. He was in fact called, to judge by the order of the enrolled depositions, immediately after his wife, Anabilla, and his stepdaughter, Alice, but it is probably unwise to read too much significance into this. Stephen had little to say about the nature of the alleged marriage between Alice de Rouclif and his brother-in-law, John Marrays. His knowledge was largely based on hearsay, though he did notice that Alice had acknowledged the contract "often" and that "she was displeased because John put off carrying forward and completing the solemnization of the marriage."

Stephen spoke more authoritatively about the duration of Alice's stay in his house—from the feast of St Andrew or thereabouts until the feast of the translation of St Thomas[25]—and was precise, almost legalistic, about the nature of her stay: she was "boarded with this witness and his wife" and this was "by John's arrangement." The point was a necessary one to the case and indeed represents the entire substance of Robert de Normanby's deposition. After her spousals, Alice was to be seen to be maintained at John Marrays's expense and to be under his authority as would be expected of any husband. Her extended stay at the Wascelynes' Kennythorpe home could not be seen to compromise this. In making this point, however, Stephen was in effect justifying his own position as a householder, who might otherwise expect to exercise authority over dependent members of his household. Alice, we are in effect told, though resident in his house, was not under his authority. It could even be read as if Stephen were distancing himself from the events that allegedly took place within his household, especially as these would have reflected badly on Stephen had Alice been under his authority and not that of her prospective husband.

Stephen Wascelyne's legalistic explanation of Alice as a boarder in his home contrasts with his wife's more matter-of-fact account of how "John took Alice to stay with this witness," an account which moreover omits any reference to Stephen as Anabilla's husband. This account has its own truth. If Alice was taken to stay in Kennythorpe at John's behest and arrangement, then it was very specifically because his married sister was mistress of the household. The implicit purpose of the stay was that Anabilla, as a married woman and household manager, would be able to train a girl, who had hitherto lived at home with her widowed mother, to be capable of assuming the role of wife and mistress of her own household.

Anabilla Wascelyne's deposition is the fullest and certainly one of the most immediate in terms of reported speech of the entire case. It served to convey some important evidence in support of John Marrays's case, but of particular interest is the way in which this is achieved. The main function of Anabilla's testimony was to demonstrate that Alice consented to her marriage, that she articulated that consent both by her words and her actions, and that she was physically mature enough for the canonical requirements regarding age of consent to be satisfied. Thus Alice was said to have slept with John and afterward declared that she wanted the marriage to be properly solemnized.[26] She also accepted various gifts from John, something that was understood to indicate consent. Anabilla also commented on her comparative physical maturity—she was at least twelve, but looked fourteen.

A substantial part of Anabilla's testimony is conveyed in the form of reported speech. This is the one place in the case that Alice purportedly speaks. This is, of course, a very deliberate strategy. If Alice's actual words of consent cannot be heard, then they can be vicariously experienced through the reported speech contained within the deposition. The apparent intimacy of the reported conversations between Alice and Anabilla, moreover, lend them an immediacy that is, even more than six centuries later, quite compelling and was presumably intended to be no less so at the time of the case. The explanation for this apparent intimacy is contained within the reported speech itself. Alice allegedly told Anabilla that "after her own mother she trusted most in this witness." The relationship between Anabilla and her brother's child fiancée that Anabilla fashions here is quasi-maternal, a relationship redolent of trust, affection, and intimacy.

An interesting contrast in the relationships between Alice and, on the one hand, Anabilla and, on the other, John Marrays is shown in regard to Alice's concern to have her marriage solemnized. She pleads first her case before Anabilla. Her supposed reported words are presented with meticulous care: "Dame, I have a secret to tell you if you will hear it." These are credibly the words of a child, uncertain how to broach a subject of particular importance. She goes on, "Dame, I should like the marriage between your brother and me to be solemnized and I ask that you persuade him to do this. . . ." What Alice is presented here as communicating is that she is upset that John has slept with her, as with a mistress, when her desire is to be his wife. Anabilla's response is encouraging, but noncommittal: "Do you want to plead these matters before him when he comes?" John Marrays's response to the same petition is very different: "You will not speak like that any more. You know the agreement between your mother and other of your friends [i.e., family] and me that I will espouse you at a future date. . . ." Anabilla thus shows herself almost as an older sister—caring, supportive, but lacking authority and unprepared to take the initiative asked of her by Alice—whereas John speaks with the firm and unquestioned authority expected of a lord to his vassal, a father to his child or a husband to his wife. By performing the roles that would be expected if the couple were lawfully married—Anabilla that of sister-in-law, John that of husband—the marriage is tacitly presented as a given. Anabilla goes on to report that the couple demonstrated their ratification of the contract every time John came to the house by embracing and kissing.[27]

Anabilla offers a particularly detailed account of the gifts made to Alice by John. The giving of gifts by a man to his intended was understood as symbolic of his intentions toward her. Conversely the acceptance of such gifts represented a form of consent. The gifts thus serve as useful circumstantial evidence in support of John's case. Anabilla's knowledge of them can be understood as another aspect of her particular expertise, namely as a household manager, well used to mentally inventorying household utensils, clothing, and the like.[28] The account of the various gifts, however, also provides a cue for another piece of remembered speech. When Alice received a gift of blue cloth to be made into a tunic, coat, and hood, she reportedly told Anabilla, "Dame, I know that I will not have any more cloths of my master before I have the veil for my marriage."

The language supposedly used by Alice as reported in Anabilla's deposition, and the sentiments expressed thereby appear authentically childlike.

This, of course, is not to undermine the credibility of the case that Alice was of sufficient age to ratify her consent to the earlier spousals, but rather to make her words seem all the more authentic and hence credible. Of more immediate concern here, however, is the quasi-maternal relationship that Anabilla presents to the court in respect of her young visitor. This mirrors the argument made in chapter 3 that mothers may be seen as expert witnesses in relation to childbirth. Anabilla's "expert" status rests on the intimacy of the relationship between herself and her charge. Alice is able, so the testimony would have us believe, to communicate with Anabilla about such potentially embarrassing and intimate matters as her attitude to having sex with John because Anabilla is able to relate to her almost as a mother: "after her own mother she trusted most in this witness."

This quasi-maternal relationship similarly authorizes Anabilla to speak about Alice's age on the basis of her physical appearance:

> She says that Alice was twelve years or more last Easter. This she learned from the account of others and does not otherwise know, but says that the whole time she was with this witness she was an adolescent and from her physical appearance [per aspectum corporis] it appears she were fourteen years. (BI, CP.E.89/27)

On one level this may appear a fairly innocuous observation—Alice was well developed for her supposed chronological age. Anabilla had, after all, a fourteen-year-old daughter of her own. The language used, however, is reminiscent of the canonical definition of puberty: "with regards to marriage, pubescents are those who from their physical condition are able to conceive and engender [puberes sunt quoad matrimonium, qui ex habitu corporis concipere et generare possunt]."[29] The text that supports this canon is taken from Isadore of Seville's *Etymologiae* (XI, ii, 13–14). It relates puberty specifically to the growth of pubic hair: "pubescents [puberes] are called from the growth of hair [a pube], that is they are named from the parts of the body of which one ought be ashamed: since these parts first develop woolly growth [lanuginem]." The capacity to reproduce is thus specifically tied to the first appearance of pubic hair.

The unspoken implication in Anabilla's testimony is that her observation went beyond the superficial, but that she would have seen Alice unclothed and seen not just her developing breasts, but also her pubic hair. This point is crucial: the case argued by John Marrays was that even if Alice might not have reached her twelfth birthday, the normal requirement under canon law in order to exercise consent, she had nevertheless achieved a sufficient level of sexual maturity demonstrated by the appearance of pubes.

From a modern, and hence anachronistic perspective it is difficult to reconcile Anabilla's supposedly caring and affectionate demeanor toward her brother's fiancée with her complicity in Alice's sexual initiation. Anabilla's testimony is at this point matter of fact:

> ...three weeks before Christmas last John took Alice to stay with this witness and about a week before they contracted marriage together. Alice stayed with this witness from that time until the feast of St James following and one night, viz. the night of Saturday before Christmas last, the said John and Alice lay together in one bed in a room in this witness's house in Kennythorpe alone and naked together from bedtime until dawn the next day. Asked how she knew this, she said by that Alice told this witness and likewise told one Joan, the witness's daughter. (BI. CP.E.89/27)

Anabilla's account offers its own strategy. It distances Anabilla from anticipation or prior arrangement of the events of that particular Saturday night; she learned of the events only afterward. It emphasizes that the initiative lay entirely with her brother: "John took Alice to stay with this witness." Lastly, it presents the events as a contract of marriage. This last follows logically from the canon-legal understanding that sexual relations serve to make a future contract of marriage, or spousals, immediately binding. This again serves to distance Anabilla from what actually happened that night—if John and Alice were lawfully married, then their lying together in bed "alone and naked" was proper, expected, and certainly not something that Anabilla or anyone else should have interfered with, let alone attempted to prevent.

Anabilla's testimony here provides useful, if second-hand evidence for the consummation of the spousals between John and Alice. It also hints at Anabilla's own inner disquiet at events she must, despite the careful phrasing of her account, have anticipated and hence been complicit in. Her complicity is in fact revealed by Dom. William Marrays's testimony, which tells us that on the night in question, the bed that Alice shared (was made to share) with John was the bed she normally shared with Joan de Rolleston, Anabilla's youngest daughter. Joan herself was displaced to another bed within the same room. This, Dom. William reported from what Joan had told him. If we accept it, then it is hard to believe that Anabilla would have been kept in ignorance about the sleeping arrangements both of John as her guest and of her own young daughter, for which she, as the mistress of the household, would normally have been responsible. If she was not ignorant, then she was complicit. In a patriarchal society where a double standard of sexual morality was commonplace, it was indeed very hard for women not to be complicit; the ethos that tolerated Gervase de Rouclif's seduction of village women—and to which Ellen de Rouclif no doubt turned a blind eye—was not one that paid much attention to women's own feelings.

In trying to discern personal feelings in the way the narrative of events told intersects with the narrative that needed to be told to further the legal case of the party for whom the deponent testifies, we necessarily enter difficult and subjective territory. It is also impossible to distinguish between the quasi-maternal role projected by Anabilla in her testimony and the way she may actually have behaved toward Alice. What we can be a little more confident of is the way in which family solidarity dictated Anabilla's reception of her prospective sister-in-law and her subsequent support of her brother's cause in the Court of York.

The third member of the Wascelyne household to testify was Anabilla's older daughter, Alice de Rolleston, presumably a child of a previous marriage. Alice's age is given as fourteen and more, no doubt to clarify that, though not yet an adult, she had achieved her canonical majority and so was legally entitled to be heard by the court. Joan de Rolleston, the other daughter noted in Dom. William's deposition, was presumably below canonical age (twelve years) or she would have been able to testify alongside her older sister. It is, however, quite exceptional to find witnesses as youthful as Alice de Rolleston giving testimony in the York court; other than for a youth of fourteen or fifteen in a case dated 1355, the present writer knows of no other witness of similar immaturity being called to testify.[30] In the case of the fourteen- or fifteen-year-old, one Robert, son of Maud Katersouth, the deposition specifically states that he was "asked by reason of his youth what age he was at the time of his examination." Robert answered by referring to what his father told him about his age. His mother was also questioned about how old he was.[31] Clearly in the case of Robert, his youth was an issue, although arguably he was closer to the canonical minimum—fourteen in the case of boys—than was Alice de Rolleston. Robert's testimony was also more essential since he was one of only two witnesses to an alleged contract of marriage, but this makes Alice's testimony all the more surprising. What, we may ask, could the testimony of a juvenile female possibly add to the case?

On one level, much of Alice's testimony adds very little: she knew of Alice de Rouclif's age only from the parties in the case and what various of Alice's neighbors had told her; she heard Alice repeatedly complain that the solemnization of her marriage was being delayed and that she was old enough to be John's wife; Alice had told her that she spent the night alone and naked in the one bed with John on Saturday before Christmas; afterward whenever John visited, the couple embraced and kissed. Its value is to reinforce Anabilla's apparently more substantial testimony—the court looked for similarities between depositions as an indicator of veracity—but also to offer yet another form of expertise, namely that of the peer, Alice's de Rouclif's sisterly confidante, another person that Alice could reasonably be thought to have trusted. Much of Alice de Rolleston's testimony is indeed in the form of Alice told her this and Alice told her that. Her mother's, in contrast, reports actual conversations.

The immediate de Rouclif kinship around Alice de Rouclif may readily be reconstructed from the evidence of the depositions. Alice's half-brothers John Fische and Robert de Rouclif have been discussed previously.[32] John Fische, who is described as "clerk" on the list of prospective witnesses noted on the verso to the articles, was said to be twenty-six at the time of his deposition.[33] Consequently he would have been born c. 1339, more than a decade before his mother's marriage to Gervase de Rouclif. Because he would still have been a boy when his father died, it is probable that, like Alice subsequently, he continued to live with his mother even after her marriage to Gervase. Alice would thus have grown up knowing him as her big brother, which may explain why John, on visiting the Wascelyne household "at Kennythorpe for a day and a night around Pentecost last...lay alone in the one room the entire night" with Alice. This was allegedly another occasion for intimate conversation under the cover of jest.

Robert de Rouclif was, at the time of the case, a married man living in Bootham. Agnes del Polles was employed as a servant in his household in Bootham for four years from the Christmas after Ellen de Rouclif's churching in respect of Alice. It follows that Robert was both somewhat older than John Fische and that he had never lived with his sister. Indeed his connection with Alice appears both slighter and rather more formal. He only knew of Alice's age "from being told by Alice's mother and her nurse." He was a witness to her spousals, which of course took place only a short walk from his home, but it was apparently only his wife Katherine, who looked after Alice the following morning prior to her departure for Kennythorpe. Robert thus appears more like a useful contact than a close family member and this would make better sense of the deduction that he was an illegitimate son of Gervase de Rouclif born prior to his marriage to Ellen. What becomes apparent from Robert's will, however, is his very close ties to St Mary's Abbey. He asked to be buried in the abbey cemetery, left money for the building of the bell tower, gave 20s. to the monks for a pittance and made provision for drinks to be shared amongst them.[34]

Alice's mother, Ellen de Rouclif, had been married before her marriage to Gervase and Alice was the youngest of her children.[35] Her first husband probably bore the name Fische. A William Fische of Horsforth, near

Leeds, is recorded in 1362, but there is otherwise nothing to indicate that he was related to Ellen's first husband.[36] Her second marriage took place at Alne around Michaelmas 1350. This probably indicates that she was then living in Alne and that it was her place of residence from her first marriage. It also suggests that her first marriage may have been terminated by her husband's death in the Black Death that had ravaged the region a year previous. Since widows were customarily allowed a year's mourning before they could remarry, we may suspect from the promptness of the second marriage that Ellen may have been put under some family pressure to marry again.[37] Her son John Fische would by this time have been about eleven, nearly old enough to go into service.[38] There is thus no particular reason to suppose that Ellen would have remarried in order to provide for her son.[39]

Ellen de Rouclif was widowed again at Michaelmas 1361, probably as a consequence of the second plague pandemic sometimes known as the Grey Death. Alice was then seven or eight.[40] This time she did not remarry. We may surmise that this was Ellen's deliberate choice: as a twice-widowed woman, it is unlikely that she would have been under the same familial pressure to marry again and so long as she were able to maintain de facto control over the lands she had shared with her late husband, she would have been well able to support herself and her daughter. Second-time widowhood may thus have allowed Ellen, for the first time in her life, a degree of personal autonomy, economic independence, and power. The ability to arrange her daughter's marriage was a reflection of this and by it she may have hoped to gain a degree of security without compromising her personal autonomy. It could be argued that some mothers would have been reluctant to impose the same fate on their own daughters in terms of early, arranged marriage as they had experienced themselves, but many, being so acculturated, would have seen this as the way things were, not something to rebel against. Besides, if Ellen did not arrange Alice's marriage, Sir Brian de Rouclif was sure to do the same—so long as she was under fifteen, and so a minor in feudal law, her marriage was effectively in the gift of her guardian.[41] Ellen may also have felt it her duty to arrange her daughter's marriage since, in the absence of a father, this responsibility fell on her. The personal preferences of a girl not yet in her teens could hardly be balanced against the imperative of an advantageous marriage.

This reading of Ellen's motivation accords well with her energetic pursuit of her cause once Alice had been abducted from Kennythorpe. Though there is no extant record of the royal letters supposedly issued as a result of her petitioning the king, we need not suppose that this is a fiction. The reference to the issuing of letters addressed directly to Sir Brian and sealed under the privy seal indicates that the king was persuaded to circumvent the normal legal processes in order to expedite a resolution. Edward III would no doubt have been moved to act in Ellen's favor precisely because her status as a widow of comparatively humble, albeit gentle social standing rendered her especially vulnerable and hence deserving of royal protection. Unfortunately the privy seal records have not survived, so we can only surmise the contents of the letters or that this was indeed the case.[42] Similarly there is every reason to think that she also approached the "Lord de Percy"—noticed by Lady Margery de Rouclif and by William Sampson, the York goldsmith—and that some kind of arbitration was attempted in the presence "of many knights and esquires." The implication is clearly that Ellen was, regardless of her gender, legally and politically savvy and also very determined. Indeed, we know about these actions precisely because witnesses for Sir Brian used them against her to show that she was partisan and hence an untrustworthy witness.

Margery de Rouclif, not to be confused with Lady Margery de Rouclif who testified for Sir Brian, was Alice's paternal aunt. She can probably be identified with the person of that name recorded in the 1377 poll tax returns for Bootham.[43] If the ordering of the returns is to be taken as a guide, she was a near neighbor of Robert de Rouclif.[44] At the time of the case she was said to be over sixty, so would have been in her seventies by 1377. She appeared before the court twice, once to give testimony about Alice's birth, and once to give testimony about the birth of her deceased older brother, John. Her depositions reflect the sort of intimate involvement in the major events of her brother's household one might expect of a close kinswoman. At the time of John de Rouclif's birth, Margery was one of those who attended, though she was unable to remember who else was present. She did not specifically testify to being at the subsequent baptism, but it is eminently possible since she was able to recall two of the godparents. She was present at the churching and a guest at the feast that followed. She was not present for Alice's birth, but came the next day "to see Alice lying in her cradle."

These four persons comprise the immediate family of Alice testifying in support of John Marrays. Beyond their kinship ties, they are a rather disparate group. Robert de Rouclif was an established householder with his roots firmly established in Bootham and hence the city rather than its rural hinterland. John Fische was a young adult who, though he may have had emotional ties to his mother and little half-sister, need no longer have had ties in Rawcliffe, but is likely instead to have inherited property from his late father in Alne. Margery de Rouclif was, by medieval standards, an old woman whose personal circumstances are unknown. Her name need not imply that she was unmarried, though, given her age and the absence of her husband's name from the beginning of her deposition, she was very likely widowed.[45] And then there was Ellen de Rouclif, the formidable mother who identified neither with her (unknown) natal family, nor the place or the family she had first married into, but with the land and the place she had become part of with her second marriage.

Although not witnesses in the case, two other member of the de Rouclif kinship should be noticed. These are brothers, both called John and both, confusingly, married to Margarets. The first John de Rouclif, senior, otherwise Master John de Rouclif, a married clerk, was evidently related to Robert de Rouclif since Robert named him as heir to his property in Bootham after the death of Robert's widow, but no indication of the relationship, not even the ubiquitous "cousin" is given.[46] John's own will, made after Robert's death in 1377, unsurprisingly makes no reference to Robert, but does note another John de Rouclif, the testator's brother, who is named as an executor alongside his widow. He left the not inconsiderable sum of 20 marks as a marriage portion for one Katherine Wacelyn once she reached fifteen. Wacelyn is not a common name and it is most likely that Katherine was related to the Wascelynes of Kennythorpe.[47] She may even have been a child born to Anabilla and Stephen. Perhaps John was her godfather. The second point of interest in John's will is provision of £20 for masses to be said for his soul and those of Alan de Schuthington and Adam de Ebor. Although John de Rouclif's close ties to the precentor of the cathedral church were no doubt professional, the implication is that the man who ultimately presided over and gave judgment in the case of Marrays c. de Rouclif cannot, at least by modern standards of justice, be regarded as impartial.[48] In 1379, some years after the case, John was to be in dispute with St Mary's Abbey when the abbey constructed a ditch at the top of St Marygate blocking John's (and other Bootham residents') access to and from the Ouse. That the city asked him to negotiate with the abbey, however, may well suggest that he was seen as generally to be sympathetic to the abbey and hence an honest broker.[49]

Master John's widow survived him by ten years, dying only in 1394. Her will adds little in general to that of her husband, though she asked to be buried next to her husband in York Minster, evidently a mark of her late husband's standing. She left 20s. to Thomas de Huntyngton, whom she described as her brother.[50] Evidently the close ties between the de Rouclifs and the Huntyngtons that can be traced back to the 1340s resulted in at least one marriage alliance.

The second, probably younger, John de Rouclif died in 1392. His will shows him to have had land, grain, and various livestock in addition to property in Micklegate, evidence of links with Huntington, but no apparent connection to St Mary's Abbey. He left clothing and a horse to William Wascelyne, whom he (and two years later his brother's widow) named as one of his executors.[51] Of particular interest, however, is his bequest of some sheep, two acres of grain, and adjacent meadowland to one John de Alne and his wife Joan on condition that he continued to serve his widow until the following Michaelmas. The bequest might suggest that he was then employed to look after John de Rouclif's agricultural interests, but this is presumably the same John de Alne who testified on behalf of John Marrays as a youth of eighteen some twenty-six years earlier.[52]

To this disparate group we can add two further names, one related by ties of spiritual kinship, the other by reason of having been Alice's nurse. Alice de Beleby, described as the wife of Richard de Warwyk, was Alice's godmother. In fact, as was normal at this period, Alice would have had two godmothers and a godfather. The testimony of Isold de Kirkeby, who carried a towel and ewer to the church so that the godparents could cleanse themselves of the holy water from the font before leaving the ceremony, confirms that there was a single godfather but plural godmothers.[53] Alice de Beleby's importance, however, is not simply as one of three godparents, but—we may surmise—the principal godparent who was responsible for naming Alice. It was not uncommon for the naming godparent to use their own Christian name and parents may well have effectively determined the name of the child by their choice of naming godparent.

It may be unwise to conclude that, because Alice de Beleby was the only one of Alice's godparents to testify that she had, as the principal godparent, maintained especially close links with the family. At least as likely is the possibility that the links were already established and that by asking her to so act, the family was merely reinforcing them. In fact Alice's testimony could be read to suggest that her contact with the family was comparatively slight. She was questioned "with the consent of the party producing her" solely on the matter of Alice's age, which rather suggests this was the extent of her useful knowledge.[54] What is surprising is that the names of Alice's two other godparents are not recorded in the case, nor was Alice de Beleby prompted to remember them by way of authenticating her remembrance of Alice's baptism.[55] Instead Alice seems to allow her status as Alice's spiritual kin, with the duties of religious instruction that are implicit in that role, to set the tone of her whole deposition. As is singularly appropriate within the context of a Church court, she presents herself as a devout woman and the authority of her testimony follows from this.

Alice's testimony commences with a statement about Alice de Rouclif's age "according to what she dares say on oath before God." All witnesses were examined under oath, but Alice is unusual if not unique in making so specific and bald a reference to the oath as a reason for giving credence to her words. She goes on to state the date of Alice's birth and baptism "and she knows no other reason to offer for her knowing other than she has thought it out in her heart, and according to what this witness has calculated from her memory." This last passage resonates with the process of spiritual reflection in preparation for the making of confession. Alice's deposition is thus presented as akin to confession; she will answer for the truth of her words before her Maker. She goes on that "she remembers that the year in which Alice was born fell in the third or fourth year at most after the great pestilence." Though the Black Death was an obvious point of reference, it is not in fact one used by other witnesses. A like absence of reference to plague as mnemonic device has been noted from Proofs of Age evidence.[56] It is almost as if this event was too traumatic for people to talk about; as a collective memory it was in the process of being airbrushed from history. In this context, therefore, it becomes more than a simple marker of past time, but a reminder of the event itself. Where a modern audience would immediately associate the "plague" with high mortality, a medieval audience associated the "pestilence" with divine wrath and punishment for sin.

Alice de Beleby's personal piety is further reinforced by her second chronological yardstick:

> this witness has a son of the Carmelite order who was made a brother in the order in the year before Alice's birth, and fourteen years or more have gone by from the year he was made a friar. She says further that at the time her son was made a friar, William la Zouche of happy memory was archbishop of York and she believes, as she says, that Alice was born in the time of Archbishop William.…(BI, CP.E.89/27)

This is a departure from the usual maternal remembrance of childbirth, but the son's taking vows as a Carmelite friar can be understood as a kind of spiritual birth. The years are then counted on from the time of this birthday in much the same way as other mothers stated that their child was or would then have been such-and-such number of years. The reckoning of time by reference to regnal years, such as is normal on documents issued by the central government, is nowhere found in this case, but here Alice de Beleby adopts a parallel dating scheme from ecclesiastical government, namely the primacy of the archbishop.

The effect of Alice de Beleby's testimony is to emphasize her role as a spiritual parent whilst masking her role as a carnal parent. The language, the sentiments, the chronological framework, all seem to have more in common with a bishop's register than any of the other depositions. By presenting herself as a singularly faithful daughter of the Church, Alice is a model witness within this ecclesiastical forum. It is, however, well nigh impossible to discern the distance between the Alice de Beleby as presented and the Alice that lurks behind the testimony. It would be too easy to see Alice's testimony solely as a matter of clever presentation—and hence to hear the voice of the ecclesiastical lawyer ventriloquized through Alice. The model of the devout matron is after all a model that only works if there are devout matrons prepared to submit to the model. Alice's responses may well have been cleverly constructed, but if they accentuate her personal piety, that is perhaps because her piety was there to be accentuated. She plays her part so effectively simply because she is playing herself.

Emmot Norice, Alice's nurse during her infancy save for the brief period when she was suckled by Ellen Taliour, may be noticed more briefly. Emmot is identified here by the diminutive or pet form of the name Emma. Such diminutives are sometimes found in listings of the names particularly of children and servants, as for example in the 1379 poll tax returns for the West Riding and for Howdenshire in the East Riding of Yorkshire.[57] The returns for Pontefract list four Emmots, of whom two were wives, one a daughter, and one a servant. This compares with twenty-seven Emmas, of whom nineteen were wives, one a daughter, three were servants, and a further four single women. Those for Eastrington parish (Howdenshire) record six Emmots. Four were married women and two were daughters.[58] The equivalent numbers of Emmas is fifteen, all of whom were wives. The implication is that the diminutive form can be indicative of youth, but there is little evidence that it denotes social inferiority: two of the Eastrington and one of the Pontefract Emmots were married to men identified as artisans and paying the tax at the higher rate. Emmot Norice was hardly an adolescent. She had become Alice's nurse some dozen years earlier and had been a mother immediately before that; she would have been at least in her late twenties. Perhaps the diminutive is to be understood in conjunction with her byname of Norice, the Middle English form of nurse. Emmot is thus not a diminutive associated with a socially inferior hireling, but the pet form used of and by children. Emmot is thus the form the young Alice de Rouclif—and Emmot's subsequent charges—would have learned and used to call her nurse, and so it was the name by which Emmot Norice as a professional nurse came to be known.

Emmot's testimony is fairly brief and unremarkable. She remembered Alice's birth by reference to her own baby boy who had been born some five months before Alice, but had died the day before Alice was born.

Emmot states that "this witness was then hired so that she should be nurse to Alice," a formula that might imply that she had been hired from the time of Alice's birth and which glosses over the interval of three weeks when we know that Ellen Taliour was in fact feeding the newborn Alice. This interval is in fact accounted for by Emmot's next statement: "and so she was, as she says, for the next three years, *excepting a fortnight only*, Alice's nurse [emphasis mine]." The effect is to accentuate the relationship between her own son's death, Alice's birth and her employment as Alice's nurse. It was probably not designed to marginalize Ellen Taliour's testimony, still to be proffered at the time of Emmot's deposition, but read in the light of Ellen's narrative it suggests that Alice was weaned around the time of her third birthday. Emmot's mental reckoning can be reconstructed as follows: Alice was weaned when she turned three; she nursed her the whole of this time save for the first fortnight; thus she nursed Alice for three years less a fortnight.

Besides the de Rouclif kinship associated with Ellen de Rouclif, there were two members of an armigerous de Rouclif family, not obviously related to the other de Rouclifs, who were opposed to the marriage arranged between the young heiress and the abbot's kinsman. The principal player here is Sir Brian de Rouclif, who, though patently the prime mover to contest John Marrays's action for restitution of conjugal rights, itself a response to Sir Brian's abduction of Alice de Rouclif, remains in the background. Indeed it would seem that he was out of the country for part of the time the case was being heard within the Court of York. In late October 1365 he made arrangements to be overseas, perhaps on campaign with John of Gaunt, but it appears from the testimonies of Thomas de Bulmer and William Sampson that he was back in residence by late March 1366.[59] His involvement in the proceedings is apparent from the number of witnesses who are described as his tenants and who testify against the validity of the marriage. Maud de Herthill, not herself a tenant of Sir Brian, stated that "she was asked to proffer her testimony by Sir Brian de Rouclif, but was not instructed." Thomas de Bulmer's testimony is especially revealing. He reports an exchange between Ellen de Rouclif and Sir Brian. Pointing to Ellen, Sir Brian is alleged to have said, "Look, here is that lady. She knows whether she promotes and prosecutes the cause against her daughter or not." Similar words are reported by William Sampson. The effect is to project Sir Brian as Alice's protector against a mother who places her own interests over those of the child she is bound by nature to nurture. It is also to invoke the canonical injunction to regard as suspect the testimony of a mother in cases where the daughter seeks an advantageous marriage.[60]

Lady Margery de Rouclif is a distinguished witness. She is distinguished both in rank and in age. The widow of Sir John de Rouclif, she was a landowner with significant interests in Rawcliffe. She was also the mother of Sir Brian. In 1364, together with her son-in-law William Fairfax and her other son Guy, a clerk in the Privy Seal Office, she purchased twenty messuages and some additional land in Rawcliffe, Skelton, Clifton, and Aton from Sir Brian for the considerable sum of 200 marks.[61] This purchase, an indication of the extent of Sir Brian's own interests in Rawcliffe for he had possessed these lands in addition to those of witnesses who were his tenants at the time of the case, was presumably designed to secure a substantial part of the family inheritance to the male line since Sir Brian's only recorded child was a daughter.[62] At the time of her deposition Lady Margery was described as aged seventy, though her own testimony demonstrates that despite this, by medieval standards, an advanced age, her mental faculties were undiminished. Her age (and rank) probably explain why her examination took place in the parish church of St Wilfrid, presumably close to her own home.[63] Lady Margery gave testimony respecting the birth of Alice's older brother John and its relation to Alice's own birth date. Her claim to expertise regarding John's birth is as his godmother. She names both the two other godparents and the location of the baptism within the abbey of St Mary's. She recalled the day of the baptism with impressive precision: John was born "one Friday three weeks and two days before Martinmas, which feast day then fell on a Sunday, thirteen years ago" and the baptism took place the next day. By remembering that this most important of calendrical feasts fell on a Sunday, Lady Margery offers compelling evidence that John's birth occurred in 1352 and not earlier.

Lady Margery provided a range of reasons for her ability to locate John's birth in time. She refers to the birth of her grandson, also called John, who was born the same year and named before baptism for fear that he would not live.[64] She goes on to describe how "she remembers by the dates of writings and indentures by which she demised certain of her lands at farm." This then is a woman of property taking an active interest in the management of her lands.[65] In fact we know that she had particular reason to have taken such an interest that year because she subsequently attempted to sue her bailiff for failing to render accounts for his time in Rawcliffe. He was outlawed for nonappearance before the justices, but in 1353 pardoned when he surrendered to the Flete prison in London. This may also help explain how Lady Margery knew that in 1352 Martinmas, the principal customary point in the year within this northern region for contracts and leases to run, fell on a Sunday. Her testimony probably also implies a degree of at least pragmatic literacy. We may note finally that the leasing out of lands "at farm" was a common strategy of land management, especially in the decades following the Black Death.[66] The likelihood here is that Lady Margery switched from direct management under a bailiff to leasing out from Martinmas of 1352, hence her concern to have proper accounts from her erstwhile bailiff.

The final reason that Lady Margery offers for remembering the date of John's birth is, as we have previously noted, her knowledge of the births of the children of her village neighbors around the same time. Lady Margery states that she was "then" living in Rawcliffe, which seems to confirm that she was now resident elsewhere. Her comparative vagueness about Alice's subsequent birth and age could perhaps suggest that she had even moved away soon after her decision to lease out her lands, even that the two went hand in hand. Her response that "she does not clearly remember this [Alice's age] at present" contrasts with her clarity in respect of John. It may also be that Alice's birth was simply less worthy of memory—as a girl baby born within an established marriage, she was unlikely to be of any importance in her own right. Instead she merely proffers hearsay testimony to the effect that Alice was not yet twelve citing "the account of many who knew well the time and date of Alice's birth." By offering compelling evidence for the date of John's birth (19 October 1352), however, Lady Margery effectively demolishes the case that Alice was born in the March of 1353 rather than 1354.

The final part of Lady Margery's testimony is her response to an article that claimed that Ellen de Rouclif had herself acknowledged that Alice was under canonical age. Again she offers hearsay evidence: "she heard well it said that Ellen de Rouclif, being in the presence of Lord de Percy, who now is, and of many knights and esquires, confessed and acknowledged just as is stated in the present article." As a member of the local aristocracy, Lady Margery is likely to have taken an interest in such quasi-judicial proceedings and to have had male acquaintances who would have been present.[67]

Lady Margery's testimony is complemented by those of her fellow godparent, John de Melsay, otherwise Melsa or Meaux, and his wife Lettice. This John belonged to a cadet branch of an established aristocratic family whose main branch had landed estates in the East Riding.[68] As such, next to Dom. William, whose status was determined not by birth, but by his office as mitered abbot of the greatest religious house in the north of England, the de Melsays probably represent the highest ranking deponents in the case. This may go some way to explain why the normal convention of requiring witnesses to appear in person in court was not followed here.

Instead, as an entry immediately following their depositions records, they were examined at Houghton, presumably at their home there.[69] The expenses involved in the pertinent employees of the court traveling to and from Houghton would no doubt have been borne by Sir Brian de Rouclif since it was on his behalf that they testified. The willingness of the court to examine the witnesses in their own home is unexplained, but it probably has a pragmatic explanation, not least that Lettice de Melsay was perhaps heavily pregnant or otherwise indisposed and unfit to travel, a suggestion obliquely prompted by her own testimony.[70]

The de Melsays are important witnesses due both to their social rank—many of Sir Brian's other witnesses were poor peasant women—and to their particular knowledge of the date of birth of John de Rouclif, Alice's deceased older brother. This time the expertise lay especially with John de Melsay in his capacity as John's principal godfather. Although John's other godfather, John de Thornton of York, was also called John, it was John de Melsay who "called him his own name John." John de Melsay thus stands in a position directly akin to that of Alice de Beleby. We may surmise that John was in fact of higher social rank than Alice since Gervase de Rouclif probably felt able to call upon a neighbor—the de Melsays were then resident in Shipton—of somewhat greater social rank in respect of the baptism of their oldest son, and hence prospective heir, than in respect of Alice's baptism, a mere daughter whose claims to inheritance were liable to be eclipsed by the births of subsequent sons. This difference is also reflected in John de Rouclif's baptism in the abbey church of St Mary, whereas his sister was baptized in the parochial "chapel" of St Olave.[71]

John de Melsay's testimony is unexceptional. He recalled John's birth both by the fact he was then living in Shipton and, more importantly, because of his role as godfather and name-giver. He named the two other godparents, including Lady Margery, and noted that he had lived at Houghton "for twelve years come a fortnight after Michaelmas next, and if his godson John had lived at that time he would have been two years of age less three weeks." Such precise and authoritative testimony was designed to impress. His deposition concludes with a logical calculation, drawn from the observations previously made, of how old John would have been had he still been alive.[72] There is no peripheral detail here, no reference to John de Melsay's own children, and no discussion of how it was that he was able to locate these past events so precisely in time. Their authority rests solely in John de Melsay's authority.

Lettice's testimony is not a simple echo of her husband's. Given that it was John and not his wife who acted as a sponsor to the infant John, and it is not even entirely clear from her testimony that Lettice was herself present at the baptism, Lettice's testimony is at first sight harder to explain: she substantiates John's statement that at the time of the birth they were living in Shipton, but subsequently moved to their present home at Houghton; she repeats that her husband was John's godfather—she makes no reference to the other godparents; she asserts the date of John's birth. She fails, however, to offer any reason for her knowledge of the birth beyond that implicit in the statement that her husband was the godfather. It may be that Lettice spoke with her authority as a coheiress of William de Houghton, a position that no doubt explains the couple's removal to Houghton some twelve years previous.[73] The real force of Lettice's testimony in fact lies elsewhere. She speaks as a mother: "in the second year after the birth of John, Gervase's son, this witness conceived by her husband and gave birth in that second year, that is to say on the feast of the Nativity of the Blessed Virgin Mary, to a son still living." She also speaks as a daughter: "she remembers otherwise because this witness's father died when she was so pregnant [ita granda] with her child that she was unable to strive to attend her father's burial [non potuit laborare ad interessendum sepulture dicti patris sui]" (BI, CP.E.89/4). Lettice thus suffered three traumatic events in quick succession: death of a parent, childbirth, and moving home. If she was not psychologically scarred by these events, she had at least impeccable reasons for remembering them and locating them in time. In so far as this triple trauma provided a benchmark against which John's birth could be set, or more simply as corroboration of her husband's narrative in respect of the couple's removal to Houghton, Lettice's testimony turns out to be as authoritative as her husband's, only differently so.

CHAPTER 6

DOM. WILLIAM MARRAYS: STORIES AND READERS

Thus far we have considered deponents and their testimonies in ways that seek to explore the social, spatial, gender, or familial ties that link one person with another. As a consequence, the emphasis has been as much on the person of the witness as on the events they describe. This present chapter seeks to shift the focus from personalities to events and one event in particular. In so doing the evidence will not be treated solely in terms of what use modern scholars can make of it, but questions will also be asked about the reception of the testimony by contemporaries.

There are four different levels of activity reflected in the case through the depositions of the various witnesses, though these are but benchmarks along a continuum. The most conspicuous level is of public activity, liable, if not necessarily intended, to be openly witnessed. When Beatrix de Morland told how her husband was killed in Bootham on the Sunday following the feast of Corpus Christi in the year of Alice's birth, she was probably describing just such a public event. The same was surely true of Ellen and Gervase de Rouclif's marriage at Alne, the baptisms of their children, or the churchings of Ellen. The concept of "public voice and report," which is often asserted by witnesses, can be seen as a public activity in its own right. The same Beatrix was no doubt justified in asserting that her testimony, which included the observation about her husband's death, was the subject of just such public voice. The exchange between villagers of news about the births of John de Rouclif, of Alice, and of other village children can likewise be described as the "public voice." Because of their public nature, the persons who might witness or hear of such matters need not be intimately connected to the party or parties concerned. The narrators of these public events or reports can include persons apparently otherwise unconnected to the activities of the pertinent parties. Thus the potter, Thomas de Bulmer, and William Sampson, goldsmith, both of York, testified to their knowledge of Ellen de Rouclif's petitioning the king. Thomas de Bulmer's testimony makes it clear that this was information he had been given by "many in the city of London." In a sense their narratives purport to be no more than relations of this public voice. Their authority lies not in the privileged position of the witness as friend, kinsman, confidante, or the like, but rather in their reporting what many folk knew and spoke of; they were in effect the mouthpiece of the "public voice."[1]

The second level of activity is less overtly public, may be located within the family home and tends consequently to be witnessed by kin, friends, neighbors, or servants rather than by comparative strangers. One example would be the spousals of Alice and John. This took place within an enclosed space and many of the witnesses were close kin. Another example would be the conversation between Alice and Anabilla Wascelyne in the Wascelyne house at Kennythorpe. There is a spectrum of intimacy apparent here. The spousals were both formal and formulaic in terms of ritual and language. The location, though not public in the sense of being accessible or visible to the many, was probably unfamiliar to most of those present. At least two of the witnesses may well have been previously unknown to Alice. The conversation between Alice and Anabilla, on the other hand, was very intimate. Alice spoke in confidence to Anabilla. She chose her own words and confided her innermost thoughts.

The third level of action is similarly intimate, but differs in that activities are secret or hidden. They invariably occur within enclosed space with the intent or at least the effect of concealing those within from those outside. Childbirth represents one such activity. Women were invariably attended only by female friends, kin, or others specifically invited to assist at the delivery. Cecily de Shupton, for example, a known friend of the de Rouclifs, testified to being in the house when Ellen gave birth to John and, more specifically, to being present at the birth of Alice. This last conflicts with Ellen Taliour's testimony, but this need not detract from the substance of either deposition. Ellen Taliour described how Ellen was confined within "a basement room [camera bassa subterraneana] of the main home of Gervase de Rouclif in the village of Rawcliffe" (BI, CP.E.89/16), a description that is remarkably suggestive of the darkened, womb-like enclosures favored for the delivery of mothers in the early modern era.[2]

Childbirth is perhaps something of a special case. It was hidden, but only from men—as we have seen, the intervention of Simon de Folifayt to revive Maud de Herthill's child was exceptional and so memorable. Sexual activity was much more likely to be secret and hidden. As such it was rarely directly witnessed, though a few other cases within the medieval archive of the Court of York contain depositions that testify to the accidental observation of couples having sex.[3]

In this present case the consummation of the earlier spousals between John and Alice is a central plank in John Marrays's argument that there was an established marriage between the couple. He had, therefore, to produce witnesses to the spousals, but also to the consummation. In this respect the case is like a fairly large body of other cases where parties attempted to enforce contracts of marriages on the basis of consummation of a future contract. In most instances, however, sexual intercourse is inferred, not observed.[4] In fourteenth-century cases this invariably followed from observations of the couple concerned naked in bed together. The formulaic phrase "solus cum sola, nudus cum nuda" is repeatedly found and it is found again here. The implication is that it was not so unusual at this period, when people normally went naked to bed, for others to have sight of other members of the household undressed when retiring for bed or even in bed.[5] It likewise implies that if an adult couple of the opposite sex retired for the night in the same bed, sexual activity was presumed to be likely to follow. Further indirect evidence, as here, is sometimes offered in the form of reported acknowledgment of sexual relations by one or both parties. The sexual act, however, remains largely unseen, hidden, and secret.

The fourth level of activity is never directly witnessed because it relates to the invisible workings of the mind and heart, to a person's inner thoughts and feelings. The chapter that follows will attempt to reconstruct something of these, particularly in relation to Alice de Rouclif, from the evidence of a number of different depositions that describe her words and actions. Without Alice's own intimate account, however, this must be a speculative and even imaginative exercise.

The present chapter is concerned with this third level of the secret and the hidden. Our particular focus will be the consummation of the spousals between the presumably adult John Marrays and the preteen Alice de Rouclif. That the couple had sex together is, as we have observed, a critical element in John's case. This readily explains the concern to demonstrate that the consummation had indeed occurred, but it does not of itself explain the particular testimony given. In one of the most startling depositions of the entire case, we are provided with an almost clinical account of the events of the occasion that John was lodged overnight in the same room as Alice. Few other cases offer direct accounts of actual sexual activity and none offer the sort of detail provided here.

The crucial deponent for the actual consummation was not in fact a first-hand witness. Rather he ventriloquizes the words and recollections of one Joan de Rolleston who normally shared Alice's bed, but was displaced on the night in question to elsewhere within the same room. The reason she was not called to give first-hand testimony is easy: she was below canonical age (i.e. twelve) and so debarred from testifying. Thus the only witness to the crucial act cannot speak. John Marrays gets around this obstacle by calling upon a senior ecclesiastic, who, as we have already considered, must also have been a close kinsman both to John himself and to Joan de Rolleston. It is he who gives voice, and hence legitimacy, to the testimony of a young girl, who in legal terms was literally an infant. This was no less than the mitered abbot of St Mary's, Dom. William Marrays. From the Church court's perspective, therefore, we have a deponent of impeccable credentials giving testimony that may make or break the case. From a modern audience's perspective, we have the distinctly uncomfortable phenomenon of a senior male cleric describing the sexual initiation of a girl of no more than twelve years. To the modern reader, encumbered by the sexual anxieties of our own age, the whole thing smacks of the sexual abuse of children.

These impressions are in no way mitigated by the abbot's actual account. He describes what Joan de Rolleston told him "in the fields of Grimston and elsewhere." The circumstances are not explained, but we must suppose that the abbot was visiting his kinsfolk and whilst visiting he went out walking or, more probably, riding with Joan from the house at Kennythorpe where Alice and Joan were staying. We cannot know whether they were accompanied or not, but implicitly the conversation was private. Indeed the force of the description of the location of the conversation is to imply the sort of privacy that would facilitate discussion of intimate and potentially embarrassing information; conversations taking place within the home could all too easily be interrupted or overheard by servants and other household members. Joan told the abbot how:

> she saw John and Alice lying together in the same bed and heard a noise from them like they were knowing one another carnally, and how two or three times Alice silently complained at the force on account of John's labor as if she had been hurt then as a result of this labor...(BI, CP.E.89/27)

These are supposedly Joan's words as reported to Dom. William, rendered into Latin by the clerk, and which I have then retranslated into the vernacular. Despite all the filters, they still have a disturbing immediacy. But that is the point. They were designed to convince the court that the event described had really happened. They are designed to demonstrate not only that John Marrays and Alice de Rouclif shared a bed, not only that they had intended sex or even attempted sex, but that John had actually penetrated Alice. This clinical detail, which is surely the implication of the references to force and to labor, clearly matters more than the implication that Alice was coerced.

A number of observations and questions are prompted. We need not be surprised that a monk should realize the implication of Joan's words. Nor perhaps should we be so surprised that Joan, a girl implicitly below the age of twelve, should have realized what was going on in the adjacent bed. But why does so much trouble need to be taken to show that a couple directly known by other witnesses to have shared a bed "alone and naked together" actually had sex? One answer is simply that John Marrays's claims over this girl and her inheritance rested on proving consummation; he simply had too much to lose. Another is that there was a recognized difference between what a couple of consenting and sexually experienced adults might be presumed to get up to if given the opportunity to spent the night alone together naked and what was true of an adult male and a girl of no more than twelve. Here the underlying presumptions would have differed. Alice would have been a virgin. She would not have wanted sex save out of duty to her husband. The court would, therefore, have expected the alleged consummation neither to have been mutually pleasurable nor painless. The entrance to a virgin's body was, in medieval thought, protected by her maidenhead (hymen) and this barrier had to be broken down to facilitate penetration. Three points may thus be read out of Joan's reported account: Alice was a virgin; penetrative sex occurred; Alice considered herself married to John Marrays and consequently allowed him to have sex with her.

The reading just offered makes sense of why the abbot's testimony was so important to John Marrays's case, but we need to ask another question. Why did John choose to consummate his marriage to Alice well in advance of the solemnization or any arrangement for the couple to cohabit and when she was still no more than (and possibly still less than) eleven? It is not because the couple were starting their new life together and that cohabitation was a simple corollary of this; it is implicit that Alice's residence with John Marrays's married sister at Kennythorpe was intended to be of some duration, even that she would live with her and learn how to run a household by way of preparation for their life together when she was some years older. Such arrangements are not uncommonly set out in aristocratic marriage contracts where the bride is still a child. Such contracts, moreover, invariably state that the couple shall not lie together until the bride is sixteen or thereabouts. Thus we are told that when in 1453, Elizabeth Clifford was married at the age of twelve to William Plumpton, his father 'sir William promised the seid Lord Clifford that they shuld not ligge togedder till she came to the age of xvi yeres."[6] Cohabitation, therefore, was not thought appropriate until after the woman had achieved a degree of sexual maturity and was old enough to bear children without serious physical risk.

It could be that John Marrays wished to secure his marriage against a background of discord over rights of guardianship. Sir Brian de Rouclif's hostility to the marriage can hardly have been unknown prior to his abduction of Alice and the likelihood is that he claimed Alice's wardship and hence control over her marriage. But John surely did not lie with her specifically because he feared that she would be abducted by Sir Brian. It could rather be because she had (or at least was thought to have) reached her canonical majority and hence that intercourse between the couple would cement the marriage. Even that suggestion appears a little less convincing in the light of the uncertainties over Alice's age revealed by the case; if Alice was too young to contract an actual marriage, but only spousals in the ceremony at St Mary's Abbey toward the end of 1364, why should she be thought to have achieved her majority only a couple of weeks later? That the only common element in the testimony relating to Alice's birth date is that she was born just before Easter only adds to these doubts. It may also be that by taking Alice's virginity John was trying to ensure that the marriage would in due course be completed and the associated dowry be paid.[7] A well-born girl who was known to have lost her virginity would have been a much less marriageable commodity and hence there would have been a strong interest to ensure that the marriage was honored.

The explanation of John's action is perhaps more straightforward. By taking her maidenhead and by his act of penetration, Marrays was asserting his authority over—in a sense his ownership of—his child bride. Medieval canonical writers appear to support this position; a betrothed man had the right to consummate his marriage even if his bride were unwilling.[8] The supposedly consensual, but secret contract between Thomas Holland and Joan Plantagenet (the Fair Maid of Kent), was likewise consummated when Joan could not have been more than twelve.[9] The issue here is not sexual gratification, but power. Normal cohabitation could wait for several more years.[10] The concern was not to impregnate the young bride—indeed she was most probably too young to conceive—but literally to impress upon her his authority. The transfer of Alice from her mother's home at Rawcliffe to his sister's home at Kennythorpe and the simultaneous transfer of authority over her from mother to husband-to-be provided both the opportunity and a kind of legitimacy. John may have been mindful of her age only so far as he thought her near enough twelve for the consummation to be socially acceptable, even perhaps customary. Only ex post facto, and as a consequence of the subsequent abduction, was there any need to try to show that Alice was actually of sufficient age for the act to validate a marriage according to the conventions of the canon law.

There is one further aspect of the abbot's testimony that merits specific comment. Invited to affirm that Alice was of sufficient age, Dom. William responded that it was true "by reason of her physical appearance, as anyone examining her can clearly see." This is strikingly similar to Anabilla Wascelyne's assertion that "from her physical appearance it appears that she were fourteen years old." Anabilla and Dom. William are the only two witnesses specifically to locate the night of the consummation precisely in time. Anabilla recalled that it was the night of Saturday before Christmas. This would have been 21 December 1364. Dom. William stated that it was the night of the feast of St Thomas the apostle, which always falls on 21 December. The congruence of the two different calendar conventions must lend weight to the credibility of this precise date. But the date also creates problems. Had the consummation been delayed until some months later, until after Alice's next birthday, then John Marrays's cause would have been much the stronger; even were it to have been the case that Alice had only been born in 1354, she would by March of 1365 have achieved her twelfth year. The canonical provision for pubescent girls in the twelfth year to marry even though they had not achieved their twelfth birthday could have been applied without too much strain. The December consummation, however, is problematic. Had Alice's year of birth indeed been 1354, she would only have been ten when she was made to spend the night with her husband-to-be. Arguments about precise chronological age thus served to introduce and focus serious doubts onto the validity of the union. What mattered was that the court be convinced that Alice was sufficiently developed physically that the court would be minded to find it credible that Alice were twelve or near enough. The function of the testimony offered by Anabilla and by the abbot was to accentuate the canonical stress on pubescence and so silently deflect attention from the potentially more fragile evidence respecting Alice's year of birth and hence actual chronological age.[11]

Dom. William's rhetorical flourish—"as anyone examining her can clearly see"—is particularly interesting. The court took evidence in the form of verbal testimony and it was the written depositions generated from this testimony that were eventually used in determining the case. Does this imply that Dom. William's rhetoric was empty? It is hard to say. It could be that Alice by the time of the case, a year on from the consummation, was indeed showing the physical signs of pubescence. It could equally be that this was a rhetorical fiction offered in full knowledge of the ways in which the court assessed evidence. Anabilla's assertion that the girl who stayed in her home when, even by her own account, no more than twelve, looked like "she were fourteen years" appears to overstate its case. In once more attempted to deflect the court's attention from chronological age, her testimony begins, to modern ears at least, to ring hollow.

Although, as we have seen, Dom. William Marrays's testimony had to do a great deal of work and we can explain something of the detail by reference to its centrality to John Marrays's case, these considerations cannot detract from the salacious, even pornographic nature of the deposition that was compiled. There are parallels here with the strikingly detailed child rape narratives noted by Kathryn Gravdal within the otherwise laconic legal records of the near contemporary *Registre de Saint-Martin*. As court accounts of alleged rapes, the record purposefully stresses the degree of violence used and the forceful nature of actual coitus. They thus differ in emphasis from Dom. William's narrative, but the graphic, almost voyeuristic detail is essentially similar. Gravdal comments on "the unusual attention to narrative development, to the reproduction of direct discourse, and to detail used for chilling effect," going on to suggest "the construction of discursive strategies that make linguistic paradigms of male violence against women acceptable to the learned legal audience and perhaps even pleasurable for the scribe."[12] The question thus arises, is to read Dom. William Marrays's text as pornography intrinsically anachronistic, or was such a reading available to a contemporary audience?

The important point here is that the personnel of the court had privileged access to this and like depositions. The examination of witnesses was a private affair. The witness's words formed the basis of the written deposition that was the currency of the court. As always, at least before the later fifteenth century, the vernacular of the witnesses has been rendered into Latin. The content of this and like documents was thus reserved solely to the Latin-educated clerical personnel associated with the court.[13] The officers of the York consistory were invariably university graduates, but were not normally in major orders.[14] We in fact enter the sexually anxious world of the clerk that Patricia Cullum has elsewhere described.[15] These were men who were uncertain as to whether to follow the celibate life of the priest or to marry. They were also men who may have found a tension between their clerical identity and the hegemonic understanding of male sexuality. Cullum's argument is that such clerks sometimes compensated for this by adopting a kind of hypersexuality, but another possibility would be their consumption of pornographic literature as a kind of vicarious sexual outlet.

The testimony of a senior ecclesiastic now begins to take on a new meaning. What previously appeared to modern eyes as a disturbing account of the sexual initiation of a girl by an older man with its implications of coercion or rape, now reads as a particularly distasteful form of pornography, obscenity even.[16] The clerical reader of the text becomes a vicarious witness to the seduction of a young virgin. There are elements here of pedophilia, of sadism, and of voyeurism. That the scene is relayed indirectly through the witness of another young girl enhances the sense of violation. Her account of events taking place in an enclosed chamber in the darkness of night, and that are as much heard as seen, likewise emphasizes that the reader is privy to dark secrets, an integral part of the pornographic lure of the text.[17] In these terms, Dom. William Marrays becomes at least as complicit in the fashioning of pornography as the female jurors whose graphic, but repetitive testimony forms an important part of extant impotence cases.[18]

The case for reading Dom. William's testimony as a form of clerical pornography circulating amongst a small group of Latin-educated canon lawyers begins to look more convincing when set within the context of a variety of other depositions from elsewhere within the archive and, in particular, the sexually explicit depositions of the female jurors in cases, as just noticed, where annulment of marriage is sought on the grounds of the husband's alleged impotence.[19] In fact these women jurors turn out not to be the honest matrons implied by the canon law, but rather sex workers.[20] The effect of these accounts of sexually voracious women effectively humiliating emasculated men was perhaps humorous, but they served also to validate the (male) reader's own sexual prowess by way of contrast. This point is reinforced by the understanding that these same clerks may well have been users of the professional services of the sort of women who testified in impotence cases.

Dom. William's testimony may or may not have circulated within the court as a form of pornography, the voyeuristic observation of the secret, the hidden, and the illicit. This is to make assumptions about their use by contemporary readers quite independent of their legal purpose or indeed of our own usage of them as documents of social history. One further perspective should be considered, however. In talking about John Marrays, Dom. William may have been talking about his own son. If this supposition is correct, he was thus talking about his son's own sexual capacity and his potential to engender children and thus continue the Marrays bloodline, a future prospect that was threatened by the actions of Sir Brian de Rouclif. This observation may go a little further in explaining the very personal intervention of the abbot in the case, but we need not stop here. If Dom. William was John's father, then John was himself conceived as a result of an illicit and presumably secret relationship between his father and the woman who was his and, we may assume, Anabilla

Wascelyne's mother. Whether this relationship took place before or after his profession as a Benedictine monk is merely to trespass further into the realms of speculation. He may even have occupied that liminal place between being intended for a monastic career, but not yet professed.[21] The relationship was located in a long-hidden past and was illicit because, whether vowed to celibacy or otherwise, Dom. William could not have been married. By describing his son's sexual initiation of Alice—an action that was illicit in that their marriage had not yet been solemnized, but may also have been illicit because Alice was underage, and was in any case morally transgressive—Dom. William may also have been reliving his own affair with a woman he was not married to and perhaps could not lawfully marry. It was perhaps the nearest he could get to talking of his secret past, his testimony before the Court of York representing a form of confession, but perhaps also a proud claim to his own lineage.

To understand some of the deposition material presented as, inter alia, a form of clerical pornography is, of course, a contentious proposition that must make certain assumptions about the circulation and readership of the depositions concerned. Copies of the depositions would, however, have to be been made available to the counsel for the contesting party and they were used ultimately by the Official or other presiding officer. The only internal evidence we have for the reading of the depositions comes in the form of a series of contemporary marginal annotations to the first two sets of depositions, which were clearly made to aid the process of evaluating the testimony given.[22] Whether these were made by Adam de Ebor in his capacity as judge or on his behalf by an assistant with a view to aiding him in his judgment is not apparent. What is clear is that these annotations were primarily designed to evaluate the merits of the conflicting evidence respecting Alice's age. Various annotations—"de etate [concerning age]" or simply "xiij·ā· [13 yrs.]" (BI, CP.E.89/27) are noted against the depositions for John.[23] "De etate" is also used against some of the counter depositions, but some testimony was pointedly qualified; two annotations note that the witness was not present at the birth and a third that knowledge depended on the "relation" of others. The process of annotation thus served to highlight both the superior number of witnesses offered by John, but also to cast doubt on the reliability of the witnesses for the other side.

The annotations just described are rare evidence for the process of evaluating the depositions once collected with a view to making judgment. How exactly judgment was reached is not recorded, but these annotations suggest that the proper canonical considerations of the reliability of witnesses and the weight of numbers were duly considered. In this respect once again, the presence of Dom. William Marrays must be seen as to the advantage of John Marrays since the abbot must surely have been regarded as a strong and (supposedly) impartial witness. This may be set against those witnesses who could be considered less trustworthy because of ties of kinship—Ellen is portrayed as striving unduly to promote her daughter's marriage to John—or dependency, as was the case with a number of witnesses identified as tenants of Sir Brian, rendered them partisan. No less significant was the implication that some witnesses might perjure themselves because vulnerable to bribery on account of their comparative poverty—hence the specific questions as to material worth asked of several of Sir Brian's deponents. Lastly there is the specific allegation of perjury leveled by John de Alne against Ellen Taliour, an attack that is compounded by the implicit challenge to Ellen's sexual morality—she supposedly perjured herself by denying that she had committed adultery with Gervase de Rouclif. It is not too hard for the modern reader to spot the irony (and the inevitable double standard) of Dom. William being presented as an exemplary witness, a pillar of the Church, but Ellen Taliour as a promiscuous and untrustworthy woman.

Repetition of the same information, the process of proof by reiteration of the same points, is thus central to the making or breaking of a case. The crucial repetition here is the number of years that had elapsed since Alice's birth. The present case has in fact many similarities to the proof of age procedures conducting under feudal law whereby a jury of local men testified to the effect that the heir or heiress of a tenant in chief of the crown had achieved his or her majority and so could legally inherit.[24] These have most recently been described by Joel Rosenthal who notes the way in which persons of comparatively humble rank are relied upon to give testimony on behalf of their superiors.[25] These jurors frequently justified their remembrance of the age of the heir or heiress by tying the date of his or her birth to some coincidental event in their own lives, just as in the present case. Even the stories the jurors tell—the events they relate—sometimes coincide with those narrated by witnesses in the present case. Thus Rosenthal observed a juror who, like Isold de Kirkeby, "took water to the church in a silver basin for the godparents to wash their hands after the. . .baptism," but notes that a common reason for remembering was by reference to the births of the jurors' own children.[26]

The procedures of the feudal jurisdiction, which were probably familiar to at least some of those involved in the de Rouclif case, seem to have shaped the pattern of evidence-giving even within a very different legal forum. In one sense the procedure is more like that found for example in tithe litigation or cases concerning parochial rights where, as Charles Donahue has described, deponents act in a manner akin to jurors rather than actual witnesses—only one deponent actually claimed to have witnessed Alice's birth—and it is as much weight of numbers as the quality of first-hand testimony that serves to establish "truth."[27] In another sense, however, the similarities between this case and the proofs-of-age cases indicate that both drew upon shared traditions of remembering and of relating information of communal interest; we have already observed how the news of the birth of Alice (and of other village children) was a matter of discussion within Rawcliffe even some time after her actual birth. The distinctive difference is that in the de Rouclif case, it is village women who are the preferred spokespersons for this shared, communal memory. If their stories carry particular weight, it is both because they have the authority of the often more immediate and compelling personal experience of childbirth and motherhood than was available to male jurors and because their narratives fit within an established and familiar cultural model. It is the very ordinariness of the events described that makes them the more credible, but it is also this same folksy mundanity that dictates the testimony of very ordinary people. In contrast, the extraordinary testimony concerning the consummation of the contract between Alice and John demanded an extraordinary narrator.

CHAPTER 7

ALICE THROUGH THE LOOKING GLASS

The chapters thus far have focused on the relationships between witnesses and the relationship between witnesses and the testimony they proffer. As such the principal parties in this case have many times been observed, but always through the report of others. This, of course, is a product of the way such cases were conducted within the Church courts, but it need not preclude our attempting to read this evidence from a rather different perspective and to attempt to understand something of the thoughts and feelings of the parties themselves. In the present chapter, I shall attempt to do precisely this in respect of Alice de Rouclif.

Most marriages, whether arranged or otherwise, in the later Middle Ages went undisputed. The marriage between John Marrays and his child bride, Alice de Rouclif, is unusual in that it was obstructed and the consequent action initiated by John in the ecclesiastical Court of York generated a mass of documentation that has survived the ravages of time. The friction was of itself neither a product of the role played by the immediate kin of one or other party to arrange the marriage nor of the relative youth of at least one of the parties. There is indeed quite a lot of evidence to allow us to locate the marriage of an aristocratic heiress in a larger context of arranged marriages and youthful marriages. Focusing on considerably higher echelons of aristocratic society, Hollingsworth's work has demonstrated that heiresses had a mean marriage age in the later teens, though closer scrutiny of his data suggests two distinct patterns. One group tended to marry in their late teens or early twenties, but another married whilst still in their earlier teens.[1] It is likely that these last represent girls who, like Alice, were wards. In such cases guardians may have chosen to exploit the window between girls achieving their canonical majority and their legal majority at about fifteen.[2]

Such marriages were not especially liable to litigation and actions for the annulment of marriages citing the canonical impediments of, as here, extreme youth (infra annos nubiles) or of undue familial pressure (force and fear), are in fact uncommon if we are to trust the pattern of litigation extant at York. The Court of York is, however, unusual in preserving to the present such a large volume of records relating inter alia to marriage litigation from the very beginning of the fourteenth century. Particularly striking is the survival of large numbers of depositions. Only the diocese of Canterbury begins to rival the York archive. Here a number of very early cases, some predating the Fourth Lateran Council, survive, but with the exception of an early fifteenth-century book of depositions, the fourteenth and fifteenth centuries are unrepresented.[3] A large body of London depositions survives from the later fifteenth century and some Norwich material from the end of the same century, but otherwise very little in the way of actual depositions survives from other English dioceses. It follows that the present case is less a freak record of entirely atypical circumstances than a rare record of a marriage that may have resonated with the experiences of numbers of other aristocratic girls and their families.

The case, as we have seen, can be explored on a number of levels. From a canon-legal perspective—the filter through which the extant evidence from the Court of York must necessarily be viewed—the case revolved around whether or not a canonically binding contract existed between John and Alice. John's case argued that there was an established marriage, which had unlawfully been impeded by the abduction of Alice. It rested on showing that the couple had contracted whilst Alice was still under age, but that Alice had subsequently affirmed the contract, and hence made a binding marriage, by willingly consummating their relationship at a stage when, even if not yet actually twelve, she was sufficiently physically mature to be considered to have achieved puberty.[4] The case presented in opposition to John's account of events claimed that Alice had been forced into the spousals and was opposed to marrying John, but, more importantly, that Alice was below canonical age and so could never lawfully have ratified any contract of marriage to John.[5]

Other ways of looking at this case have stressed the solidarities of kinship and of locality that underpin the evidence of litigation. On one level this looks like a conflict between families and even within a family. On another level it looks like a power struggle between, on the one hand, St Mary's Abbey and, on the other, the tenants of Rawcliffe and their lay lord. We move further and further from what may at first sight appear to be a struggle for the affections of Alice de Rouclif, although as we have seen, her consent and her ability in law to consent is central to the action in the Court of York. Ironically, we in fact know very little of the two parties at the center of this case. As the principal parties, neither were examined in the way their witnesses are and so we are left with no depositions to analyze. Both appear, from a documentary perspective at least, comparatively obscure. In the case of Alice, an underage heiress drawn from the lowest echelon of landed society, such obscurity is unremarkable. That of John Marrays is perhaps more frustrating than surprising. Even his putative kinsman—we may suspect his father—is comparatively obscure beyond his office as abbot of St Mary's. We know something about him as the officeholder, but apparently nothing about the man.

How far can we reconstruct the motives and intentions of John and Alice from this limited and necessarily loaded evidence? In one sense, we cannot. We may have evidence relating to their actions, but the feelings that lie behind these cannot be known. The evidence in respect of Alice is, however, more complex because her feelings are actually central to the case. Consent, the central plank of the Church's teaching since the late twelfth century on what made a binding marriage, might normally be expressed by the exchange of words or where, as here, spousals already existed, by (supposedly) consensual sexual relations, but it still had to be shown that the parties were motivated by reasons other than fear or coercion. On another level, we can at least offer readings of the evidence that attempt to make sense of the couple's actions without claiming that any one reading is more "true" than another.

John Marrays's reasons for bringing an action for restitution of conjugal rights, an otherwise obscure action within the ecclesiastical courts, can be seen as a logical response to the abduction of Alice de Rouclif by Sir Brian de Rouclif.[6] Such an action had the advantage that it demanded more of the defendant to disprove the marriage than of the plaintiff to prove it, unlike a simple suit to enforce a contract of marriage where "the burden of proof was on the person who sought enforcement of the marriage contract."[7] The decision to initiate an action in the Church court has to be seen alongside an energetic attempt by Ellen de Rouclif to interest the king in Sir Brian's actions, which reportedly resulted in the issuing of letters under the king's privy seal and some kind of attempted arbitration more locally by various members of the regional aristocracy under "Lord de Percy," presumably Henry, third lord Percy (d. 1368), a leading magnate and experienced administrator.[8] Both were in effect different strategies to the same end. Clearly the marriage was a matter of considerable importance to John as to his would-be mother-in-law. Much energy and expense were to be invested in securing the same.

For John the marriage brought the prospect of material advantage, both in terms of the dowry offered (£100 or 100 marks), but also control over Alice's inheritance and the income to be derived from this. It would also have given him a stake in the local community and, if our surmise that he was the illegitimate son of the abbot of St Mary's is correct, have lent him status as a member of the landed classes, albeit at the very lowest level. Whether or, as is more likely, not he is the same John de Marrays, franklin listed in the 1379 poll tax returns for Burton Salmon, the descriptor would be an appropriate indicator of his status. We need hardly suppose that John was motivated by any particular affection or desire for his child bride. His contact with her, so far as the depositions allow us to see, was slight and much of his courting, evidenced by the giving of gifts, was done by proxy. As Noël Menuge has argued, Alice's consent was not an issue until the court action retrospectively made it one.[9] John did not have to try too hard to win her or please her. When, on his visiting Kennythorpe, she begged him to hasten the marriage celebrations, he told her to be quiet. Anabilla Wascelyne's deposition here probably intends this exchange to show not just Alice's desire to be married, but also the power relationship between husband and wife. To modern ears it sounds more like an irritated adult telling off an overexcited child. It is emphatically not the relationship of a devoted lover to his mistress.

What then of Alice? Menuge succinctly summarizes the role of the court in "paradoxically" attributing "to her an autonomy which its procedures deny her: it assumes she is under age and cannot speak for herself and then decides that she can and did. It first silences her and then creates its own voice for her."[10] We know what others wanted her to have said and done: John's case was that she wanted the marriage and demonstrated her consent at critical moments; the counterargument, supposedly in Alice's name, denied that Alice was of sufficient age to be able to exercise her consent one way or the other. We are in a looking-glass world in which we learn of Alice's supposed thoughts and actions only as selectively presented by others whose agenda is to present her as having consented to the marriage and always to have been in favor of the marriage. It would be too easy to conclude, therefore, that the real Alice also wanted the marriage or that her consent was unambiguous. The evidence needs to be marshaled and evaluated with care, but whatever we do, Alice's own feelings must remain enigmatic.

There are three different occasions that the depositions focus on to make the case that Alice wanted the marriage. Two are specific moments crucial to demonstrating that the canon-legal requirements for a marriage had been satisfied, namely, the initial spousals made at St Mary's Abbey and the subsequent consummation at Kennythorpe. The second also served to prove that the marriage was a consummated and hence established marriage for the purposes of an action for restitution of conjugal rights. The third is not a specific moment, but rather a more general observation of Alice's time at Kennythorpe and her social interaction with a number of different persons. Of these, the first is the least informative of Alice's feelings. We are presented with testimony concerning the spousals in terms of the day and time, the precise location, who was present, the ritual actions performed, and the precise words used. Ellen de Rouclif remembered the words exchanged as "Here I take you Alice to my wife to have and to hold until the end of my life and to this I plight you my troth," to which Alice replied in like words merely substituting "John to my husband" for "Alice to my wife." The couple held hands for their vows, but released them and kissed after pronouncing the words. The words and the ritual actions were entirely formulaic. It would not have been necessary specifically to remember John and Alice's spousals in order to know what supposedly (and probably in fact) happened.

In anticipation of the subsequent counterargument that Alice went along with the spousals only unwillingly or under duress, the witnesses were specifically asked about her demeanor. John Fische, probably the closer of Alice's two half-brothers, asserted that "Alice contracted marriage willingly and with a cheerful countenance, compelled neither by force nor by fear." Robert de Rouclif, her other half-brother, in a deposition that is so clipped that it has surely been edited, stated merely that the couple "contracted marriage together by words of present consent of their free will without either force or fear placed on either party." That Alice was in fact forced into the contract through threats and fear was asserted in "Alice's" exception and associated articles, but no deponent was able to offer any evidence for this since all the witnesses to the spousals had already testified in support of John.[11] In fact we should be wary of putting an anachronistic gloss on consent. Alice was socialized in a world in which, in Waugh's words, girls of gentle birth "had the right of refusal, not the right of choice" but where in fact "complete refusal...seems to have been rare."[12]

The second specific moment, the consummation of the earlier spousals, is, of course, less well documented. We are largely dependent on Dom. William Marrays's testimony as discussed in the last chapter, but his account is itself second-hand. A number of other witnesses refer to the consummation. Beatrix de Morland, who ran the Bootham hostelry patronized by the family, for example, said "that she certainly heard say that after the contract she was obedient to John as to her husband because she lay with him in one bed alone and naked together." Anabilla Wascelyne, in whose home the consummation occurred, claimed to have known about it because she was told of it both by Alice herself and by her own daughter Joan, who was also Dom. William's authority. Ellen de Rouclif, Alice's own mother, likewise knew of it, but only through "the relation of John Marrays and Anabilla, his sister." William Pottell, John's factotum, knew about it "because this witness made the bed in which John and Alice lay together at Kennythorpe alone and naked together in a certain room." This observation leaves it ambiguous whether he knew of his master's intentions or whether he saw evidence of the night's activities; it is unclear whether we have a hint here of the practice long established in some Mediterranean cultures of using the blood-stained sheet as proof of virginity. The narrative could, however, be read to indicate that he merely made up the bed against his master sleeping in it with Alice, but that the ambiguities introduced are deliberate.

The third "occasion" is really a series of encounters witnessed by various deponents concerning Alice's time at Kennythorpe beyond the night of the consummation. Most important is Anabilla Wascelyne's account, but John Fische also visited his half-sister at Kennythorpe and slept in the same room as her, and William Pottell visited a number of times at John's behest. We also have the testimony of Katherine, the wife of Alice's other half-brother Robert, about a conversation she had with Alice hours before she first came to Kennythorpe. This last is perhaps the logical chronological starting point.

Katherine de Rouclif looked after Alice on the morning of her departure for Kennythorpe. During her stay, she asked Alice if "she was quite willing to go to Kennythorpe away from her mother." Alice's reported reply was "yes...she wanted to go wherever John wished her to go." Katherine then added the interesting statement that "she was never able to examine why Alice was, from the time she first saw John, always so well disposed to have him as her husband." Katherine's observation could anticipate or answer an unasked question; the point that is made is that Alice wished to be married to John, that the attachment was strong even if unexpected.

The various testimonies of Anabilla Wascelyne, Alice de Rolleston, John Fische, and William Pottell make sense in the light of the consummation that reportedly occurred fairly soon after Alice's arrival in Kennythorpe. John Fische "jesting" asked Alice when he spent the night alone with her in the same room whether she would rather be married to John or remain single. "Jesting" was presumably the way John Fische felt able to ask his young half-sister about so intimate a matter. We cannot but be struck also by the fact that the question would have been posed as Alice was again confronted by a naked adult male since the wearing of night attire was unknown; John reiterates in the main part of his deposition that Alice was "his sister" implicitly to explain what might otherwise appear an impropriety. There would thus have been an inevitable sexual edge to John Fische's question. Alice replied she wanted to be married to John.

The same teasing approach was adopted by William Pottell. He asked Alice if "she was happy with John as her master [contenta de dicto Johanne magistro suo]" (BI, CP.E.89/27). Her reply was again affirmative; Alice wanted John for a husband. Pottell then responded, somewhat crudely, with the retort, "May you grow up so he is able to do with you as is fitting [crescas bene sic quod posit facere tecum sicut decet]" (BI, CP.E.89/27). Alice's reply does not duck the sexual insinuation, but meets it head on: "I am adequate [satis sufficiens] to be his wife, but not his whore" (BI, CP.E.89/27). The purpose of this testimony is clearly to reinforce the position that not only was Alice willing to be married to John, she had implicitly already had sex with John, and that she was physically sufficiently developed, that is she had reached puberty.[13] This is not, of course, the spin that Alice herself necessarily intended.

Alice's retort that she was mature enough to be John's wife, but not his mistress is reiterated elsewhere. The first part (about being a wife) is found in Alice de Rolleston's testimony, but the whole phrase is recalled by Alice de Rolleston's mother, Anabilla de Wascelyne. In private conversation between the two, Alice complains, "I am old enough and mature enough [sum in sufficienti etate constituta et satis senex] to be his wife, but not his mistress [amica]—in English 'leman'"[14] (BI, CP.E.89/27). Some time later she confronts John with the same charge, "I am mature enough to be a true wife, but not a mistress." Alice's repeated assertion is of course very useful for John's cause, but that it is reported, in whole or in part, by three different witnesses and Alice supposedly uttered it on a number of different occasions tends to lend strength to the supposition that these are words that Alice really spoke. Of course, that is the intention.[15]

Alice's reported conversations and actions go beyond this one phrase. The principal source here is Anabilla Wascelyne's deposition, though the substance of it is confirmed by Alice de Rolleston's less detailed testimony. It is to Anabilla that Alice nervously opens her heart with her "Dame, I have a secret to tell you" gambit. This, as we have remarked before, sounds like the authentic voice of a child struggling to find a way to share with another her innermost concerns. The credibility of the testimony of course depends on the contemporary reader(s) of the deposition finding the same note of authenticity. But just because the testimony is presented in a manner designed to make Alice's reported words sound credibly her own, does it follow that they are necessarily to be distrusted? Anabilla would have no need to remember any words of Alice's that might undermine John's case, but equally she hardly need perjure herself by "remembering" words she did not in fact utter if some of Alice's actual words served the same purpose. It is our contention that Anabilla's testimony, though selective and partisan, is essentially a reliable record of some of what Alice said.

Alice's concern, as suggested by her reported words, was for the speedy solemnization of her marriage. As we have seen, the reason she gives for this desire is her repeated assertion that she was old enough to be John's wife, but not his mistress. There are several observations that follow from this. Alice clearly did not feel that the consummation of her earlier spousals constituted of itself a valid marriage: by having sex with John, Alice became merely his mistress. That Alice had little understanding of the finer points of canonical teaching on marriage is unsurprising. What is also suggested here is that Alice in fact understood solemnization, the public ceremony at which vows were exchanged *in facie ecclesie*, that is at the church door in the presence of a priest, was what was needed to elevate her status to that of wife in the eyes of the wider community and indeed her own eyes. Alice's concern for her sexual reputation, which must reflect the values in which she and many other girls of her day were socialized, thus displaced any essentially anachronistic concern about the inappropriateness of a girl not yet in her teens having sex with an adult male chosen as her husband by her own mother.[16] The desire for solemnization also accords with Alice's reported statement to Anabilla, "Dame, I know that I will not have more cloths of my master before I have the veil for my marriage." This assertion was recounted by way of reinforcing the message that Alice wanted to be married to John, but it in fact also tells us that Alice understood marriage in essentially ritualistic terms. She was looking for the medieval equivalent of the white wedding.

This last observation might also make sense of Alice's response to John's explanation of his reason for delaying the solemnization of their marriage. John reminded Alice, "You know the agreement between your mother and other of your friends [family] and me that I will espouse you at a future date and I will stand by the agreement because I do not want to lose a hundred marks."[17] John thus presents the marriage as a business transaction in which (from Alice's perspective) the desired objective is relegated to some "future date." Anabilla Wascelyne went on to recall that "Alice kept on repeating unreasonably this reply." What Alice might have been railing against is her sense that John was placing financial and legalistic considerations above her sexual honor. But there is probably more here. If Alice understood marriage in romantic, "white wedding" terms, she would have found John's logic incomprehensible. For her, marriage was too important to be postponed indefinitely because of such worldly considerations as money and legal contracts.

If Alice understood the public ceremony of solemnization as the only proper form of marriage and saw sex with John as tantamount to being his mistress, the question arises as to why she allowed him to have sex with her soon after her arrival at Kennythorpe. One possibility is of course that she did so unwillingly.[18] The evidence contained in the testimony of Dom. William Marrays is inevitably partisan and so presents the consummation as implicitly consensual, but in striving to indicate that actual penetrative intercourse occurred, Dom. William relates "how two or three times Alice silently complained at the force on account of John's labor as if she had been hurt as a result of this labor." The silent complaints could be read other ways. A scared and bewildered child faced with the forceful advances of an older and much stronger man need not have cried aloud and could hardly have resisted to any effect. She may well have frozen, a common response on the part of rape victims.[19] Her sense of shame, of confusion at the behavior of the man she was supposed to honor and obey, her impotence in the knowledge that somehow she was expected to endure this ordeal and that the adults elsewhere in the house were complicit in the nightmare she was experiencing, that ultimately no one would help her, all would have stifled her cries and reduced her response to the silent complaints witnessed from across the room by (a presumably equally scared) Joan de Rolleston.

There is perhaps much truth in the interpretation just offered, but it would be possible to modify certain elements of it. Rape, coerced sex, where the pressure may be psychological rather than physical, and consensual sex represent points along a continuum. More importantly, following Nicola Gavey's recent discussion of "(hetero)sex," Alice ought still to be understood as a victim even if she neither considered John's behavior inappropriate nor did anything to resist him or signal her unwillingness.[20] Again we are confronted by the problem that we know something of what Alice did, albeit from the partisan and hearsay testimony of Dom. William Marrays, but we do not know what Alice's thoughts and feelings were. Beatrix de Morland's words—"she was obedient to John as to her husband because she lay with him in one bed alone and naked together"—may be useful here. If Alice understood she had a duty of obedience to John as her husband, then she may have thought she had a duty to allow him to have sex with her. Once again we can be reasonably sure that Alice would have been socialized to look to a husband as her lord or master, this last being the term used by William Pottell. Obedience in a wife was a womanly virtue valued alongside chastity. Alice may have felt obligated to yield to John's desire because she did not consider that she had any option to refuse.

Two other aspects of Alice's behavior in the Wascelyne household may militate against the notion that the consummation constituted rape. First, Alice appears to have told others about the consummation. Certainly she told Annabilla Wascelyne and Alice de Rolleston, but interestingly not apparently her own mother. This may simply be a product of her lack of contact with her mother following her removal to Kennythorpe, but it may also represent embarrassment at discussing such matters with her own mother. It need not imply that Alice did not get on with her mother. We do not, however, know in what terms Alice discussed the consummation since the purpose of the testimony was merely to bolster the understanding that it had occurred. The second aspect of Alice's conduct we should notice is her reported affectionate behavior toward John whenever he visited Kennythorpe. The couple were said to have embraced and kissed, hardly the behavior of a victim toward her assailant. Obviously the witnesses who testified to this effect had a vested interest in so doing and consequently their words may be suspect. Equally Alice could have been going through the motions of behaving appropriately toward her "husband," but her outward actions may have hidden her inner feelings. It could be, however, that a lonely girl, taken away from her natal home and her childhood friends was merely trying to find affection from a man who was prepared to take notice of her. If we see Alice as an abused child, we need not expect her actions to be those of an emotionally undamaged adult.

Alice's "consent" may not have depended solely on a sense of duty and of obedience. She may also have understood sex as integral to marriage. This makes sense of Alice's reply to Pottell's crude exhortation "May you grow up so he is able to do with you as is fitting." In retorting with her catchphrase "I am adequate to be his wife, but not his whore," Alice reveals an explicitly sexual understanding of the duties of a wife and the nature of the marital relationship. It follows that Alice may have felt that consenting to sex with John was a necessary stage in their marital relationship and that, by so consenting, the process toward solemnization would be greatly accelerated—hence her uncomprehending frustration at John's vague "I will espouse you at a future date."

Another consideration is Alice's liminal position as a child on the verge of adolescence. Leaving home might symbolically mark the end of childhood, but marriage conferred a form of social adulthood.[21] Part of Alice may, in her desire to be considered grown up, have welcomed her marriage to John, her leaving her childhood home at Rawcliffe and her departure for Kennythorpe. Within this context she may well have agreed to sex with John because that was part of what being a wife, of what being grown up was about. Similarly the kisses and embraces exchanged between the couple reported by Anabilla Wascelyne and her daughter Alice can be seen as Alice's attempt to behave like a wife and an adult, and this is precisely how this evidence is used within the case.

Our argument thus far depends on Alice's simultaneously holding two positions that are from a strict canonical perspective incompatible;

however, Alice was no canon lawyer, but rather a girl not yet in her teens, and the capacity to hold conflicting beliefs at the same time is very human.[22] These two positions are that Alice was bound to John as his wife (and had been since the spousals) and that the couple were not properly married until the contract was formally solemnized. Within this logic, the consummation of the earlier spousals had no particular impact on the validity or otherwise of their marriage, though it did make the need for solemnization the more urgent. Canon law would in fact have made a distinction between a clandestine marriage and a canonical marriage and this perhaps has some parallels with Alice's own position. According to the provisions of the fourth Lateran council, only marriages publicly contracted before a priest and after due notice through the publication of banns were licit, but any consensual contract between a couple free to marry could potentially make a valid marriage.

The reason that from a very early stage Alice may well have considered herself actually married to John depends not on her understanding and sharing the canonical notion that a consummated future contract constitutes a binding marriage, but rather on the initial spousals. The adults present and especially Richard Bernard and Adam de Thornton, who were probably both well-versed in the canon law, must all have understood the spousals as no more than a legal commitment to a future marriage. This is not necessarily how Alice would have understood it. First, the occasion was hardly routine. The spousals were conducted within the precinct of St Mary's abbey. Present were two, presumably unfamiliar, but authoritative men—Richard Bernard, who can be identified as the abbey's steward, and the notary public Master Adam de Thornton. Richard Bernard, whose clerical status may in Alice's eyes have lent him priestly authority, presided, guiding the couple in the words to use as at any marriage ceremony conducted *in facie ecclesie*—and was not St Mary's *in facie ecclesie*?[23] Finally, the words used directly followed the marriage rite must surely have been familiar to Alice. The vows, moreover, were in the present tense—"I take you"—not, as she might have expected if the ceremony was merely a kind of engagement, "I will take you." Alice, who would have been more conscious than anyone else in Richard Bernard's chamber that evening that she was not a little girl, but a young woman about to embark on the career that all well-born and well brought-up girls were taught to aspire to, must surely have felt that the words she exchanged with John bound the couple for the rest of their lives.

The foregoing discussion has tried to explain Alice's actions and words in the light of her immediately previous experiences. It has offered a speculative interpretation of Alice's thoughts and feelings as experienced at the time, which presents Alice as having consented to her marriage because she had so completely internalized the social and familial expectations of her age. In retrospect, as an adult, she may perhaps have agreed with Katherine Willoughby, married at fourteen to Charles Brandon, Duke of Suffolk, thirty-five years her senior, that "I cannot tell what more unkindness...than to bring our children into so miserable a state not to choose by their own liking."[24] We likewise, from our own retrospective and arguably anachronistic perspective, see Alice as a victim and see her marriage as a form of child abuse. It is, however, possible that rather than understanding the child Alice to have imagined her relationship to John up to the time of the case as "consensual," whilst leaving open the (surely rather slender, because also essentially anachronistic) possibility that an adult Alice may have seen things differently, that the process may in fact have worked in reverse. The Alice who was betrothed whilst still only ten or perhaps eleven, who was taken to live with strangers and was then forced to sleep with her new "husband" only a couple of weeks later—an act that we may legitimately label as rape—may have attempted to rationalize these events over which she had no control as a romantic, affectionate and consensual relationship as a way of regaining some sense of control over her life. Her urgent appeal to Anabilla Wascelyne and subsequently to John to hasten the solemnization of their marriage was part of this effort to take control. If the marriage were solemnized, somehow her life would have been placed once again within a familiar and comfortable paradigm, but so long as the solemnization were delayed Alice would see herself as the whore that her pathetic, but deeply felt refrain "I am mature enough to be a true wife, but not a mistress" implies.

PART II

SEX AND THE CITY

CHAPTER 8

BREWING TROUBLE: THE DEVOUT WIDOW'S TALE

Early in 1411 a matrimonial cause was heard in the Court of York between John Dale, otherwise John del Dale, on the one hand and Agnes Grantham and John Thornton on the other.[1] All the parties were resident in York. Agnes was a very eligible widow. Her husband, the mason Hugh de Grantham, had died in March of the previous year leaving a net estate, less property, worth just short of £150.[2] Agnes, who is described unflatteringly as "a woman of great age," herself managed a significant brewing business.[3] John Thornton, otherwise John de Thorneton, was a well-to-do draper who had served as chamberlain earlier in his career.[4] He enjoyed a long-standing business partnership with William Pountfret, his next door neighbor in Coppergate; Pountfret in his testimony claimed to have known John Thornton for some forty years, that is to say his entire adult life.[5]

In essence the case required the court to determine which of two contracts of marriage was valid and enforceable according to canon law. The contract between Agnes and John Dale was slightly the earlier of the two. Dale appears to have argued that this was a marriage made by words of present consent before witnesses which was subsequently consummated. Agnes challenged Dale's suit for enforcement of this contract claiming that it was achieved only under duress—"force and fear" to use canonical terminology—and was therefore null.[6] In its place a second contract, again using words of present consent and in the presence of witnesses, between Agnes and John Thornton was presented. That these two contracts had both occurred was not subject to challenge: Agnes acknowledged her contract to John Dale, but challenged its validity; John Dale had no need to question the existence of Agnes's contract to John Thornton since his own contract to Agnes had preceded it and thus would take precedence if upheld by the court.

The documentation that survives from this case is comparatively substantial; David Smith in his published handlist counts twenty-four separate items and these include several sets of depositions.[7] It is apparent, however, that the extant documentation is incomplete. A number of depositions are apparently lost, including some that would have been central to John Dale's case. Aspects of John Dale's case can consequently only be surmised. The larger picture can nevertheless still be reconstructed from the fairly full series of articles or surmised from the tone of the testimony presented by Agnes Grantham's witnesses.

As the action was initiated by John Dale as a suit to enforce a contract of marriage, it is reasonable to assume that it was prompted by news of Agnes's own subsequent contract to John Thornton.[8] A common strategy in defending such petitions was to deny that any such contract had in fact taken place: the defendant was elsewhere at the time; such a marriage would be far more advantageous to the plaintiff than the defendant; the plaintiff's witnesses were tainted and untrustworthy. All these strategies can be found in the Court of York and elements of the last two play a secondary role here, but the gender dynamic is normally the reverse of that within this case. Usually it is the woman who attempts to hold a reluctant lover to his word and it is the man who provides an alibi—he was playing football at the time, he was away for the weekend, he had never promised marriage. Agnes Grantham's strategy is very different. She acknowledges that a verbal contract was made between her and John Dale. She asserts, however, that the contract was forced from her through actual violence, sexual assault, and the imminent and continuous threat of rape. Agnes's defense was thus not to challenge the existence of an alleged contract of marriage, but to challenge the validity of an actual contract. Given that in general terms it was easier to get a judgment against the enforcement of a disputed contract than it was to annul a canonically established marriage, this was a difficult strategy. That it is the strategy Agnes—or her legal counsel—preferred may serve to lend credibility in our eyes at least to Agnes's narrative. For the purposes of the actual case, however, it meant that Agnes had to work especially hard to convince the court that John Dale's petition should be rejected.

There are two strands to Agnes's strategy. The first, crucially, goes to the heart of the canon law of marriage. From the time of Pope Innocent II, it was the consent of the couple alone that was held to make a valid marriage. This understanding was formally laid down in the canons of the Fourth Lateran Council of 1215. By asserting that she had been forcibly abducted and made to pronounce the words of contract under duress and attempted rape by her would-be spouse, Agnes offers a travesty of what might normally be expected of marriage making: the bride is carried unwillingly to the place of contract; her contract is made with words unwillingly uttered by a cowed and tearful bride bereft of the support of her family or friends;[9] sexual relations represent not the looked-for consummation of mutual love and the desire to procreate, but a violent threat symbolic of the man's power over the woman. Agnes "married" John Dale, but the words and actions are hollow without her consent. The "marriage" can have no canonical validity. If the court were to give credence to Agnes's account, necessarily ventriloquized through her witnesses, then John Dale's petition would fail and Agnes's contract to John Thornton would by default be allowed to stand. Some other factors are offered, notably according to one set of articles that Agnes was a woman of advanced years whereas Dale was a penniless young man, the implication being that she would not willingly contemplate such a marriage.[10] John Thornton also claimed that John Dale's witnesses were untrustworthy.[11] Ultimately, however, as is so often the case where rape or attempted rape is alleged, it was Agnes's word against John's. The only reason why the court should believe Agnes would be because Agnes appeared a woman of unimpeachable integrity. It follows that the second strand of Agnes's strategy was to present herself to the court as just that.

There were many different facets to Agnes's life. She was an apparently successful businesswoman with her own established brewing business. She was a householder with responsibilities for the servants she employed to assist her in her business and help run her home. She was an established member of the parish and community of St Michael le Belfrey: this is where she had her home, elsewhere specified as being in Petergate; it is the location of some of her witnesses; and it is where she contracted John Thornton. It is likely, however, that her network extended more widely. Her late husband must have been quite a well-known figure within the city. Another of Agnes's deponents hailed from the parish of St Margaret at the opposite end of the city from St Michael le Belfrey's. We do not know how she came to meet John Thornton, whose home was in the central parish of All Saints, Pavement, but, as we shall see, it must have been through John Thornton that she came to be given shelter in William Pountfret's house. She was a recent widow. This is hardly an exhaustive list and it tells us nothing about her character or personality. It does, however, provide the framework from which Agnes, the wronged party, could draw in order to construct her case. It may be useful here, however, to begin with a discussion of some evidence relating to her late husband.

We have the will and associated probate inventory of Hugh Grantham.[12] As we have already observed, these reveal the Granthams to have been a prosperous couple. Hugh had been a mason and some of the places he had worked are apparently reflected in his inventory—the Dominican friary, All Saints', North Street and St Giles's in York, probably also the Minster, Pocklington church, and Nun Monkton nunnery. The will, however, highlights Hugh's piety, which may well have been shared with his widow. It commences with an unusually full preamble that commends his "wretched soul" to the "great mercy" of God and Mary, the mother of Christ who redeems "by his precious blood." He leaves to his executors the choice of place of burial for "my wretched body" and, in making provision for a wake, asks that it be done "without any kind of worldly pomp," a desire that would appear not to have been honored to judge from his funeral expenses. He makes particular and comparatively generous provision to the poor of Marton, Grafton, Minskip, and other places in the vicinity of Boroughbridge, some dozen miles to the northwest of York and presumably the locality in which he grew up.[13] He remembers the nuns of Nun Monkton, also northwest of York. Both his witnesses and two of his four executors are clerics.

Hugh Grantham's pious provision provides a context for Agnes's own devout persona. His comparative prosperity and his substantial bequests to her likewise underpin Agnes's own social and economic standing. In his will Hugh specifically bequeathed Agnes £40 and "the entirety of vessels and utensils of my house." The extent of Hugh's prosperity is, however, only revealed in his probate inventory. His net estate was valued at little short of £150, though part of this was in the form of debts owing. He appears to have held land for growing barley to the west of York, but this may well in fact have been in part to support Agnes's brewing business. The home he shared with Agnes was patently comfortable and well-equipped by bourgeois standards of the day. The inventory lists a certain quantity of silver plate and seventeen silver spoons. The chamber had painted cloths, a large collection of sheets, and various chests. The hall boasted cushions, basins, and ewers. The kitchen contained a variety of brass pots and pewter dishes. It was also an industrious place. There were two spinning wheels plus cards for carding in the hall. There was a cow and calf, four hens and a cockerel, four capons and two ducks. There was also a brewhouse full of utensils. All these presumably represent work activities carried out by Agnes and various household servants under her direction.

Agnes the businesswoman and brewster is a conspicuous part of her identity as revealed in the depositions made on her behalf. As we have already seen from her late husband's probate inventory, her brewing interests clearly predate his demise. The contents of the brewhouse were appraised at just over £54, of which £42 was accounted for in malt alone.

Lead brewing vessels accounted for most of the remaining sum. It was on a scale that she needed to employ women servants to assist her. Thomas Catton testified that "he often saw...the said Agnes's servants take away and carry ale to the master of St Leonard's Hospital."[14] Her contract to supply William Feryby, the then master of St Leonard's hospital, at his official residence at Acomb Grange must have been something of a coup. It was noted in the testimony to explain how Agnes came to be traveling between York and Acomb Grange in response to a dinner invitation, conveyed by Feryby's employee, John Dale, from his master. Her business—dependent on heavy brewing equipment and large quantities of malt—was also used to explain or justify her repeated visits back to her own home from her temporary lodging in William Pountfret's house "to see her household...and her chattels, so that nothing unpleasant or detrimental should occur or be suffered." For Margery Kempe, Agnes's contemporary and a woman of only slightly more elevated rank, her foray into the brewing business is presented as worldly vanity, her motivation to make money being presented as essentially selfish.[15] Agnes, in contrast, is presented as a householder, a woman with responsibilities to others. Where Margery's business fails, Agnes's apparently prospers. Agnes's brewing activities are thus presented in very positive terms. She engages in honest labor to support herself and those over whom she exercises as a duty of care as a parent, an employer, a householder.

Most householders were male and the ordinary assumption was that it was male householders who exercised discipline and authority over their dependents—wives, children, servants, and journeymen. As we will see in the following chapter with the case of the Doncaster widow, Alice Brathwell, the ability of widows to manage their households without male aid was open to question. Agnes's deponents here work hard to assert her capacity to so act. As has just been noticed, Agnes is described by Roger Marschall and other witnesses as visiting "her household" to look after not just her material possessions and the brewing equipment by which she pursued her trade, but the welfare of her dependents. Indeed Marschall talks of "her household, which she kept there, and her chattels" as distinct entities. Much the same is true of Agnes Kyrkeby's statement that Agnes from time to time visited her own house "to see her household and goods left by her there." Alice Rayner, one of Agnes's witnesses, is described both as her servant and—unusually and lest there be any ambiguity created by Agnes's temporary relocation to William Pountfret's home—"household member." John Watton tellingly refers to Agnes as a "materfamilias" to her household in Petergate.

Marschall does not merely record Agnes's solicitude toward her household. Her periodic visits to her home in the parish of St Michael le Belfrey were also undertaken "to give alms to the poor by bringing them wood, fuel and other necessaries." This serves to reinforce the perception of Agnes as the dutiful woman householder, for such provision for less fortunate neighbors seems to have been customary. A number of York women requested in their wills that fuel be distributed to their poor neighbors in what was presumably an extension of the kind of provision they ordinarily provided within their lifetimes. As household managers responsible for ensuring their own homes were stocked with fuel for warmth and cooking, women were particularly associated with this form of material provision.[16] To anticipate the suspicion that Agnes's conduct was motivated only by a concern to appear in a good light against possible litigation, Marschall goes on to explain that Agnes's giving on these occasions was "just as she was wont to do in the year of habit to the observation and knowledge of this witness."

Agnes is thus constructed as a capable and virtuous householder who is solicitous to poor neighbors. She is also to be seen as virtuous in the narrower sense of protecting her sexual honor. During the course of the alleged abduction, Agnes was repeatedly subject to violence or the threat of violence and to actual sexual assault and attempted rape or the threat of rape.[17] Thus we learn from the testimony of Thomas Catton that Agnes was lifted up and placed across the back of a horse "like a sack" deliberately exposing her genitalia. Agnes was made to understand that if she tried to escape, she would be raped and similarly it was the imminent threat and fear of rape that compelled her unwillingly to pronounce the words of contract with John Dale. Agnes's articles specifically allege that John Dale actually tried to rape her. The detail and its reiteration may, like Dom. William Marreys's testimony in the Rouclif case, have made for salacious reading on the part of the court lawyers, but it serves a more immediate double function for Agnes's action. In respect of the canon law, it makes the case that Agnes did not consent, but was subject to force and fear. Had Agnes suggested that she had in fact been raped, then John Dale's claim that consensual sex had occurred—giving further strength to an allegedly consensual contract—would ironically have been rendered more credible. By placing emphasis on how real the threat of rape was if she tried to escape and how close John came to actually raping her, Agnes as a woman and respectable widow in fact draws attention to how ultimately she valued her honor and her chastity over her ability to choose a spouse for herself. Here she understands that her culture likewise valued female "honor" over their right to choose.

The Agnes who is charitable toward her poor neighbors and who sets such high store over her chastity and sexual honor is also the Agnes who is devout. This is carefully demonstrated by the various details recorded in Agnes Kyrkeby's deposition ostensibly designed to show that Agnes Grantham had transferred her place of residence, and hence her parochial affiliation, from St Michael le Belfry parish to that of All Saints, Pavement. Not only does Kyrkeby, then a servant employed in Pountefret's house, describe how Agnes Grantham shared a room and bed with the vowess Dame Christiana or Christine, a kinswoman of the head of house, she also describes her worship in the parish church. Vowesses were women, almost invariably widows, who took formal vows of chastity before the bishop or his nominee.[18] They were an established part of later medieval aristocratic and mercantile society and in that sense would hardly demand explanation within the Court of York, yet Kyrkeby explains that Dame Christine "by taking the mantle and ring, entered a vow of chastity." The effect is to accentuate Dame Christine's status, and by implication Agnes's own sexual honor through such close association with her.

It is Agnes's devout conduct as one who is seen to frequent her parish church "on weekdays and holidays...to be present at divine services, listen devoutly to them, make oblations at masses celebrated, and receive holy water and blessed bread from the hand of the parish priest" that is most fully presented in Kyrkeby's deposition. John Watton, the parish clerk, also testified to seeing Agnes regularly at mass and at vespers.[19] On one level, the point is simply that because Agnes availed herself of the full range of worship within the church, she clearly identified All Saints as her new parish. One does not have to look too much further to realize, however, that Agnes is here presented to be a singularly devout woman, whose attendance at services is not confined to holidays, that is, holy days. Kyrkeby's testimony goes on:

> Lately also, when brought down by serious illness and being on the point of death, she was confessed in the dwelling house of William Pountfret by the aforesaid parish priest and would have received the consecrated Host from the same if the said illness had not proved worrying, particularly because she was unable to hold down for long any foods or liquids taken by her, but by reason of her illness quickly expelled them by vomiting...(BI, CP.F.36/roll 7)

This part of Kyrkeby's testimony offers detail that is surely superfluous to make the case that Agnes had become a parishioner of All Saints. Rather, its purpose is to reinforce the message that Agnes was a devout believer. That whilst apparently on her deathbed she confessed her sins in preparation to receive the Host shows that as a good Christian she was aware of how to make a good death, it indicates her reverence for the Host as the body of Christ, but at the same time it also cleverly signals just how sick she was. The

Official reading the deposition must have been intended to feel only sympathy for this devout widow and the tribulations she had endured. But Kyrkeby too presents herself as a devout and hence intrinsically credible witness for her knowledge of Agnes's frequent presence in the parish church depends on her own observation—"she very often saw the same Agnes on weekdays and holidays in the said church of All Saints."

Agnes's persona as the devout widow that Agnes Kyrkeby sets out to create tallies with the previously noticed observation made by several witnesses regarding her care for her poor neighbors and her concern to safeguard her chastity. It also makes better sense of the reason given in John Eberston's testimony for Agnes's keenness to attend a dinner invitation from the Master of St Leonard's accompanied by her son, Thomas: Agnes wanted to ask Master William Feryby to help secure an ecclesiastical benefice for her son. As the master of one of the largest and richest hospitals in the country and as an ecclesiastic with substantial administrative experience in the diocese, Master William would indeed have presented a good contact and possible patron for Thomas Grantham.[20] This explanation of Agnes's interest in the dinner invitation simultaneously signals the pious leanings of Agnes and her immediate family and also presents her as a good mother and household head in that she is seen to be promoting her son's career.

As the foregoing discussion demonstrates, Agnes, through the testimony of her witnesses, is able to present herself as a devout and chaste widow. This was the platform needed to lend credence to her claims that her marriage to John Dale was made unwillingly and as a consequence of his violent actions. The account of Agnes's abduction—her "raptus" or rape to use medieval terminology—is set out in detail in a series of thirty-four articles put to a group of Agnes's witnesses and is further reiterated in their depositions. Agnes was said to have been traveling through fields between the village of Acomb, west of York, and Acomb Grange, the residence of the master of St Leonard's Hospital in the company of her son, Thomas, and her servant, Alice Rayner. She and her companions were there ambushed by three armed men. Agnes was seized and beaten. Her son and her servant were forced to flee out of fear—her son was threatened with a drawn dagger. Agnes was tied up and taken into the darkness of the surrounding woods. There, as previously noticed, she was bundled onto a horse and, because she would not stay on, she was held on laid crossways "like a sack." Part of this narrative has already been commented on, but the detail is striking. That Agnes was held against her will and there was no means of escape is clearly established. The comment about her being unwilling to stay on the horse may be designed to reinforce that it was her will to escape even if she had not the means so to do.

The narrative here has some striking parallels with abduction or rape narratives found in two cases before royal justices and others from the patent rolls. Thus, from a King's Bench case dated 1336 we hear how a group of men abducted the Countess of Lincoln from Bolingbroke Castle at night by lifting her up onto one of her palfreys, but the countess resisted by falling from her horse. They then lifted her on again and had a groom sit behind her to hold her on.[21] Similarly a case heard by the Suffolk Justices of the Peace in 1362 records how Alice le Dimeigne was abducted by Geoffrey le Wolmonger and John de Causton by being lifted onto a horse behind John, but she fell to the ground and was hurt. They then took her to a wood, pulled her into the bushes and brambles and gagged her with her glove and hat to stop her crying out, and so mistreated her that they left her all bloody.[22] This case and the associated narrative are strikingly reminiscent of Agnes's own circumstances since the abduction was allegedly precipitated by Alice's refusal to agree to marry Geoffrey.

The patent rolls, at least in their calendared form, are much less informative, but some telling examples may still be cited. From a case dated 1320 we learn of how a large party of men broke into the house of Isabella, the wife of Walter Gacelyn, who was alone at the time, "abducted her by night and placed her across a horse, and against her will conducted her to Ocle by Newent in the forest of Dene." Like Agnes, Isabella was thus taken into a forest, but, more frighteningly, at night. In a case from 1358, Sir John de Cokeryngton and his servant allegedly seized Joan de Fletewyk and (to cite the modern calendared text) "set her on an horse against the peace, so that for fear she fell off the horse whereby she nearly suffered death." In another case dated 1384, Maud, widow of John Fullere, complained that she had been attacked by a group of six men, including a parochial chaplain and one William Wlips, the servant of the parson of the same parish, who "ravished her outside her house there, put her on a horse to abduct her, and, because she would not sit or lie upon it, beat her, brought her back into her house and threatened her that if she would not marry him [William Wlips] they would immediately kill her, made her promise and compelled her to go to bed with him, and that he (the said William) feloniously knew her against her will."[23]

The motif of the woman bundled onto a horse—the medieval equivalent of being bundled into a car—probably serves to signal the powerlessness of the woman and the intention of her attackers to abduct her. This action in itself signals abduction if not intended rape in the modern sense, though the detail that Agnes's genitalia were deliberately exposed not only constitutes actual sexual assault, but signals a real threat to her chastity. The latter case has some further parallels with that concerning Agnes Grantham. Both Agnes and Maud Fullere are widows and, if the byname is significant in Maud's case, perhaps widows of artisan. The assailants in both cases are employees of clergy and they work as part of a gang. In both instances the victims' nonconsent is indicated by their unwillingness to remain on the horse. In both, violence and the threat of greater violence is used to obtain an agreement to marriage. There is, however, one significant difference between the narratives. Whereas Agnes loudly protests that she pronounced the words of matrimony only in order to save herself from rape, Maud here alleges that actual rape followed the forced marriage. The patent roll indicates that rape was indeed confessed by her assailant—"he having acknowledged before the coroner the truth of the premises." This difference illuminates the different strategies between different legal jurisdictions. Agnes uses a defense of "force and fear" to nullify a contract of marriage that her alleged assailant looks to the court to enforce. Maud's case is known to us by reason of a royal grant of pardon to her assailant for the felony of rape, for which he would otherwise, in theory at least, have hung. The validity or otherwise of the marriage between Maud and William is not the issue and is beyond the competence of the royal courts or even the king, but it might be seen as a mitigating factor, and certainly an explanatory factor, in how William came to rape Agnes. As I have already argued, for Agnes to have claimed to have been raped could perversely have been open to the interpretation that she actually consented to her marriage.

The narrative of events following Agnes's initial abduction is known largely from one very full set of articles, though these are confirmed to a greater or lesser degree by some of the recorded depositions that were made in response to these same articles. The articles imply that Master William Feryby was implicated in the abduction: when Agnes's servant Alice fled the attackers she sought help from Master William and his household, but apparently without response; Robert Kyrkham, one of Dale's two accomplices, allegedly went to Acomb Grange to consult with him whilst Agnes was still being held. These allegations are not discussed by Agnes's witnesses, though they of course represent matters known only to master William and to the abductors. When Agnes, on first escaping, confronted Master William at his home, he is reported to have denied any complicity.

John Dale "forcibly abducted [violenter rapuit]" Agnes and led her "captive, grieving...to frightening and wooded places [et sic raptam captivam dolorose abduxit ad loca terribilia silvasque]" (article xvi for Agnes Grantham in Dale c. Grantham, BI, CP.F.36). Agnes is thus taken from the roadway running between the village of Acomb and Acomb Grange into the surrounding woods.[24] To the medieval mind, this represented not a transition from the bustle of town life, Acomb being but a couple of miles outside York, to the tranquility of countryside and nature, but something much more threatening, as the epithet "terribilia" implies. Woods were the haunt of wild animals and outlaws. In woods, travelers are attacked, women violated. They were frightening and threatening places.[25] In describing how she was taken into wooded places, Agnes tacitly signals that her abductors were like outlaws and that she, already raped in the medieval sense of having been abducted, should also fear physical rape; this was the fate of the maid lost in the forest in *Sir Degaré*, a romance that was popular in this era and, like other romances, probably enjoyed a bourgeois readership.[26]

Alice, Agnes's servant, ran to seek help at Acomb Grange, her son likewise looked to find help within the neighborhood, but Agnes was led on into the wood. She was brought in time to the lodge of Thomas Forester, Dale's other accomplice, in Healaugh Park and held there for a couple of hours. Agnes's articles go on to state that she offered inducements to Thomas Forester to let her go, but to no avail. This assertion could not, of course be proven, since Agnes and Thomas were the only two persons in a position to know its veracity or otherwise, but it serves to show that Agnes's options were fast being closed down. The point is reinforced by the next article that alleged that John Dale then threatened and even attempted to rape Agnes [tempore predicto minabatur et conabatur extorquere carnalem copulam de eadem Agnete] (article xx for Agnes Grantham in Dale c. Grantham, BI, CP.F.36). The threat of rape was here evidently being used to intimidate and coerce Agnes and the claim that actual rape was attempted serves to reinforce the threat.

The articles go on relentlessly, dramatically ratcheting up the threats and so recreating Agnes's emotional state in the minds of the court's clerical personnel. Agnes is told that she would not be released unless she married John. Her three captors then took her, so the articles allege, into the Forest of Knaresborough "and other remote and hidden places." This would seem an exaggeration, for the forest's boundaries appear to have lain some miles to the west, and it is in tension with a subsequent article (number xxvi) that implies Agnes was held the whole time in Healaugh Park. Maybe Healaugh Park can be seen as an extension of the Forest of Knaresborough, but Agnes's narrative purpose is clear enough; Agnes is removed from the orderly world signaled by the king's highway, open fields, and village settlement into a dark and threatening environment signaled by "forest" and the epithets "remote" and "hidden." Again they piled on the threats to Agnes's person and her body unless she agreed to the marriage. It is at this point (article xxvi) that we are told there was negotiation between Robert Forester and Master William Feryby, which Robert then reported back to his two confederates.

Although the precise nature of Robert Forester's interview with Master William is not elaborated upon, article xxviii asserts that on Robert's return the three men again threatened Agnes, demanding that she agree to the marriage and publicly acknowledge the same before various people. She would be taken into the Forest of Knaresborough in order to contract *in facie ecclesie* with the understanding that he would know her sexually afterward. Agnes was then taken to the village of Healaugh and forced to acknowledge and even repeat her contract of marriage to John Dale. Finally she was taken back to the village of Askham at which point Agnes was able to use blandishments and flattery to escape her captors and hurry to Acomb Grange. There she stoutly denied that she had ever consented to the marriage forced upon her. John Eberston, testifying on her behalf, claimed that she had asked to commend her soul to the devil should she have actually consented. Subsequently she returned to York in Eberston's company.

The abduction and forced marriage occurred on Thursday 30 June 1410. The previous day, the feast of St Peter and St Paul, the patronal saints of the cathedral church, Agnes had been at the house of Richard Ulskelf and had told him of her dinner invitation with Master William Feryby the next day.[27] Agnes's subsequent contract of marriage to John Thornton was remembered to have taken place on the Saturday before the feast of St Margaret, which fell on 20 July, otherwise described as the Saturday before the feast of St Mary Magdalene, which fell two days later on 22 July.[28] Immediately following this second contract, Agnes took up residence in William Pountfret's house. There was thus an interval of only some two and a half weeks—30 June to 19 July—between the abduction and the allegedly forced marriage and Agnes's subsequent consensual contract to John Thornton. This interval represents something of a lacuna in the narrative of events reflected in the case, but it raises two possibilities: Agnes was prompted to hasten her marriage to John Thornton in order to provide herself with protection from John Dale; alternatively John Dale abducted and coerced Agnes at the end of June precisely in order to preempt a contract of marriage with John Thornton. The first of these is implied by Agnes's witness, Roger Marschall, otherwise Tayliour. He related that Agnes moved to Pountfret's house precisely "because she feared that John...had access and entrance through the grammar school situated next to her at the house she then lived in and should thus any time by force and armed might seize and abduct her."

At the time of Dale's attack, Agnes had only been a widow for some three months. On balance it would seem more likely that Dale's action was opportunistic rather than a calculated attempt to anticipate John Thornton. Thornton would have been expected to observe the social convention that allowed the widow a year of mourning before she might remarry. Nothing is explicitly made of Dale's failure to respect this convention, but in a sense his violation of this social norm pales into insignificance against his alleged violation of Agnes's right to consent. We may read the contract between Agnes and John Thornton, therefore, very much as a betrothal designed to offer Agnes immediate protection, but that presumably was not intended to be solemnized before March 1411. This explains the comparatively informal setting—"in a certain arbor within the garden of John Laxton"—and the unconventional timing—"after the vespers hour." It also explains why the couple did not immediately cohabit, but instead arranged that Agnes lodge in the house of Thornton's close friend and next-door-neighbor. It would seem that she left immediately after the betrothal, implicitly under cover of darkness.

The choice of the garden arbor as the venue for the couple's exchange of words of matrimony is no accident. A similar venue is recorded in the deposition of William Prudmay in a London marriage case of some sixty years later. Here John Bedeman and Agnes Nicholas "went out into the garden, and there in the garden, beneath a vine, this deponent asked Agnes whether she could find in her heart to have John Bedeman...to her husband."[29] Sylvia Landsberg suggests that "vines and roses were the most usual plants for medieval arbours," which often also provided a shaded and comparatively intimate seating area.[30] The garden was often associated in literature and art with love and beauty.[31] As such it was an appropriate setting for the betrothal of a loving couple. The ordered and disciplined environment of the garden—symbolizing consensual matrimony—contrasted moreover with the wild and untamed woodland or forest—symbolic of ravishment and forced marriage—into which Agnes had earlier been unwillingly snatched.[32]

The Pountfret home in Coppergate has been located by Sarah Rees Jones as at around modern number 26 and next door to a still partly surviving property that occupied a frontage of five bays on the east side of Coppergate opposite the parish church of All Saints, Pavement.[33] This last may be a clue to the quality of buildings along this clearly affluent street frontage.[34] We have then a possibly substantial and centrally located property—the grain market of Pavement, the hall of the Holy Trinity guild in Fossgate, and St William's chapel on Ouse Bridge, the then seat of city government, are all but a short walk distant. What we can be confident of is that there would have been adequate space to accommodate the separate room occupied by the vowess Christine and subsequently shared with Agnes as well as the various servants employed within the household. Its location opposite the south side of All Saints, Pavement also goes a little way to explain the frequency with which both Agnes Grantham and Pountfret's servant, Agnes Kyrkeby, visited the parish church.

The Pountfret household, its intimate association with the Thornton household, and Agnes Grantham's association with the two may be illuminated by a number of sources, not least probate evidence. The timing of the case means that it coincides with a significant break in the main Exchequer court probate series for York. This probably explains the absence of recorded wills for either William Pountfret or John Thornton. We do, however, still have the will of Avice de Pontefract. She was the wife of William de Pontefract, draper of the parish of All Saints, Pavement, who died in 1404, that is seven years before the case.[35] She remembered two sons and two daughters, one already dead. Since one of her sons is named William, it is not immediately clear whether this is the wife or the mother of our William Pountfret (to reiterate the spelling that happens to be found in the court record). We can, however, be confident that she was his wife. A William de Pountefracto, junior, draper, was admitted as a citizen in 1371, which would suggest that this William, if still living, would have been around sixty years of age in 1411—old enough to have outlived his wife and sufficiently old to deflect suspicion of impropriety by harbouring Agnes in his home.[36] This is precisely the age attributed to William Pountfret (this time rendered as Pountefret) when his deposition was recorded.

Avice's will certainly reflects the social standing of the family as is suggested by the fact that she names four female servants, to the most senior of whom, Joan Staynton, she bequeathed clothing and the comparatively generous sum of 20s. Interestingly she also remembered one Christine Pontefract, described as a blood relation of her husband who can only be the same Christine described in like terms and living in the Ousegate home in 1411. Her will also hints at the family's piety. She provided torches to burn on the feast of Corpus Christi in her parish church. She left money to Mount Grace Priory and to purchase bells for St Agatha's Abbey, Easby, which may also suggest family roots in the Richmond area. She bequeathed 12d. "to each small hospital for the poor called maisondieu [masyndow]" and 6d. to the recluse anchorite by the parish church of St Cuthbert.[37] To the hermit in Gillygate she left 6d "to repair the roads." Some of her bequests were even more personal. She left 4d. to her former servant Agnes who had subsequently become an anchoress in Hungate and 12d. to Anabilla in the Holy Trinity guild hospital of St Mary located underneath their guildhall in Fossgate. She also left 4d. "to a poor woman staying in the cemetery of my parish church"—very much the poor (wo)man at the gate.

The most intriguing reference in Avice's will is to one Katherine, wife of John de Thornton. She is described as "my faithful friend [fidel socie mee]" and was named, alongside her husband and Avice's own husband, as her executor. The appointment of women, other than where husbands nominate their widows, as executors is unusual. This together with the description implies an unusual degree of intimacy and trust between the two women and indeed, since John Thornton was also named, between the two families. As we have seen, it is Rees Jones's work on York property deeds that further clarifies this relationship: the Thorntons and the Pountfrets were neighbors whose properties adjoined.[38] It was, moreover, not just the wives who were so intimate. The eighteenth-century antiquary Francis Drake records the two men were buried side by side in their parish church, the inscription on John Thornton's memorial slab reading "here lies buried John Thornton, lately draper of York, and Katherine his wife next the tomb of William Pontfract their friend [socii eorum]."[39] It is noteworthy that the same Latin term "socius"—here perhaps something more than just associate—is found both in Avice's will and the Thornton memorial. William Pountfret's own testimony recorded that he had known Thornton for some forty years. John Watton, the parish clerk of their church of All Saints, deposed that Thornton and Pountefret had for many years sold woolen cloth together as partners in their shared shop. The ties between the two houses were thus of long standing and continued after death; the two men together endowed a chantry at the altar of St Katherine, the name saint of Thornton's (first) wife, in their parish church of All Saints.[40]

Ties of some standing between the Pountfets and the Thorntons are further reflected in Agnes's late husband's probate inventory: among the debts owing to Hugh de Grantham at his death was the sum of £4 owed jointly by John Thornton and William Pontefracto. The implication of this must also be that there were ties between these men and the Grantham household even before Hugh Grantham's demise, though Pountfret's own deposition implies that he did not know Agnes herself until around the time she came to live in his house.[41] The close ties between Pountfret and Thornton must explain the reason for Agnes Grantham's removal to Pountfret's house immediately following her contract of marriage to John Thornton. It would have been deemed inappropriate, even scandalous, for a widow of Agnes's standing to have simply started to cohabit with a widower of similar social rank prior to any formal solemnization of the marriage, but for Agnes to live next door to her betrothed under the protection of an eminently respectable and probably devout draper and in the company of his devout kinswoman would surely have satisfied the social conventions of propriety appropriate to their status.

The mention of Katherine as wife of John Thornton at the time of Avice Pountfret's will in 1404 tallies with the inscription on Thornton's grave slab, which, as we have seen, commemorates Thornton "and Katherine his wife."[42] We must surmise that Katherine died sometime between 1404 and 1410. But the inscription conspicuously fails to notice Agnes as a second wife. There are two possibilities. One is simply that the marriage that Agnes and John Thornton tried to establish in the Court of York and which was upheld by that court, but was immediately appealed, never came to fruition. Another possibility is, however, simply that Agnes chose to be buried with her first husband; it is unlikely that this second marriage would have lasted many years since we presume that John Thornton at least would have been of a similar age to William Pountefret and so, by medieval standards, already quite old when he betrothed Agnes.

Agnes and John Thornton contracted matrimony not as the product of a lengthy courtship. Until but a couple of months or so previous, Agnes had been wed to Hugh, a successful mason. Thornton was himself so intimate with his neighbor William Pountfret that had he had much association with Agnes prior to the contract we might expect Pountfret to have known of it and to have met Agnes prior to that day. We do know that Pountfret and Thornton together had some commercial dealing with Hugh Grantham, but Pountfret's testimony suggests that, whatever he may have known or heard, he had not previously met Agnes. Social mores dictated, moreover, that a widow be allowed a year's mourning before finding another husband; courtship within that period, and especially so early in that period, would surely have been frowned upon. We can only conclude that Agnes betrothed herself to Thornton solely to protect herself from the man who a couple of weeks before had attacked her and in order to obtain shelter and safety in the home of his friend and neighbor.

The advantage to Agnes is easy enough to discern, even if our understanding of the fuller story remains patchy and enigmatic. Much harder to grasp is what John Thornton got out of it. Even allowing that Thornton and Pountfret together owed Agnes £4, a bad debt noted in her husband's inventory, this would seem an improbable form of compensation. Thornton (we must presume) and Pountfret were both widowers and men of comparatively advanced age. Pountfret had living with him his kinswoman, Dame Christine, the vowess, but the two men may have valued the presence of another woman, especially one so business-savvy and capable as Agnes. Again this is hardly sufficient to explain the suddenness of the contract.

Ultimately we cannot know. We must enter the realms of speculation. What Agnes Grantham, John Thornton, and William Pountfret had in common was their shared business acumen, albeit in different areas of trade, their conspicuous piety, and the fact that, by medieval standards, each would have been considered old. (Agnes, moreover, we know had been very ill, near even to death, in the weeks before the case came to court.) Thornton and Pountfret were also indebted to Agnes, but the debt was recorded in her husband's probate inventory as one that was unlikely to be returned; it may be indicative of previous association rather than a reason for guilt. Thornton and Pountfret together enjoyed a close homosocial relationship within a contemporary tradition of such close bonds between male friends. Pountfret also provided a home for a kinswoman vowed to chastity. The two households thus formed a sort of small lay devout community. By contracting herself to Thornton, Agnes was effectively joining this community, sharing room and bed with the vowess and home with Pountfret. By living with Pountfret, moreover, Agnes was preserving her chastity even within marriage. We cannot know if this arrangement was intended to go on beyond the anniversary of her first husband's death or the resolution of the action within the Court of York, but there are in fact reasons for suspecting so.

Chaste marriage was a recognized and valued social arrangement adopted, for example, by Agnes's much better known contemporary, Margery Kempe, but would have been deemed especially laudable for a widow past child-bearing age.[43] It is possible to take this a little further. Margery Kempe may have been influenced by the examples of Dorothea of Montau and of Brigit of Sweden, but it is eminently possible that one or both these examples of married bourgeoises would have been known in the devout Pountfret—Thornton household. Indeed Brigit of Sweden may have enjoyed particular devout interest precisely at this time in York.[44] Chaste marriage may also have been both an acceptable and convenient arrangement for Thornton and Pountfret. They would gain the companionship, the domestic management skills, and the business acumen and resources of a mature, but somewhat younger woman within the context of a joint household comprising two widowers and a vowess. Such a marriage may also have served to defuse any adverse comment about the relationship of Thornton and his "socius" William Pountfret that had surely been thrown into relief once both men had become widowers. Our speculative conclusion is, therefore, that the marriage between Agnes Grantham and John Thornton was a mutually convenient arrangement, which offered protection to Agnes, companionship to all parties, and social legitimacy to Thornton. Having fought to preserve her chastity in the forest, Agnes secured it by her vows made in a garden. It was these same vows she looked to the court to uphold.

CHAPTER 9

PATRIARCHY, CIVIC IDENTITY, AND THE WIDOW OF DONCASTER

The business of the Church courts was adversarial. The parties contesting an action necessarily told contradictory stories that were retold through the words of their witnesses. This is amply demonstrated in the disputed marriage case from 1391 between the widow Alice Brathwell of Doncaster and William Dowson of North Cave, a village some twenty-five miles to the northeast across the River Ouse in the East Riding of Yorkshire.[1] As always in matrimonial cases, the central point of contention related to consent. Witnesses for Dowson attempted to show that Alice had by words of present consent agreed to marry Dowson and hence was lawfully married. Following the contract, the couple had allegedly drank together in a tavern run by her neighbor Thomas Taverner. Alice, through her witnesses, claimed that she had merely agreed to think about his proposal. Although at first a guest in her house, her witnesses explained that Dowson was confronted by a group of burgesses who told him he must lodge elsewhere precisely because he was not in fact Alice's husband. Alice herself appears to have wanted to marry one William Roger of the nearby town of Pontefract.

Doncaster, the setting for our case study, was a middle-sized town of well in excess of a thousand persons in the later fourteenth century.[2] It was a significant market and trading center, with leather and textiles trades especially prominent. It was also a seigneurial borough whose inhabitants had little formal political role.[3] A charter secured from Richard I in 1194 had effectively granted the fee farm to the burgesses,[4] but over two centuries of rule by the de Mauley family appears to have largely frustrated further moves to self-government. Peter de Mauley IV issued letters patent in 1331 recognizing the right of the burgesses to collect a levy in respect of baking and brewing and Richard I's charter was confirmed by his royal namesake in the troubled year of 1381. It was, however, not until the borough passed to the house of York with the death of Peter de Mauley VIII in 1415 that real signs of change become apparent. In 1467 a charter of Edward IV finally recognized the election of a mayor and allowed for the burgesses to run their own court. These constitutional changes, culminating in the charter of 1505 whereby the lordship of the borough was finally vested in mayor and commonalty, disguise a history of political action and resistance on the part of a number of the leading burgesses. Such activity seems to have been especially marked in the second half of the fourteenth century and at the very time of our case.

Our initial focus, however, is the personal and the domestic. The case heard in the ecclesiastical Court of York in 1391 required the court to decide the competing claims of William Dowson and William Roger for the hand of Alice Brathwell or Braythewell. Of William Roger's claim we know nothing save that it was judged by the court to prevail over that of his rival. It is evident from the surviving depositions that Alice was totally opposed to Dowson's claims. The discussion that follows must necessarily focus on the disputed contract between Alice and William Dowson. This is in fact the more puzzling of the two contracts.

Whereas, as we shall discover shortly, William Roger was of like status to Alice and resident of the neighboring town of Pontefract, Dowson is a more ambiguous figure. From the depositions we learn that he is supposedly rich and powerful in his own locality. He employs a manservant who rides with his baggage and carries his sword. The implication is that he belongs to the lesser aristocracy, a rank soon to be called gentleman.[5] But how and why such a man from a different part of the same county should find himself in Doncaster proposing marriage to an eligible bourgeois widow is unexplained. Alice's witnesses contrive to cast doubt on the veracity of the claims made on Dowson's behalf in respect of his social rank and they draw attention to his being an outsider. Dowson's own witnesses are conspicuously silent on all these points, concentrating instead on the proper focus of the case, namely the words and actions that symbolized matrimony.

It would be helpful if we were able to match the persons and places described in the present case to other sources. This is possible to a modest degree. No court rolls survive for Doncaster before the later fifteenth century, but two wills are extant before 1430, dated 1390 and 1398 respectively.[6] Fortuitously they are both of some interest to us. There are also a few pertinent entries in the Chancery rolls and there is the extant poll tax return for the second tax of 1379.[7] The sources, therefore, if a little scanty, allow us to go rather further than would be possible armed only with the disputed marriage case.

The 1379 poll tax, dating to only twelve years before the present case is particularly helpful. The West Riding returns vary considerably in quality, but those for the Strafforth Wapentake, which encompasses Doncaster, are some of the better. They invariably list tax payers in groups by reference to an individual named first and others described relationally to that individual as wives, sons, daughters, or servants. Because only persons over sixteen were liable to be taxed and because this is a quintessentially an urban community, children are in fact uncommon, but servants are somewhat more numerous. Likewise, because the 1379 tax was levied according to a predetermined schedule whereby artisans, merchants, and the like paid higher rates than the standard minimum of 4d. per individual or married couple, some tax payers are recorded as paying 6d., 1s., or more and an occupational designation is provided by way of justification.[8] Thus we are fortunate to locate "Willelmus de Braythewell et Alicia uxor ejus, souter [shoemaker]" assessed at 6d. Of Alice's three deponents, Thomas Knyght is not found, but John Clerk, a bowyer, is listed together with his wife Agnes, so too is John Marschall and his wife Alice. Clerk is assessed as an artisan at the higher rate of 6d., but Marschall and his wife pay the standard rate of only 4d. Alice's neighbor, Thomas Taverner, is likewise listed with his wife Emma. Taverner and Alice Braythwell are found roughly within the same part of the returns and this could well be compatible with his description within the case as Alice's neighbor. The deponents that Alice called upon were (in two out of three instances) established members of community and one at least belonged to an artisanal elite.

This then is the world in which Alice, herself an artisan's widow, may be located. But these are not the only Doncaster men noticed in the case. Of the group of burgesses that confront William Dowson, Thomas Messyngham and William Spyser are specifically named. Both are listed in 1379. William Spyser and his wife Margaret are listed, assessed at the standard rate, midway between Alice herself and Thomas Taverner. Thomas de Messyngham, merchant, is listed with his wife Margaret assessed at 2s. Only fourteen other individuals or married couples were assessed at the same or a higher rate within the entire town. Messyngham was evidently a man of substance, but it may well be that Spyser, despite his unremarkable assessment, followed the occupation suggested by his name and thus had related mercantile interests. Serendipitously he is also recorded, along with William Millott and the testator's widow, as one of the executors of the will of William Braithewell.[9] Millott, whose will of 1398 is also extant, is recorded as a merchant assessed at 40d. in 1379.[10] These are shards of evidence for a closely connected group of persons with trading interests who constitute a privileged group within Doncaster society. We can be confident that the widowed Alice Braithwell was part of this group.

The equivalent returns for Pontefract also allow us to locate William Roger. He is recorded as a walker (or fuller), assessed at 6d., but interestingly even in 1379 listed alone and so probably a widower.[11] Much harder to identify are William Dowson of North Cave and his witnesses John Bukton and John Clerk of Greenoak. Of these three, it is perhaps William who is most interesting to us. There are no medieval manorial records for North Cave, but we have extant poll tax returns of the East Riding in 1381.[12] The 1381 returns are usually regarded as the least satisfactory of all three taxes, but Dowson at least ought to be recorded. He is not. A William Dowson, assessed with his wife at 3s., is recorded at Wheldrake and there is an extant probate act recorded for his widow Agnes in 1394.[13] Wheldrake was by the River Derwent some fifteen miles north-west of North Cave, but unless our Dowson was intent on bigamy, this is unlikely to be our man.

Of Dowson's two key witnesses, the identification of Greenoak is reasonably certain.[14] It was a village, now a hamlet, not far off the road between North Cave and Doncaster and is but six miles distant from North Cave. Greenoak, unlike North Cave, fell within the Liberty of Howdenshire, so we have some rather good normative listings surviving from the 1379 poll tax returns.[15] Neither John Bukton nor John Clerk are listed, though both were of sufficient age to have been taxed twelve years before. The name Bukton is not noticed at all, though the (admittedly common) name Clerk is associated with two households in this comparatively small community. The problem of identification is compounded by the fact that servants are often identified only by first name and would often move about. If John Bukton were, as is stated, thirty in 1391, then he would have been only eighteen in 1379, precisely the age he might have been in service. John Clerk, on the other hand, is presented as being in Dowson's service at the age of forty, evidently a ballpark figure, so must be understood as a career employee rather than a life-cycle servant. It follows that his association with Greenoak may have lasted no longer than his employment by Dowson.

The only substantial information we have about Bukton and Clerk is in fact that provided by the three character witnesses, Adam Scrase, Richard Bythekyrk, and Robert Dowlenay, brought by Dowson to counter attacks on the credibility of his two key witnesses. All gave their age as forty and all allegedly came from the North Cave area. Two claimed to have known Bukton for fourteen years, but none claimed to have known Clerk more than four years. Bukton they said was a man of modest substance, enjoying an annual rental income of 5m. from lands and tenements and worth 100m. in total. Dowlenay further added that he was in good standing with, among others, Sir Thomas Metham and Thomas Aske, esquire, both local gentry. Clerk was described as a victualling trader dealing primarily in meat and fish. None of these three character witnesses, however, is recorded in the North Cave poll tax returns of only ten years previous; in essence Alice Brathwell's witnesses and the people they describe are independently documented, Dowson's are not. If even Dowson's character witnesses are untrustworthy, then perhaps Dowson was not the man he claimed to be. Perhaps he was an adventurer and would-be bigamist after all.

The dramatis personae have been set out. They set urban bourgeois against (alleged) rural landowner, town against country. As we shall see, they will also set those whose claim to authority is based on morality and a concern for godly order against one whose claim to authority is rooted only in his alleged wealth and power. This is thus the larger conflict between the burgesses of Doncaster and their lord in microcosm. It is now time to explore the action. The deposition evidence highlights two separate tableaux, though the first is contested and the second is dependent on one version of the first. According to Bukton and Clerk, on Thursday before Pentecost, that is, Thursday 11 May 1391, Alice Brathwell contracted marriage with William Dowson before Bukton and Clerk using words of present consent—"Here I take you Alice to be my wife and to this I plight my troth"—and then sealed the contract over a drink of ale in the neighboring tavern. Had Bukton and Clerk been deemed credible witnesses and had Alice not objected, this would have been sufficient to make a binding marriage. There is, however, an alternative version of events on this day. This is provided by Thomas Knyght and (confusingly) a different John Clerk. In their version, there is no actual contract, merely an agreement that Alice would think about Dowson's proposal. This alternative narrative takes us to our second tableau, also testified to by John Marshall. According to this account, on the Monday after Pentecost, that is, 15 May, William Dowson acknowledged that he had not yet been given an answer to his proposal of marriage and was instructed by a party of Doncaster burgesses to move to different lodgings in Doncaster. It is this alternative narrative that will now engage our focus.

Unlike the Court of York, our present concern is not with the veracity of the events described per se, though it is tempting to conclude that Dowson was given to invention and elaboration. Rather our concern is with their social, cultural, and political resonances. It matters not whether they actually happened, but rather that they plausibly happened. In the first tableau, strictly two sequential events on the same day that take place in Alice's own home, Alice was put under a lot of pressure to agree at once to marry William Dowson. She resisted this pressure initially by pointing out that she had not been widowed a year. Subsequently she demanded a period of grace in which to think the offer over. She also appealed to a sense of what was right and proper, which is of course culturally specific.

The first objection, that Alice had not yet been widowed a year, relates to the custom, traceable back to the pre-Conquest era, that a widow be allowed a year of mourning before she might remarry. There is some evidence to suggest that widows were mindful of this custom and, as in this case, used it to resist pressure to remarry. Patricia Cullum has likewise noticed a tendency for some gentry women to enter into vows of chastity with their diocesan as their year of mourning drew to an end.[16] Again it is possible some of these women were using this as a strategy to resist family pressures to marry again. We know from the dates of making and of probate of his will that Alice's husband died in later June, so by May of 1391 her period of grace would be fast running out. Her plea to be allowed a period of six weeks to reply would thus have taken her to the anniversary of her husband's death and hence to the point at which social convention would have permitted her to remarry. Alice's request would thus have seemed to the court eminently reasonable and proper and, by implication, Dowson's subsequent insistence that she be allowed only a month, precipitous, improper, and insensitive.

In urging that she be allowed six weeks to give a response to Dowson's pressing demand for her hand in marriage, Alice is reported to have argued "that the matrons of the town of Doncaster and other of her neighbors would roundly criticize her about it if she were to contract marriage so hastily with an outsider of whom she had never before had knowledge." Alice here conjures up two groups whose views carried (or could be believed to have carried) weight with her, namely, "the matrons of Doncaster" and "other of her neighbors," these not being mutually exclusive categories. Matrona" is the Latin term that lies behind our translation and so hides the original vernacular used by Alice and ventriloquized by John Clerk. The term Alice most likely used is "wif," a term that need not define marital status, but can be used to denote the mistress of a household (definition 1a(b) in the *MED*), but when used collectively—the wifs or the wives—carries the sort of resonances well represented in modern English by the archaic "matrons." To give two examples, the wives [*uxores*] of Winchester carried a torch in city's Corpus Christi procession according to a record of 1437, and it was "mulieres et honeste uxores [the women and honest wives]" of Windsor who in 1517 took it upon themselves to examine Alice Ridyng and so discovered that she had given birth to and subsequently disposed of a baby fathered by a local priest.[17] This last perhaps, despite its late date, provides a clue as to the moral authority of "wives." Interestingly a bequest noted in a Doncaster will of 1430 reinforces the sense of "wives" having a collective identity. In that year Agnes, the widow of Richard Stanssall left 6s. 8d. to the "wives of Doncaster."[18]

The second, potentially overlapping group, whose opinions were presented as a control on Alice's actions were her neighbors. This is important in two respects. First it suggests a cultural context where kin and neighbor tend not to occupy overlapping categories. The poll tax evidence reinforces the point. High proportions of rural immigrants seem to have militated against any significant kinship density. Doncaster in 1379 was essentially unlike 1950s Bethnall Green or the Sicilian village of Milocca in Chapman's classic study.[19] The corollary is that Alice perhaps did not have any close kin living in Doncaster. Second, the observation and critical comment of neighbors was deemed a sufficiently powerful influence that Alice could appeal to this by way of justifying her refusal of an immediate answer to Dowson's proposal. Neighbors could not police as such what went on under an individual's roof, but they could watch who went in and out and at what hour, they could notice faces at windows or overhear heated conversations, they could overlook yards or gardens, they could notice household members in the street or engage in neighborly conversation.

The neighbors are at first constructed as an impersonal collectivity—as much an idea as an entity, though an idea that has real moral authority that can impinge on the lives of households and their members. Our second tableau, on Monday 15 May 1391, sees the idea take on a very real presence. A group of men, including the witness John Clerk, Thomas Messyngham, and William Spyser, both of whom are named in Clerk's deposition, and a number of other burgesses came to Alice's house and confronted Dowson. It may well be that this group did not itself comprise Alice's actual neighbors, but it is almost certain that it was her neighbors who alerted this group or at least tacitly supported its presence. Spyser may be the key intermediary here since he was one of the executors of Alice's late husband's will.[20] It is at this point that the concerns of the neighbors for order and propriety come to be consumed into the concerns of government and of a governing elite. This is where this Doncaster case becomes especially interesting.

As we noted earlier, prior to the later fifteenth century Doncaster was essentially a seigneurial borough. Somewhat unusually the town was ruled almost continuously by the same de Mauley family from 1214 until almost the middle of the fifteenth century. There were, however, a comparatively small number of years when de Mauley lordship did not prevail and 1391 is one such. Between 1383 and 1399, during the minority of Peter VIII de Mauley, the town was held by Thomas de Percy as Peter VIII's guardian. We know that de Mauley lordship had provoked increasing friction with the town's burgesses in the decades following the Black Death. The likelihood is that the burgesses of this middle ranking town came to resent the debilitating effects of seigneurial authority on their economic and political ambitions at a time that numbers particularly of royal boroughs were being granted ever increasing degrees of self-government. The de Mauley monopoly over the borough court was a particular bone of contention. Trouble had been especially acute during the rule of the dowager, Lady Margaret de Mauley, from 1355 until her death in 1382. How far this represents a greater willingness to exploit the perceived weaknesses of a female lord or simply an optical illusion created by the greater recourse of a dowager to assistance from royal government and hence to record is hard to assess.

A history of friction and resistance to de Mauley lordship can be readily documented from the 1360s. A generation later those most active in this movement included Richard Lewer, apprentice at law, William Staynford, merchant, Richard Ash, sergeant, Richard de Edlyngton, and the merchant, Thomas de Messyngham.[21] This is a comparatively illustrious group of persons. Lewer helped endow the town's Carmelite friary and was assessed at 20s. for the 1379 poll tax. Between them, they shared considerable experience of law, administration, and commerce. Messyngham is, of course, of particular interest to us since it is his name that crops up in the group of burgesses who confronted William Dowson. Messyngham was evidently still an activist in the early 1390s, for in 1392 he was indicted and then pardoned for releasing a felon from the stocks. He subsequently died an outlaw.[22]

The interregnum created by the de Mauley minority may have made the activities of a burgess "opposition" less visible, but there is no reason to suppose that they were any the less active. Indeed the absence of a local lord may well have allowed these men greater de facto influence. The confrontation with William Dowson can indeed be seen as a manifestation of that influence. The issue here is one of order and morality. By the later fourteenth century the household was coming to be seen as a basic unit of government.[23] Householders, understood primarily as adult, male burgesses were expected to exercise a policing role in respect of their dependents—wives, children, servants, and other employees. The widow Alice Braythwell could be seen as unable to exercise such a role in her own right or at least unaided. For a respectable unmarried woman to shelter an unmarried man (and a stranger to boot) was seen as undermining the good order of the community. The self-appointed leaders of the community thus asserted a quasi-patriarchal authority in order to protect the widow's good name and ensure that godly order was upheld. These burgesses can thus be seen attempting to legitimate their authority by using morality as their justification. This morality is not some transhistorical abstraction, but rather a specific late medieval bourgeois morality. It is a morality that is concerned with the good governance of households, the sexual honor of women, the good name of burgesses, and a distrust of the outsider, the stranger. As in the case of John Deynes prosecuted by the civic authorities in Norwich in 1465 described by Philippa Maddern, it is a morality that extends beyond the public world of the borough and the street and into the more intimate space of the home.[24]

The case also raises questions about trust and reputation. Alice Brathwell had standing and credibility within her community as an artisan's widow and householder. This standing is implicit in her appeal to the opinions of her neighbors and of the town's "matrons"; Alice here simultaneously locates herself as property holder and a woman of standing within the community. She reinforces these twin identities performatively by asserting the customary year of mourning allowed to the widow and by looking to her neighbors for support. This last implies something about Alice's standing within the community; it shows both that Alice is known and that her reputation is worthy of protection. William Dowson, on the other hand, as an outsider has to work harder to assert his identity. This is again done in part performatively by a show of status: Dowson and his two supporters come to town on horseback and John Clerk carries Dowson's sword for him. We would also expect Dowson to dress the part. John Bukton described his dress at the time of the alleged marriage contract as "a short garment one part of which was of green motley cloth and the other part of white russet covering." The russet fabric hardly suggests especial wealth, but the green motley and the short, particolor costume may at least mimic high-status costume for the period.[25] Dowson's standing is also asserted: John Bukton stated that "William was one of the most powerful and wealthy in their parts."

Dowson's position depends ultimately on what his supporters say. All the deponents in this case were male, but whereas Alice relied on but three comparatively young men—two were said to be thirty, one only twenty-five—Dowson backs up his two principal witnesses (aged thirty and forty) with three character witnesses, all said to be forty. Perhaps it would have been to Alice Brathwell's advantage had she called upon

William Spyser or Thomas Messyngham, but they could not have provided crucial testimony to what words were said at the time of the alleged (non)contract. Dowson can produce only the minimum two witnesses to the alleged contract—though that would suffice in canon law—but has to produce additional witnesses simply to shore up their credibility. In crucial respects, however, the testimony of Dowson's two key witnesses can be viewed as untrustworthy. Both denied they were servants of Dowson—all deponents were asked if they bound to either party by ties of kinship or employment—and both hailed from a place whose obscurity invited challenge; the fourth of six articles to which Alice's witnesses responded specifically claimed that John Clerk was Dowson's servant, the fifth that the location of Greenoak was unknown to Alice.

The clash of cultures that underpins this case is here revealed. Alice occupies a bourgeois world in which reputation is a carefully nurtured commodity. It is, as Gervase Rosser has argued, part of the rationale for the guilds that proliferated particularly in towns in later medieval England.[26] For women it is given a specific sexual construction. Dowson represents a perceived threat to the chastity of a respectable widow. His mere presence in the same house as her is destabilizing, a challenge to the moral order of bourgeois respectability. Dowson, in contrast, nominally represents a world where reputation depends more crudely on the possession of land and the assertion of authority, backed ultimately by the threat of violence symbolized by his sword; it is his wealth and his power, not his pedigree or fine manners that his supporters assert. In practice we may suspect that Dowson is a charlatan. If he were who he claimed to be—"one of the most powerful and wealthy in their parts"—he is hardly likely to have disappeared so completely from the historical record. As an impostor, therefore, his position depends on his being unknown, a stranger from a distance, a man whose property exists only in boasts, whose power rests in bullying vulnerable widows, whose reputation is an invention of his lackeys and coconspirators.

The clash of cultures—bourgeois respectability versus aristocratic pretensions—is of course only a metaphor for and microcosm of the larger dispute about the claims of the burgess residents, substantiated by their commitment to the prosperity and orderliness of their own community and mindful of ancient rights and chartered privileges, and an absentee lord, nominally a mere infant incapable of personal authority, but in practice an unrelated guardian for whom the borough represented solely a source of income and profit. Consent thus emerges again as a contested issue. Alice Brathwell's burgess protectors intervene to ensure that her will to resist William Dowson's heavy-handed attempt to get her to marry him is given succor. In similarly resisting their own lord, Messyngham and his allies were asserting their own right to have a voice in the government of their own community. They sought government by consent of the burgess body in opposition to the arbitrary will of a man whose authority ultimately rested not even in hereditary right, but in his purchase of the wardship of a minor.

CONCLUSION

The themes that run through this book pertain to consent—particularly women's right to choose to marry or have sex—and the power that men may exercise over women. We see these issues played out through the lens of cases within the ecclesiastical Court of York. The power dynamics of aristocratic and bourgeois society are thus retold in a series of scripts that privilege the rather different conventions of canon law. The aristocratic imperatives of lineage and patronage that underpinned the practice of arranged marriages are thus occluded by the canonical emphasis on the consent of the contracting parties. Likewise, the frictions between bourgeois and aristocratic ideologies or bourgeois concerns with order and good governance that emerge from these cases are in fact entirely peripheral to the court's concern with the validity of disputed marriages. These are matters that can nevertheless be reconstructed from the court record.

Later medieval theologians and canonists made consent the lynchpin of marriage. Only by the verbal articulation of consent, freely and willingly expressed, might a canonically valid marriage be made. Consent is, of course, not the same as free choice. Canonists assumed that families would take an interest in and exercise a degree of influence over the marriages of their children. Canon law merely sought to ensure that such influence was not abused: children could not (or at least were supposed not to) be betrothed as small children and no marriage was to be recognized as binding until both parties had achieved their canonical majorities, namely, twelve years for girls and fourteen for boys; no contract was permitted to be made by force or threat; marriages to close kin (often a hallmark of arranged marriage) were disallowed. Any contract that allegedly breached any one or more of these stipulations could be challenged within the Church courts and annulled if the court was satisfied that canon law had been breached. This, of course, is the rationale behind arguments found in respect of Alice de Rouclif. The child Alice, it was claimed, fell below her canonical majority (also known as age of consent) and so could not lawfully be the wife of John Marrays.

The same canonical rationale underpins our other two cases. Although, as reasonably prosperous urban widows without apparent family ties, neither Agnes Grantham nor Alice Brathwell were under obvious family pressure to marry, the same legal caveats are pertinent in their cases. Agnes Grantham claimed she was forced by fear and actual physical violence to enter into words of matrimony with her alleged attacker. Alice Brathwell asserted that she had been put under some pressure to agree to marry William Dowson, but her argument was essentially that she had never said anything that could be understood as a promise of marriage, let alone a binding contract. Put simply, Alice de Rouclif was too young to be able to consent, Agnes de Grantham yielded to force and so did not consent willingly or freely, and Alice Brathwell simply did not consent.

The case of Alice de Rouclif is known to us because it was brought by John Marrays as an action for the restitution of conjugal rights before the Court of York. The action was precipitated by Alice's sudden and dramatic abduction by Sir Brian de Rouclif from her married sister-in-law's home. Because the action brought by John Marrays was conducted within the Church court according to canonical conventions, the issue of consent was placed center stage: was Alice of sufficient age to have consented to marrying John? Did she in fact consent to marry him? It is, however, very hard not to read this case as a conflict over control of Alice's person as a minor in feudal law. There is reason to believe that Ellen de Rouclif, Alice's mother, simultaneously attempted to secure the king's agreement that Sir Brian had no rights over Alice and that she should be returned. The conflict was thus not about consent, but about who controlled Alice's marriage. The case thus highlights and is a microcosm of the differences between canonical and feudal ideologies.

The niceties of canon law were in tension, even at times conflict, with the mores of the landed aristocracy. Elizabeth Robertson characterizes this as a clash between "feudal assumptions about female choice in marriage (that she has no choice)" and "ecclesiastical assumptions (that she does have a choice)."[1] Where canon law stressed consent, and hence the necessity of both parties being of sufficient age to exercise this consent, aristocratic families tended to undermine this by arranged marriage, including the marriage of minors. Probably the most frequent violation of canonical norms was the tendency of the aristocracy to arrange marriages between kin. This is apparent from the numerous papal letters granting retrospective dispensation for couples who had already contracted marriages to remain married despite having "discovered" that they were related within forbidden degrees. Perhaps one of the better known examples is the marriage of Sir Geoffrey Luttrell, patron of the famous Psalter, and Agnes Sutton, his second cousin.[2] By only declaring the relationship after the marriage had been solemnized, families knew that a dispensation would likely be issued as the Church was reluctant to dissolve established marriages; the Luttrell case is unusual in that the petition for a dispensation came many years after the actual marriage. If, however, a dispensation were requested before any formal contract or solemnization, there was much more chance that the request be refused.

As the case of Alice de Rouclif demonstrates, the betrothal of children whilst under canonical age was a known practice. So long as the child was over seven, however, such betrothals were perfectly licit in canon law. It is certainly possible to point to examples of betrothals where one or both parties were under seven, though they were probably comparatively rare by the later Middle Ages. The case of Sir William Plumpton who cynically betrothed his little granddaughters, his heiresses apparent, only subsequently to reveal an heir by an alleged clandestine marriage features disproportionately in the secondary literature and is almost certainly quite atypical.[3] Rather more common were marriages arranged when one or both parties were still children, but not necessarily quite of canonical age—as was true of Alice de Rouclif. Using data extracted from the *Oxford Dictionary of National Biography* relating to a sample of fifty-two almost exclusively high aristocratic or royal women active in the period 1250–1500 whose age at first marriage is known, seven were betrothed before their eleventh birthday and a further eight were married when aged between eleven and twelve years, that is to say more than a quarter of the women within this sample had had their marriages arranged even before their teens.[4]

Another of the aristocratic mores that conflicted with canonical teaching on marriage was the use of abduction—"raptus" in contemporary Latin, a usage that is ambiguous and liable to be rendered as rape or the no less ambiguous ravishment when translated into English—as a vehicle for effecting marriage.[5] To cite one famous example, Elizabeth de Burgh, the widowed coheiress of Gilbert de Clare and subsequent founder of Clare College, Cambridge, was forcibly abducted from Bristol Castle by Theobald de Verdun who promptly made her his wife and fathered a daughter by her.[6] Alice de Rouclif, the only surviving child of Gervase de Rouclif, was likewise abducted by Sir Brian de Rouclif ostensibly to protect her from an underage marriage to John Marrays, but presumably to transfer control of her marriage from her mother to her seigneur. Had Sir Brian succeeded, we can have little doubt that he would have arranged his own marriage for Alice—protecting Alice from an arranged and perhaps unwanted marriage was almost certainly not what Sir Brian had in mind when he ordered his men to Kennythorpe in the summer of 1365.

We know that Sir Brian was ultimately unsuccessful in his actions, but there is also an ironic twist to this narrative. Sometime before November 1375 Sir Brian appears to have died leaving only an underage daughter to succeed him. This we know because commissions were issued on 6 November concerning the abduction of his daughter and sole heiress Ellen. One was a commission "to find by inquisition…who the evildoers were that ravished Ellen, daughter and heir of Brian de Rouclif, a minor, at Pykeryng [Pickering]"; one of the four named commissioners was Richard Bernard, the steward of St Mary's Abbey. By ravished we are here presumably to understand abducted. The second was a commission of "oyer" and "terminer" issued at the petition of Margery, widow of John de Rouclif and in response to her charge that "John de Langton and others ravished the said Ellen, whose marriage pertains to her, at Pykeryng."[7] This Margery must be Ellen's grandmother, who would then have been nearly eighty.[8] Once again it is left to a widow and head of the immediate family to petition the king to secure the restitution of her abducted daughter or, in this case, granddaughter, and so retain control over not just her person, but the family lands and property that attach to her.

That two heiresses connected with Sir Brian de Rouclif should have been abducted within the space of only twenty years must warn us that such behavior, alongside the abduction of widows who were also likely to have lands associated with them, was perhaps not so exceptional within the ranks of landed society. As Scott Waugh, writing of a slightly earlier era, puts it, "tales of abduction were not frequent but were common enough to spark legislative remedies and to be a reminder that violence was never far removed from the realm of social relations in medieval England."[9] Abduction presented a way for a man to achieve a marriage or to effect control over a marriage that circumvented familial hostility or the problems of dowry negotiation. It represents, as Pollock and Maitland long ago observed, a continuation of a long tradition of marriage by capture.[10] A woman, viewed legally as in effect the property of her lord or her father, might thus be abducted with or without her consent. Indeed, in marked contrast to canon law, the consent of the abducted woman was not really an issue in common law, but the lack of consent of the father or husband, who had legal authority over her, certainly was. When Thomas de Thurmaston abducted ("rapuit") Maud, wife of Roger de Oxenford from her Lincoln home in 1351 and took a gold ring and various goods with her, it was done "against the said Roger's will."[11]

A number of cases of alleged ravishment or abduction of heiresses, of widows, and of wards, both female and male, are documented, for example, in the patent rolls. In several instances we may suspect that disputes over wardship, and hence control of marriage, underpin reported acts of violence. In 1358, for example, Joan, the widow of John de la Berwe was pardoned for escaping prison, but she had been imprisoned in the first place because she had abducted her own son and heir from the prior of Worcester "whose keeping pertained to the prior as he pretended."[12] This case has obvious parallels with that of Alice de Rouclif since it is an example of a widowed mother fighting to secure the custody of her child. Another abduction that further highlights the entanglement of religious in the politics of aristocratic marriage is the 1386 case of Beatrix Sheldon snatched from the custody of the prior of Chicksand, for which action one Edmund Randolf, esquire, was pardoned.[13] In 1356 it was alleged that Bishop Trillek of Hereford had headed a band of men who broke into Sir Thomas Moigne's home and abducted Joan, the kinswoman and heiress of William Muntrich, who was his ward.[14]

The reports of abductions of heirs and heiresses recorded in the patent rolls invariably specify that the victim was a minor, but no further indication is given of actual age. One exception to this is the abduction of Emma, daughter of Alice de Bourdon, forcibly taken from the house of John de Swyneford the elder, by Robert, the servant of John de Tiryngham, who was subsequently pardoned. Emma is specifically described as being "of eleven years of age."[15] The detail is striking because the rolls are otherwise unspecific about age. As our earlier discussion of the marriage of Alice de Rouclif shows, eleven years was the youngest age at which a girl could in effect be married and that marriage could be made to stick in canon law. The implication is that this detail was added by way of tacitly explaining the abduction, where abduction itself was understood as a means to control marriage. This is also reflected in the frequent note of who owned the marriage of an heir or heiress that had been abducted. Sometimes this was the immediate guardian of the heir or heiress, but in a number of instances it was a superior lord. In 1391, for example, a commission was appointed to discover who had abducted Alexander, the heir of Sir Thomas de Mountford. His marriage was said to belong to the queen who had already granted it to Richard le Scrope.[16] The presumption that the abduction of heirs and heiresses was primarily about controlling their marriages is made rather more explicit in the case of Roger, the kinsman and heir of Margaret Senche, a tenant in chief, whose marriage consequently belonged to the king. A commission was appointed to find out the perpetrators, but also to discover "whether he has been married, and, if he has, what is the value of his marriage."[17] Alice de Rouclif's abduction at the behest of Sir Brian de Rouclif fits this established framework. Alice's probable rape at the hands of John Marrays a few nights before Christmas 1364 does not.

The medieval legal concept of "raptus" is frequently stated to conflate the essentially different phenomena of abduction and of rape.[18] Though there is some truth in this, modern scholarship has sometimes introduced ambiguities, not least in respect of the terminology used, that were never intended. As Henry Ansgar Kelly has observed, "the basic meaning of the Latin raptus and rapere is 'seizing.'" He notes "two kinds of seizure, one preceding sexual violation, and the other preceding abduction."[19] "Raptus" on its own, without any elaboration that forced coitus followed, need not imply more than abduction. Similarly the verb "rapere" is only used to signify abduction, though abduction may precede actual rape and indeed was understood as a necessary preliminary to the act of forcible coitus.[20]

Confusion is brought about by the distinction made in law between abduction—where the underlying Latin specifies "rapuit"—with and abduction without the consent of the party abducted or ravished. This is true of the provision made within chapter 34 of the statute of Westminster II (1285) which refers to the acts of ravishing and of forceful ravishing ("si homme ravise femme...ou homme ravise femme...a force").[21] J.B. Post understood the Statutes of Westminster (of 1275 and 1285) to have been framed against rape and in time to have been used to deal with abduction.[22] Kelly conversely understands their concern always to have been directed at abduction and regards the limited evidence of contemporary attempts to use this legislation in actual rape cases as exceptions.[23]

The abduction of a woman was largely imagined as theft from a father or husband. A woman who eloped with another man taking even the barest of personal possessions with her, as in the case of Margaret de Oxenford noted above, was liable to provoke a legal action for abduction and damages. Thus when in 1356 Maud, the wife of William Lenegor went off with William de Rothewell "by her own will" taking clothing, jewelry, and money with her, William was said to have ravished her and caused 100s. of damages to her husband.[24] Evidently there was nothing oxymoronic to the medieval mind about the juxtaposition of "raptus" alongside the consent of the party so ravished. Other cases suggest that the abduction was accompanied by force. In fact, a number of such cases probably represent a legal fiction designed to reinforce the sense that the woman's father or spouse had not consented and was therefore being wronged. In an unusual case, one Robert de Flete, initially charged with the abduction of Elizabeth, the then wife of Matthew de Clyvedon and breaking his house, was subsequently pardoned when it transpired that he was Elizabeth's servant and that he had gone with her on her orders "and so abducted her with her own will."[25] Many other abductions, however, were apparently violent and implicitly in violation of the consent of both the victim and her male protector. This was evidently the case when in 1360 armed men entered Richard de Wodeford's manor, beat the lord of the manor and three of his staff and "abducted Elizabeth wife of John de Wodeford [Richard's son] with a robe worth 5s. with which she was clothed, and ravished her against her will, and killed William Cartere."[26] Even in this case, "rapuit" still only meant abducted.

"Raptus" in the sense of abduction thus took a variety of forms. It could represent consensual elopement. Equally it could represent actual kidnapping—abduction in its modern sense. In such cases abduction could herald arranged marriage—as was almost certainly intended in the case of Alice de Rouclif's abduction—or even forced marriage, the fate allegedly suffered by Agnes de Grantham or that lay behind the case of Alice le Dimeigne.[27] "Raptus" in the sense of abduction could, moreover, preface actual rape. Thus in 1349 a gang abducted Agnes, daughter of John de Loukare from her home by night and took her to Basing Park "against her will," where one William Bacoun "lay with her against her will."[28] In an unusual office case before the Capitular court of Lincoln in 1339 relating to alleged fornication, one Margaret, the daughter of Richard son of Geoffrey claimed that Richard de Benetby "took her by force against her will and held her thus taken against her will for forty days [rapuit eam contra voluntatem suam manu armata et tenuit sic raptam contra voluntatem suam per quadraginta dies]." "Raptus" here again implies only abduction. She went on "and he knew her [cognovit eam] against her will for the whole of that time." By claiming rape, Margaret was able to convince this Church court that she had not sinned by fornicating with Richard since she had done so without her consent, a concept integral to the canon law, but here, although the abduction clearly served as a preface to actual rape, the rape is spelled out as nonconsensual sex.[29]

In a number of cases "rapuit" is used within a sequence of verbs where the action described culminates in rape in the modern sense. It follows that "rapere," though continuing to signify taking, comes to have resonances that signify nonconsent, violence, and sexual violation. Thus, in a case before the Lincolnshire Justices of the Peace dated 1396, the nature of the alleged felony is given rhetorical emphasis by the juxtaposition of three related verbs: one Robert "forcefully seized, lay with and violated [vi et armis rapuit concubuit et violavit]" Margaret, the wife of William Lenyng.[30] In another slightly earlier case from the same source one Robert was outlawed after it was found that he had "seized and known carnally against her will [rapuit et cognovit carnaliter contra voluntatem suam]" a twelve-year-old girl he had first "took [cepit]" and then cut with a knife.[31] "Rapuit" here is evidently something more than the initial "cepit." In like fashion John Helwell tied up [ligavit] Alice, the daughter of Robert Couper, before "he feloniously took her there and violated her body [ipsam ibidem felonice rapuit et corporaliter violavit]."[32] Alice was already bound before Robert "seized" her, so "rapuit" here seems not so much the capture, but more the violation, yet it occupies a position between (and perhaps linking) the two other verbs. Here "rapuit" seems to act as a necessary stage in a narrative of rape where the ability of the attacker to move his victim—indicative of his control and her powerlessness—is integral to the understanding of the crime, just as narratives of women being thrown onto the backs of horses become a common feature of the narrative of abduction.

What emerges is that the woman's consent was recognized as a pertinent issue both in respect of abduction and of rape. In the former case the woman's consent comes, however, to be occluded by consideration of the consent of a father or husband, such that a woman could be abducted even though she consented to her own abduction. The same is not true in respect of rape. Here the woman's lack of consent is repeatedly, if only implicitly, emphasized in rape narratives by reference to the force or violence used against her.[33] Indeed the late-thirteenth-century legal treatise known as *Britton* defined rape as "a felony of violence by a man inflicted on the body of a woman, whether she be a virgin or otherwise [une felonie de homme de violence fete au cors de femme, quele qe ele soit pucele ou autre]."[34] The legal framework that underpinned medieval rape narratives, however, required more than just an assertion that force or violence had been used against the victim. It demanded proof. The appeal of rape contained within the undated Office of the Coroner demanded a "signum veritatis, per ampnum sanguinolentum, vel hutesium levatum [proof by a bloody flow or the hue raised]."[35] *Britton* likewise advised coroners to look for "telling evidence, such as blood stains and torn dress [les signes presumptives, cum de saunc espaundu, et de robe decyré]."[36]

More detailed legal narratives of rape combine three elements—abduction, violence, and the issue of blood—so as to mirror this legal framework. Thus in a case dated 1282, Rose, the daughter of Nicholas le Savage, was forcibly taken from her father's house and put on the back of a palfrey—the archetypical forced abduction motif—before being stripped, held down, and raped of her virginity, and finally left bloodied.[37] Similarly in a case from the 1321 Eyre of London discussed by Barbara Hanawalt, Joan, daughter of Eustace, is said to have been abducted from by her father's house, forcibly held down and raped of her virginity such that she bled.[38]

It is thus mistaken to suggest that medieval people did not distinguish between abduction and rape; that the medieval term "raptus," though sharing some resonances, did not coincide in meaning with the modern term "rape," but instead often signified abduction, is of little matter. Of more importance is that rape was differently constructed, although there is in fact less distance between modern lay perceptions of rape and medieval understandings as between the modern law and that prevailing in the later Middle Ages. As Kim Phillips has observed, high and later medieval legal practice tended to construct rape as "a crime against the body." By emphasizing the powerlessness of women to protect their bodies from their assailants—hence the emphasis on force and violence—the law tended to marginalize consent; the crime lay in the violation of the body, not the violation of the will.[39] There is thus a difference between canonical notions of consent, which emphasize the capacity of the individual as a sentient being, regardless of gender, to express (and to express verbally) their will and common law conventions that rather reduce women to bodies over which others may have control.

In proving that a woman had not willingly consented to marriage, but, as was alleged by Agnes Grantham, had been forced into it, canon law offered the yardstick of the "constant man" or the "constant woman." This notion placed emphasis on the thoughts, feelings, and fears of the individual and recognized that a "constant" man or woman could be moved by threats or fear as much as by actual physical violence.[40] This allowed Agnes Grantham to argue that it was the fear and threat of rape that moved her to agree to marry John Dale as much as any actual violence. Canon law allowed Agnes a will and recognized how that will could be violated even whilst her body remained unviolated. Similarly canon law provided that Alice Brathwell could say no when pressed by William Dowson to agree to marry her. The action within the Church court revolved around what Alice said, not what Alice did.

The same story is not true of Alice de Rouclif. By providing that marriages could be made as much by words of future consent followed by coitus as by words of present consent, the canon law effectively undermined its own principle of consent. Alice, it was argued in court, was married to John Marrays by virtue of words of betrothal spoken before Alice had achieved the canonical age of majority, but rendered immediately binding by her having sexual intercourse with John whilst sufficiently close to her majority that this was construed as present consent to what had previously been only a future intent.[41] This argument was accepted by the court in a legal process that formally silenced Alice by presuming her a minor and therefore debarred from testifying in her own right. Though Alice's words at the initial betrothal are carefully reported to the court by various witnesses and duly recorded within the resulting depositions, the subsequent coitus is documented not in terms of words, but actions.

In an earlier chapter, I presented Alice's sexual initiation by John Marrays as rape. Here I followed modern legal and feminist perspectives that place absolute emphasis upon consent, frequently characterized as the woman's right to say no. What happened to Alice one night just before Christmas 1364 is within the case implicitly characterized as consensual sex. Indeed, that sexual intercourse followed an earlier contract of marriage would have created the presumption that sex was consensual. The narrative provided by Dom. William Marrays, ventriloquizing what he had been told by a little girl who had witnessed the events from elsewhere within the same room, emphasized that actual penetration had occurred, not whether Alice wanted sex. As in rape narratives, Alice is reduced to body. But not entirely so. Allegedly she "silently complained at the force on account of John's labor as if she had been hurt then as a result of this labor."

In challenging John Marrays's case that Alice was his lawful wife who had been unlawfully snatched away, the contesting party—in effect Alice's abductor, Sir Brian de Rouclif—made the argument that Alice was too young to have consented to marry. The case, therefore, was not that Alice had not in fact consummated her relationship with John, nor that Alice had been coerced into sex. The former might be hard to deny—Alice seemed too ready to acknowledge it. The latter was equally problematic. In a cultural context that understood rape primarily as involving forcible abduction by a person, who, if not a stranger, then certainly not a kinsman or fiancé, a degree of violence, physical injury marked by the issue of blood, and culminating in the raising of the hue against the assailant, what happened to Alice would not have sounded like rape: she was not abducted; she was betrothed to her assailant; John's "labor" may have exercised a degree of "force" over her, but violence is otherwise played down; though Alice was presumably deflowered, the narrative chooses not to specify any bleeding; and if Alice cried out it was "silently" and not to raise the hue.

It may be that Dom. William's testimony was colored by an awareness of the medieval law on rape and a concern to ensure that Alice's sexual initiation be understood as consensual rather than coerced. Indeed, because youthful victims claiming the rape of virginity were such a significant subset of rape victims reported to the courts—and hence so central to the medieval conception of rape—Dom. William had to be especially careful. If the account appears to modern eyes deeply disturbing—and perhaps to the eyes of the court, salacious and even pornographic—it would not then have seemed so. There was nothing unusual in pubescent aristocratic girls being married, nothing deeply shocking in the idea of an adult man having sex with a girl not yet in her teens, nothing problematic in the notion that a girl may have consented to sex in such circumstances.

The medieval law on rape that constructs women as bodies is consonant with broader aristocratic and patriarchal notions that construct women as property. The dispute played out between Alice's mother, Ellen,

John Marrays, and Sir Brian de Rouclif is for control of Alice's body. Her marriage is arranged for her by Ellen and John, *pace* the canonical principle of consent; if Ellen and John had not succeeded, then Sir Brian would surely have arranged his own marriage for her. Having contracted marriage in the gatehouse of St Mary's Abbey, Alice was then taken to Kennythorpe. There she was made to share a bed with her "husband" and obliged to let him have sex with her. Sir Brian, eager to act before Alice reached her canonical majority, then had her abducted from Kennythorpe. Alice is reduced to being a pawn and a parcel in aristocratic games about power, influence, property, wealth, lineage, and inheritance.

We know about Alice de Rouclif because her marriage was the subject of lengthy litigation within the Court of York. Because the canon law on marriage privileges consent, Alice's words are several times reported in depositions as evidence of her will. This serves to highlight the tensions implicit between canonical and aristocratic conceptions, but there is a certain irony here. Alice is presented as having a determining voice in one of the most critical decisions in her life, but in fact all the key decisions have been made for her. In being presented by John Marrays's witnesses as wanting the marriage—a sentiment that she quite probably expressed—Alice appears to be exercising her will, where in fact she is only doing what is expected of her; her underlying needs and concerns go unaddressed. When confronted by John in the bed she had previously shared with another girl, she can only comply with his will. This contrasts with the case of Agnes Grantham. As a widow and capable independent business woman, Agnes is much better able to express her will and hence it is easier to recognize when that will is violated. In presenting her case, however, Agnes draws upon a discourse of forced abduction that is reminiscent of that found in the royal courts. She is abducted by a gang whilst traveling between Acomb and Acomb Grange; she is thrown on the back of a horse and taken into the woods; she is held against her will. The forced abduction and the rapid entry into the woods is in fact reminiscent of rape narratives.[42] The narrative strategy lends credence to Agnes's case that as a constant woman she was forced to yield to John Dale's demands that she consent to marriage.

Agnes Grantham's strategy was designed to present her as a virtuous woman who had sacrificed her right to consent to marriage—her right to say no—so as to preserve her honor. Her narrative—contained in a lengthy list of articles—stresses the threat of violation, even that violation was attempted, but denies actual violation. John Dale's response, noted on the articles, is that Agnes in fact had consensual sex with him. This is, of course, a logical facet of Dale's case that Agnes willingly contracted marriage with him; if Agnes willingly contracted marriage, consensual sex would be an expected outcome. As I have argued previously, for Agnes to claim that she was raped by Dale, would in fact have weakened her case within the Church court. It would also have damaged her standing within the community and may even have undermined her business and hence her livelihood and her capacity to support her son. The possibility thus arises that Agnes's non-rape is in fact a legal fiction; Agnes was just as much a victim of rape as was Alice, but both these rapes remained hidden and unacknowledged because prevailing social attitudes demanded that they be kept hidden and unspoken.[43]

Alice de Rouclif as an aristocratic minor below canonical age had little effective power to exercise her own voice, to assert her own will. The same is less true of Agnes Grantham and Alice Brathwell. There are in fact some interesting parallels between the cases of these two bourgeois widows. Just as with heiresses, their marriages are sought after because of the wealth and property they control. They are thus the objects of attention by ambitious men eager to possess that wealth and property. Canon law and custom afford them limited protection. Canon law required consent to marriage, custom permitted the widow a year of mourning before she might marry again. Because these are disputed marriage cases, and the issue of consent is central to determining the canonical validity or otherwise of marriage, then it is upon the question of consent that these cases inevitably focus. The custom of a year's mourning is more marginal to the way these cases are presented—indeed it is invisible in the case of Agnes Grantham—but may be of considerable significance in understanding their broader context.

Alice Brathwell, pressed by her impatient lover to contract marriage, properly demands time to think over his proposal. The space is proper because, as she notes, he is a stranger to her and she knows nothing of his character or standing; by implication she will have an opportunity to make enquiry. The more telling reason why the delay is proper is, however, because she had not yet been widowed a year. In asking for period of reflection, Alice in fact asks to delay her response until immediately after the end of this period of mourning. The custom here works in Alice's favor, making more plausible her account that they discussed marriage, but that she gave no actual response rather than that, as William Dowson claimed, actual words of contract were exchanged. Indeed the alleged delay works more to Alice's credit than would an outright refusal, just as Dowson's apparent insistence that there was an immediate contract, or—as Alice alleged—that any delay be kept comparatively brief, works to his discredit.

What emerges is that Dowson was in a hurry. John Dale, who attacked Agnes Grantham at the end of June 1410, was also in a hurry. He required that Agnes publicly acknowledge a marriage between them within hours of ambushing her on the road between Acomb village and Acomb Grange. He attacked her at the end of June 1410. Agnes had only been widowed in March of that year, so would not otherwise have expected to remarry, if at all, for another eight months or more. Looked at another way, John Dale may have seen the customary year of mourning as an opportunity to forestall other potential suitors. In both cases, it is the argument here that widows were targeted precisely because they were still within their customary year of mourning. These men, therefore, were trying to secure marriages before anyone else could and to anticipate any rivals who might prefer the courtesies of courtship and negotiation. This is in fact not so far removed from the abduction or coerced marriage of eleven-year-old heiresses or even the arranged marriages of wards below the age of legal majority.

A petition dated 1439 outlines an abduction and forced marriage that is strikingly reminiscent of Agnes Grantham's circumstances, though here it would appear that the forced marriage was followed by imprisonment and actual rape. Margaret Malefant claimed that she was tricked into going from her home in Wales to London with one Lewis Leyson in order to visit Sir Thomas whom she believed to be sick, but was in fact already dead. Whilst traveling through a park within the Gower peninsular she was ambushed by Lewis's men and taken into the mountains and held there without food. She was then taken to an accomplice's house, threatened further, and made to marry Lewis in the local church. She was then taken back to the accomplice's house where he "against her will ravished her."[44] Lewis thus exploited Margaret's widowhood, a status still unknown to her, with greater alacrity and ruthlessness than even John Dale.

Another parallel between these two cases is that the two widows were assailed not so much by individual men, but by, in effect, small gangs. Dowson was supported in his time in Doncaster and in the subsequent court hearing by John Bukton and John Clerk. John Dale was accompanied in his attack on Agnes, her son, and her servant by Robert Kyrkham and Thomas Wakfeld, otherwise Forester, of Wighill, who is described as the forester of Healaugh Park. Thomas Wakfeld is described as playing a particularly active role in the events following Agnes's abduction, holding her in his lodge at Healaugh Park and allegedly going to Acomb Grange to consult with William Feryby. For Dowson, his accomplices constitute the two witnesses needed according to canon law to prove a contract of marriage. The same may be true of Dale's accomplices, though only Thomas Wakfeld is noted as a deponent; the probability is that other witnesses were used to prove the contract between Agnes and John Dale.[45] More likely is that Dale's accomplices were just that. This is very much the pattern found from judicial records of assaults and housebreakings. To take a couple of examples from the Peace sessions for Lincolnshire in the latter part of the fourteenth century we find John at Bek, Robert de Yorke, and William de Irland, all of Dalby, allegedly assaulted one Thomas Doddy of Calceby on the road one night intending to murder him. Similarly three clerks, William Wyssyndeyne, Roger Beuc, and William Bouay supposedly forcefully imprisoned John, the heir of Sir John Roos of Dorrington until he agreed to marry Elizabeth de Brynkill.[46] Many other assault cases and the like name one man as the instigator, but add vaguely "and others."

Such group activity, felonious or otherwise, is indicative of the functioning of homosocial relationships within later medieval English society.[47] Such groupings were an integral part of the social fabric. They were, for example, fundamental to the governance of medieval communities since women were formally excluded by reason of gender. The Doncaster burgesses who assembled to confront William Dowson acted in the absence of any formal administrative or policing response on the part of the borough's then lord and in so doing claimed responsibility for ensuring moral order and, ultimately, government. In challenging Dowson so as to protect Alice Brathwell's honor, they were in effect also regulating Alice's own conduct, specifically her sexual conduct. When Agnes Grantham escaped her attackers and hurried to Acomb Grange, it was to protest before a group of notable males that she had consented to marry John Dale only under extreme duress and to protect herself from being violated. In a sense Agnes was not only laying the foundations of her subsequent stance within the Church court against John Dale's petition for the enforcement of a contract of marriage, she was also defending her honor before a de facto jury of men.[48] The leading burgesses of Doncaster effectively serve a like function for Alice Brathwell. This collective male affirmation of female honor functioned in effect as a force for stability, just as male affronts to female honor—as threatened in different ways by Dowson and Dale—were seen as destabilizing and a threat to the wider community.

Of particular interest in exploring homosocial relationships is the partnership between John Thornton and his immediate neighbor William Pountfret. The two men had known each other for forty years by the time of the case relating to Agnes Grantham. They are described as business partners who traded in woolen cloth out of a shop they jointly owned, but the business relationship was clearly rooted in close ties of friendship. It explains how Agnes, immediately on contracting marriage to John Thornton was allowed to move into William Pountfret's house even though, according to Pountfret's own testimony, he had not previously known Agnes. Most remarkable, however, is the evidence of Thornton's burial next to his "socius" in the parish church that stood opposite their houses.[49] This is very reminiscent of the ritual bonds of brotherhood signified by shared graves described by the late Alan Bray. Pountfret and Thornton thus stand as mercantile bourgeois counterparts to Bray's contemporary aristocratic and clerical exemplars and suggest that the model of sworn brotherhood enjoyed wide cultural dissemination in the later fourteenth and earlier fifteenth centuries.[50] It may be that popular romances, understood to have enjoyed a bourgeois as much as an aristocratic readership, played a particular role here for sworn brotherhood is a motif common to several.[51]

Though Pountfret and Thornton clearly enjoyed a commercial partnership, their conduct glimpsed through this case and their subsequent burial side by side bears out Bray's broader thesis concerning the spiritual significance of this kind of alliance. Pountfret was almost certainly a man in tune with contemporary devotional interests. As we have seen, his house was home to his vowess kinswoman, Dame Christiana, and the two gether joined the York Corpus Christi guild in the very year of its foundation.[52] Agnes Grantham's residence within this household is apparently characterized by conspicuous piety, a quality shared to a degree by one of Pountfret's household servants. The wills of both Pountfret and Thornton, obvious sources for their devotional interests, are lost, but we do have the will of Pountfret's wife, Avice, who predeceased him. This too suggests devout enthusiasm manifested in both the diversity of pious bequests in fulfillment of the Seven Works, her numerous bequests of prayer beads, and her interest inter alia in the cult of Corpus Christi and the Carthusian house at Mount Grace.[53]

In the context of a social norm of the male-headed conjugal household, the precise domestic arrangements of the functionally conjoint Pountfret-Thornton household may well have been unorthodox.[54] At the time of the case, their two homes contained a widower who resided with a presumably widowed kinswoman and a widow, who was probably a rape victim and who had recently remarried, but was apparently not cohabiting with her husband who lived next door. The home next door comprised a recently remarried widower, who was not cohabiting with his wife, who lived next door. The widower's home also housed female servants and the same was likely to have been true of both homes. Such an arrangement could even have been portrayed as subversive and hence disruptive. There are reasons why it was not. These may be illustrated by reference to an example of a superficially orthodox, because simple conjugal, household that was in fact characterized by disorder.

In the 1440s, another well-to-do York citizen, the goldsmith William Snawschill, presided over a household where the servants, both male and female, were presented for fornication both with others and with each other and where even his wife was conducting an adulterous relationship.[55] The Snawschill household was dangerously dysfunctional because William himself failed to exercise control over his dependents. His wife's affair and his servants' sexual misconduct destabilized not only his own household, but those other households implicated in the web of illicit sexual relationships consequent on William's impotent headship. Unchecked, the canker could spread still more widely. William's failure to exercise patriarchal authority is here specifically manifested in a failure to regulate the sexual conduct of his wife and servants. His delinquency can be contrasted with the reaction of John Bown, Poutfret's contemporary, on discovering his male apprentice, John Waryngton's seduction of a fellow servant: John first considered having Waryngton imprisoned, implicitly for breach of his indenture of apprenticeship, but soon after, resolved on making Waryngton marry the young woman and so restore the social harmony.[56] The Pountfret-Thornton household, in contrast, offered a model of sexual control: Dame Christiana was vowed to chastity; Pountfret and Thornton were intimately bound in friendship, but we need not read this as anything other than a chaste relationship; Agnes Grantham was a devout widow who was able to use the court of York to assert her chastity; the marriage between Agnes and John Thornton appears not to have involved cohabitation and can be construed as a chaste marriage. Within a contemporary religious culture that promoted the virtues of chastity, the household, including the women servants, were conventionally, but conspicuously devout.[57]

The Pountfret-Thornton conjoint household thus emerges not so much as an unorthodox arrangement viewed from a historical-demographic perspective, but as a model of bourgeois respectability, where the values of sexual restraint, otherwise chastity, mirror the values of good government and the social harmony that so follows. Within this model we can more clearly comprehend why the regulation of female sexuality came to be seen as so central to contemporary magisterial understanding of godly governance and the maintenance of social order. This is implicit in Marjorie McIntosh's brilliant survey of small town court records.[58] It is manifest in the assertion of the civic government in Norwich in 1465 that their duty was to prosecute and imprison "dicers, gamblers, adulterers, fornicators, burglars, pimps and housebreakers," and it lies behind the radical reform agenda targeting adultery and prostitution pursued in 1492 in Coventry.[59] It explains the intervention of Thomas de Messyngham and his fellow burgesses to confront William Dowson and protect Alice Brathwell. It explains Agnes Grantham's urgent concern to defend her virtue and, supposing she was in fact raped by John Dale, to reassert her virtue publicly by her marriage to John Thornton and by her vigorous defense against Dale's petition to enforce a contract of marriage within the Court of York.

If bourgeois society sought to regulate women's sexuality by an insistence on chastity, a virtue in which women were socialized from an early age and which women clearly internalized, a similar point may be made in respect of aristocratic society. This is echoed in Alice de Rouclif's repeated and plaintive demand that her "lover" solemnize their marriage. There are, however, significant differences in the degree of agency allowed to women, even young women. Child marriage, an extreme manifestation of arranged marriage, is not a bourgeois phenomenon, but is found within the aristocracy; even, as in Alice's case, at the level of parish gentry. Orphans and particularly orphaned heiresses were especially vulnerable. Similarly marriage following abduction—whether with the woman's consent or otherwise—is again much more of an aristocratic phenomenon; Agnes Grantham's case is unusual, though her assailant was a clerk rather then a burgess.

It is tempting to conclude that the combination of aristocratic concern with family and lineage and an aristocratic masculinity that emphasized martial and sexual prowess demanded a correspondingly compliant femininity, of which Alice de Rouclif was a product.[60] Bourgeois society, with its emphasis on trade, the workshop, on sociability and trust, constructed a less aggressive masculinity and a correspondingly more assertive femininity, which is precisely what we find in Alice Brathwell and Agnes Grantham.[61] Certainly we may contrast *The Book of the Knight of Tour-Landry*, composed in France in the early 1370s, but circulating widely thereafter, with its relentless emphasis on modesty, chastity, and restraint in speech with the still conservative, but more pragmatic values found in "How the Goodwife taught her Daughter," a slightly earlier text that likewise circulated over many years.[62] Equally it is well nigh impossible to imagine the quintessentially bourgeois Margery Kempe in any other guise.[63] The three cases discussed in this book tend to accentuate these differences because Alice de Rouclif was only a girl not yet in her teens, whereas Brathwell and Grantham were both widows of mature age. But they also reflect an underlying truth. Consent, the issue that came to be central to these three cases as presented in the canon-legal forum of the Court of York, has a variety of meanings. In the bourgeois world of negotiation, credit, trust, and contract, the notion of consent was understood to demand an agreement willingly entered into by both parties. In the aristocratic world of land, lineage and political rivalry, where violence and intimidation were readily resorted to, consent was more an imperative than a choice.

NOTES

Preface

1. Emmanuel Le Roy Ladurie, *Montaillou: Village Occitan de 1274 à 1324* (Paris: Editions Gallimard, 1978), published in an abridged English translation the same year. The description is from the cover of the 1980 paperback edition. Carlo Ginzburg, *The Cheese and the Worms: The Cosmos of a Sixteenth-Century Miller*, trans. J. and A. Tedeschi (London: Routledge and Kegan Paul, 1980). Ginzburg's work was first published in Italian in 1976.
2. Natalie Zemon Davis, *The Return of Martin Guerre* (Cambridge, MA: Harvard University Press, 1983); Gene Brucker, *Giovanni and Lusanna: Love and Marriage in Renaissance Florence* (London: Weidenfeld and Nicholson, 1986); Richard Wunderli, *Peasant Fires: The Drummer of Niklashausen* (Bloomington, IN: Indiana University Press, 1992); Robert Bartlett, *The Hanged Man: A Story of Miracle, Memory, and Colonialism in the Middle Ages* (Princeton: Princeton University Press, 2004). Another work worth noticing is Robert C. Palmer, *The Whilton Dispute, 1264–1380: A Social-Legal Study of Dispute Settlement in Medieval England* (Princeton: Princeton University Press, 1984), which has some resonances for this present study, but although some of the sources used relate to legal proceedings, there is nothing akin to the witness statements or testimony used in the other studies.
3. Natalie Zemon Davis, *Fiction in the Archives: Pardon Tales and their Tellers in Sixteenth-Century France* (Cambridge, UK: Cambridge University Press, 1987).
4. John H. Arnold, *Inquisition and Power: Catharism and the Confessing Subject in Medieval Languedoc* (Philadelphia: University of Pennsylvania Press, 2001); Noël James Menuge, *Medieval English Wardship in Romance and Law* (Woodbridge: Boydell, 2001).
5. The population of Rawcliffe is not known. Seventy persons are recorded as paying the 1377 poll tax for the neighboring village of Skelton together with that part of Rawcliffe that fell within the Liberty of St Peter: TNA (formerly PRO), E179/211/30/15; *The Poll Taxes of 1377, 1379 and 1381*, ed. Carolyn C. Fenwick, Records of Social and Economic History 27, 29, and 37 (Oxford: British Academy, 1998–2005), 3:242. No tax population for the remaining part of Rawcliffe survives among the returns for the

liberties of St Mary and of St Leonard (regularly listed together for taxation purposes) or elsewhere for the wapentake of Bulmer. The same is apparently true of Clifton, but Bootham at least is included within the York returns under the parish of St Olave. In 1334, Skelton and Rawcliffe within the Liberty of St Peter were assessed at 18s. and Rawcliffe within the Liberty of St Mary's at 10s. In fact the first Ordnance Survey map would suggest that most of the then settlement of Rawcliffe (as opposed to the associated lands) fell within the parish of St Michael le Belfrey and hence within the Liberty of St Peter. This might explain the apparent absence of a separate return for the Liberty of St Mary. It follows that a very crude estimate of the total number of taxpayers for Rawcliffe in 1377 might be, therefore, in order of thirty to forty, hence a total population of something below seventy.

6. Unless otherwise stated, all references and quotations in the first seven chapters of this book are derived from this case, which is BI, CP.E.89. The depositions, but not the other materials in the case, have been largely translated in *Women in England, c. 1275–1525: Documentary Sources*, ed. and trans. P.J.P. Goldberg (Manchester: Manchester University Press, 1995), pp. 58–80.
7. R.H. Helmholz, *Marriage Litigation in Medieval England* (Cambridge UK: Cambridge University Press, 1974), pp. 67–9.
8. Dorothy M. Owen, "White Annays and Others," in *Medieval Women*, ed. Derek Baker, Studies in Church History, subsidia I (Oxford: Blackwell, 1978), pp. 331–46 (especially pp. 338-9). Owen makes useful observations about the role of women in the remembrance of past events. Frederik Pedersen, *Marriage Disputes in Medieval England* (London: Hambledon, 2000), pp. 128–33. Pedersen's account is limited to one set of depositions (CP.E.89/27) and his reading is sometimes erroneous. To cite two examples, he describes William Pottell as "the carpenter on the Wastelyn estate" on the basis that he prepared ("made") John Marray's bed, and elsewhere states that Alice stayed with Katherine de Rouclif "on the night preceding the ceremony [spousals]," whereas she stayed the morning after.
9. Menuge, *Medieval English Wardship*, pp. 95–9, 104. It may also be possible to see some parallels between this case and Linda Mitchell's account of Alice de Lacy, betrothed at eleven and formally married two years later, but abducted after a number of years of marriage. Linda Mitchell's discussion of this case debates the degree to which Alice de Lacy colluded with her abductors, as suggested by some of her chronicle sources, and hence explores the problematic territory of Alice's own feelings: Linda E. Mitchell, *Portraits of Medieval Women: Family, Marriage, and Politics in England 1225–1350* (New York: Palgrave, 2003), pp. 107–14.
10. Owen, "White Annays," in *Medieval Women*, p. 334.
11. Chris Given-Wilson, *The English Nobility in the Late Middle Ages* (London: Routledge, 1987), pp. 71–3.

12. This conclusion is predicated on Sir Brian's role in the case and in the events that precede it. For genealogies of the two families of de Rouclif see figs. 1 and 2.
13. Indeed the boundaries are fuzzy and porous: cf. Nigel Saul, *Knights and Esquires: The Gloucestershire Gentry in the Fourteenth Century* (Oxford: Oxford University Press, 1981), pp. 19–20, 25–6, 242, 244–5.
14. As we shall see (chapter 4) even the status of St Olave's as a parish church is questionable. Strictly St Olave's seems to have functioned as a chapel, the parochial rights being possessed by St Mary's Abbey.
15. In my 1995 translation of this case I transcribed "Wascelyne" with a "t" rather than a "c" since the down stroke of the long "s" joins the "c" in a manner that makes it almost indistinguishable from a "t." In the case of Stephen Wascelyne, Anabilla's husband, however, the name is rendered Waceleyn. A near contemporary will, written in a clearer hand, renders the name Wasscelyne.
16. There are three versions of the cartulary extant, but the copy in the York Minster Archive has been used here since it records property in Rawcliffe: YML, St Mary's Abbey Cartulary, XVI A.1, 2.
17. The records of 17 sessions of the court in 1445–46 survive: YML, F 1/3/1.
18. The archive was temporarily moved by a chain of tradesmen whilst the fire was raging in 1829 to rest on the pews of the neighboring church of St Michael le Belfrey and again by a convoy of carriages and carts to the registrar's house in Monkgate: Katherine M. Longley, "Towards a History of Archive-Keeping in the Church of York," *Borthwick Institute Bulletin* 1 (1975): 63–7 [59–74]. I am grateful to Dr. Philippa Hoskin for this reference.

Chapter 1 Alice de Rouclif: An Eventful Childhood

1. No separate population figure survives for Kennythorpe from the poll tax of 1377, but together with the neighboring hamlet of Thornthorpe a total of only forty-five taxpayers are recorded. The much less satisfactory 1381 returns record fifteen taxpayers for Kennythorpe as against fourteen for Thornthorpe, a total of only twenty-nine. Kennythorpe was assessed to pay 12s., but Thornthorpe only 10s. toward the subsidy of 1334, so a crude estimate might suggest a total population of less than fifty: *The Lay Subsidy of 1334*, ed. Robin E. Glasscock, Records of Social and Economic History, New Series, 2 (Oxford: British Academy, 1975), p. 365; TNA, E179/202/61/7; *The Poll Taxes of 1377, 1379 and 1381*, ed. Fenwick, 3:160, 210, 212.
2. This is in fact the earliest of three possible dates for the events described here. Stephen Wascelyne thought it was around the feast of the translation of St Thomas (presumably Thomas of Canterbury), so about a week later on 7 July. His wife Anabilla remembered it to have been the feast of

St James, that is, 25 July. The date used here was that remembered by Cecily de Shupton. There is little reason for preferring one date over another, though Frederik Pedersen takes 25 July observing that this "coincided almost perfectly with the York court's summer recess": Pedersen, *Marriage Disputes in Medieval England*, p. 133.

3. The house was excavated by the York Archaeological Trust in the course of a series of small-scale digs during the first part of the 1990s prior to the development of formerly agricultural land for housing. The final report of these excavations is still awaited. The house, located to the east of a more prominent moated site apparently abandoned in the thirteenth century, was itself first occupied around the middle of the same century. It can be tied to the de Rouclif family from the discovery of the seal matrix of Thomas de Rouclif. Gervase was Thomas's grandson, but he had an older brother, Thomas, who leased the house to one Philip de Gillyng for twelve years in 1332. Since this appears to be the last record of Thomas, it is possible that he died unmarried or childless in or before the Black Death and hence his property would have passed to Gervase. Certainly this would help explain Gervase's possibly advantageous marriage to the widow Ellen shortly after the Black Death and indeed how Alice came to be an heiress with land and tenants to her name. The house appears to have been used until the mid-sixteenth century. The hearth excavated within the hall below the most recent hearth was in use in the period c. 1340–80: K. Hunter-Man, "Rawcliffe the 5th," *Interim* 17, 3 (1992): 2 [2–6]; idem, "Rawcliffe: Hall's Well that Ends Well," *Interim* 19, 2 (1994): 4–7 [4–9]; Nicky Rogers, "Signed, Sealed and Deciphered," *Interim* 19, 2 (1994):10–12; Chris Daniel, "The Family Seal," *Interim* 19, 2 (1994): 13–17. It should be noted that the excavated structure as reported does not immediately tally with the "basement room [camera bassa subterraneana]"referred to in Ellen Taliour's account of Alice's birth. For a reconstruction of the de Rouclif genealogy see fig. 1.
4. The account that the unnamed woman had become senile was implicitly offered to explain the failure to use her as a witness in the ensuing court case.
5. For a discussion of baptismal practice see Nicholas Orme, *Medieval Children* (New Haven: Yale University Press, 2001), pp. 21–9; Robert Dinn, "Baptism, Spiritual Kinship, and Popular Religion in Late Medieval Bury St Edmunds," *Bulletin of the John Rylands Library* 72 (1990): 97 [93–106].
6. St Mary's Abbey in fact did not recognize St Olave's parochial status at this date.
7. Cf. Didier Lett, "Adult Brothers and Juvenile Uncles: Generations and Age Differences in Families at the End of the Middle Ages," *The History of the Family* 6 (2001): 391–400.
8. Men were supposed to abstain from sex with their wives for an extended period following childbirth: Becky R. Lee, "The Purification of Women after Childbirth: A Window onto Medieval Perceptions of Women," *Florilegium* 14 (1995–96): 44–7 [43–55].

9. The propensity for the aristocracy to father illegitimate children seems not to have attracted much scholarly attention, but see Emma Hawkes, "Younger Sons, Illegitimate Sons and the Law: A Study of Three Yorkshire Gentry Families, 1480–1540," *Parergon* n.s.17 (2000): 125–46.
10. *Chronica Monasterii de Melsa*, ed. Edward Augustus Bond, 3 vols., Rolls Series 43 (1866–68), III:159; *The Anonimalle Chronicle 1333 to 1381*, ed. V.H. Galbraith (Manchester: Manchester University Press, 1927), p. 50. Very high mortality in 1361 is also suggested by the significant peak in wills proved within the court of the Dean and Chapter that year: P.J.P. Goldberg, "Women in Late Medieval Society: Some Demographic Evidence from the York Region," unpublished University of York MA dissertation (1982), fig. 2.3.1 and p. 25.
11. Kim M. Phillips, *Medieval Maidens: Young Women and Gender in England, 1270–1540* (Manchester: Manchester University Press, 2003), pp. 32–4.
12. Menuge, *Medieval English Wardship*, ch. 5, esp. pp. 103–4.
13. Menuge, *Medieval English Wardship*, p. 104.
14. Scott L. Waugh, *The Lordship of England: Royal Wardships and Marriages in English Society and Politics 1217–1327* (Princeton: Princeton University Press, 1988), pp. 217–20.
15. The prefix "St" seems to have been used into the eighteenth century, so it is not specifically a pre-Reformation usage.
16. The medieval gatehouse, which still largely survives, though substantially rebuilt in the fifteenth century and remodeled internally in the nineteenth, housed inter alia a court room. Richard Bernard's chamber is also described by Master Adam de Thornton as "le StyWard chaumber" from which Bernard's occupation may be deduced.
17. Adam de Thornton was also the parson of Potter Brompton, a church appropriated to St Mary's Abbey: Sarah Rees Jones, "Property, Tenure and Rents: Some Aspects of the Topography and Economy of Medieval York," unpublished University of York D.Phil. thesis, 2 vols. (1987), 2, tenement 24.
18. A matrimonial cause of 1398 records a marriage contracted between Alice Park of Moor Monkton and William Robynson, the servant of Adam Brynand of Cattall in the room of Adam Clerk, an employee of St Mary's Abbey. Also testifying in this case was another employee, William Brenhand, then aged twenty-two. It is tempting to surmise that this man was the son or close kinsman of Richard Bernard and that Adam Brynhand was likewise related. An Adam Brennand is listed as a spicer at the head of the 1379 poll tax listing for (Kirkby) Cattal. BI, CP.E.238.
19. Barbara J. Harris, *English Aristocratic Women, 1450–1550* (New York: Oxford University Press, 2002), pp. 46–7.
20. Helmholz, *Marriage Litigation*, p. 98.
21. Using the *Oxford Dictionary of National Biography* as a reference, the following later medieval high aristocratic females were married as eleven-year-olds: Elizabeth Berkeley, Isabella de Forz, Margaret of England, and Katherine

Neville. Alice Chaucer was about ten: http://www.oxforddnb.com. Accessed on 29 June 2005.

22. Katherine de Rouclif's deposition does not make it explicit that her brief visit to their Bootham home took place the day immediately following the spousals, but there is nothing to indicate that any longer interval occurred.
23. This arrangement was in effect a variant of the more common practice of placing persons betrothed at a young age to live in the homes of their prospective in-laws: Waugh, *The Lordship of England*, p. 198.
24. Stephen Wascelyne remembered that Alice came around the feast of St Andrew (30 November). Anabilla Wascelyne recalled the day to be three weeks before Christmas, but Ellen de Rouclif remembered the spousals to have taken place only a fortnight before Christmas. These are still unusually precise indicators.
25. In my translation of this case in *Women in England*, p. 62, I erroneously stated that it was the feast of St James the Apostle.
26. Gift giving was a common aspect of marriage making. The giving and receipt of gifts thus constituted evidence for the intentions of the parties concerned. Clothing, kerchiefs, and knives all appear in Diana O'Hara's analysis of early modern marriage cases: Helmholz, *Marriage Litigation*, p. 127n.; Shannon McSheffrey, *Love and Marriage in Late Medieval London* (Kalamazoo: The Medieval Institute, 1995), pp. 42–3; Diana O'Hara, *Courtship and Constraint: Rethinking the Making of Marriage in Tudor England* (Manchester: Manchester University Press, 2000), ch. 2.
27. Cf. Simon Payling, "The Politics of Family: Late Medieval Marriage Contracts," in *The McFarlane Legacy: Studies in Late Medieval Politics and Society*, ed. R.H. Britnell and A.J. Pollard (Stroud: Alan Sutton, 1995), p. 24 [21–47].
28. License to go beyond the seas was issued on 26 October 1365 and attorney was granted to his brother Guy and another man: *CPR*, 1364–67, p. 175. Evidently Sir Brian had returned before the subsequent Church court action had been completed as he is noticed in the case.
29. Helmholz, *Marriage Litigation*, p. 68.
30. Helmholz, *Marriage Litigation*, p. 67; X 2.13.8.
31. BI, CP.E.89/26. The libel that precedes these articles talks merely of Alice ratifying the contract: BI, CP.E.89/25.
32. Michael M. Sheehan, "The Formation and Stability of Marriage in Medieval England: The Evidence of an Ely Register," *Medieval Studies* 33 (1971): 228–63.
33. R.H. Helmholz, *The Oxford History of the Laws of England, I: The Canon Law and Ecclesiastical Jurisdiction from 597 to the 1640s* (Oxford: Oxford University Press, 2004), pp. 542–3.
34. Edward de Cornubia was appointed on 27 September. On 8 October he was joined by Henry de Haxholm as Alice's proctor for the case: BI, CP.E.89/13. John was represented by his proctor, John de Staunton, appointed 4 October: BI, CP.E.89/28.

35. BI, CP.E.89/12, 14.
36. Cf. BI, CP.E.76, F.119.
37. Many were of peasant stock. Joel Rosenthal shows, using Proofs of Age material, that persons of humble rank may still have been seen as trustworthy repositories of communal memory: Joel T. Rosenthal, *Telling Tales: Sources and Narration in Late Medieval England* (University Park: Penn State Press, 2003), pp. 150–1. Chris Wickham describes the role of "gossip" in constructing group identity: Chris Wickham, "Gossip and Resistance among the Medieval Peasantry," *Past and Present* 160 (1998): 11 [3–24].
38. See "Preface," note 1 above. Two Rawcliffe witnesses were married to one another, but most of the others were probably mistresses of households. The extant poll tax returns for Rutland in 1377 would suggest that households there contained a mean of a little over two taxpayers (including solitaries).
39. Most, but not all the depositions are dated, so these represent the earliest and latest recorded dates.
40. *Handbook of Dates for Students of English History*, ed. C.R. Cheney (London: Royal Historical Society, 1978), pp. 73–4.
41. BI, CP.E.89/12, 14, 16, 25, 26, 27.
42. BI, CP.E.89/2, 3, 4, 18. The argument about John's birth was reiterated in a document dated 31 January: BI, CP.E.89/9.
43. BI, CP.E.89/17, 19, 20.
44. BI, CP.E.89/6.
45. Thomas de Buckton, LL.D. had seen the pope by 28 June and was to die on his return journey. A change in the headship of the court whilst the case was ongoing, though atypical, would have been relatively unproblematic; the actual process of judgment depended solely on an evaluation of the depositions after these had all been collected in: BI, CP.E.89/23, 24; *Testamenta Eboracensia*, vol. I, ed. James Raine, Surtees Society 4 (1836), pp. 77–9 and note, p. 77; Durham, Durham University Archives, 1.3.Archiep.2. Adam de York, a bachelor of canon law, had been appointed precentor the previous year displacing Hugh de Wymondeswold. His appointment was ended after five years and Wymondeswold was reinstated in 1371: B. Jones, *Fasti Ecclesiae Angicanae 1300–1500, vol.VI: Northern Province* (London: The Athlone Press, 1963), p. 11.
46. YML, Dean and Chapter probate register 1, L2(4), fols. 65 (Robert de Rouclif, d. 1377), 79 (John de Rouclif, sen., d. 1384). For fuller discussions of Master John de Rouclif, senior, and Robert de Rouclif see chapter 5 below.
47. X 2.20.32.
48. X 4.2.6: "Si autem fuerit aetati proxima, ut in undecimo vel circa XII. annum, et cum suo assensu et voluntate parentum desponsata et benedicta fuerit, et cognita ab eodem viro, separari non debet."
49. BI, CP.E.89/24.
50. YML, St Mary's Abbey Cartulary, XVI A.1, fol. 322.

Chapter 2 William Pottell: Stories and Storytellers

1. For a lucid and authoritative discussion of the way the Church courts operated see Helmholz, *Marriage Litigation*.
2. This informs both Helmholz, *Marriage Litigation* and Pedersen, *Marriage Disputes*.
3. Bartlett, *The Hanged Man*, p. xi.
4. Bartlett, *The Hanged Man*, p. 116.
5. Elizabeth S. Cohen, "Court Testimony from the Past: Self and Culture in the Making of Text," in *Essays on Life Writing: From Genre to Critical Practice*, ed. Marlene Kadar (Toronto: University of Toronto Press, 1992), pp. 83–93.
6. Arnold's thesis, which draws heavily on Foucault's notion of discourse, is most succinctly articulated in John H. Arnold, "Inquisition, Text and Discourse," in *Texts and the Repression of Heresy*, ed. Caterina Bruschi and Peter Biller (Woodbridge: York Medieval Press, 2003), pp. 63–80.
7. Arnold, "Inquisition, Text and Discourse," p. 63.
8. Arnold's approach is in fact no less pertinent in respect of canonization proceedings than to heresy trials; both demanded particular kinds of knowledge reflected in particular discourses on the part of those framing the questions.
9. Helmholz, *Marriage Litigation*, pp. 17, 19–20. The court may partly have been acting in deference to de Melsa's gentility, but the canon law allowed for such examinations where witnesses were sick, old, or disabled: X 2.20.8.
10. On BI, CP.E.89/27, which consists of several membranes stitched end to end, the depositions of Agnes Fritheby and Isold de Kikeby dated 6 December follow immediately and on the same membrane those of Beatrix de Morland and Margery Gregson, dated 1 [*p*° = *primo*] November. Depositions on the immediately previous membrane are dated 26 November.
11. The concept of "common report [communis-fama]" was a regular feature of cases within the ecclesiastical courts. The concern was to show that various aspects of a witness's narrative were known at the time and so could not have been fabricated ex post facto for the purpose of the court action. This is a somewhat different argument to that made in Bartlett, *The Hanged Man*, p. 108.
12. Bartlett, *The Hanged Man*, pp. 53–7; Barbara Harvey, "Work and *Festa Ferianda* in Medieval England," *Journal of Ecclesiastical History*, 23 (1972): 289–308; Ronald Hutton, *The Rise and Fall of Merry England: the Ritual Year, 1400–1700* (Oxford: Oxford University Press, 1994).
13. That Alice Porter knew about Alice's birth only from the relation of others was, as was noted in the previous chapter, the subject of a marginal annotation, a reflection of the clerical eye for what was or was not important.

14. Helmholz, *Marriage Litigation*, pp. 17–19.
15. Helmholz, *Marriage Litigation*, p. 17.
16. The articles are BI, CP.E.89/26 and were drawn up on the basis of John Marrays's original libel (BI, CP.E.89/25). His deposition appears not to be dated, but two depositions slightly higher up the roll are dated 6 December, but see note 4 above.
17. See note 6 above.
18. X 4.2.9. The canon law is concerned with the growth of pubic hair, not the onset of menstruation, but it is the latter that is historically documented. For a discussion of age at menarche in the English later Middle Ages, see J.B. Post, "Ages at Menarche and Menopause: Some Mediaeval Authorities," *Population Studies* 25 (1971): 83–7. Post would suggest that menarche often commenced at about fifteen, that is, at an earlier age than was true of much of the nineteenth century, though in practice there would have been considerable variation around this modal age. The development of such visible secondary sexual characteristics as breast budding (representing stage two of Tanner's five-stage model of female puberty) and the first growth of pubic hair (stage three) would have preceded actual menstruation by two or more years. In this sense the canon law anticipated a possibility that was not solely hypothetical. Tanner's stages are described in W.A. Marshall and J.M. Tanner, "Variations in Patterns of Pubertal Changes in Girls," *Archives of Disease in Childhood* 44 (1969): 291–303.
19. As discussed in the previous chapter, the canon law laid down that a properly contracted marriage that had been consummated whilst the girl, though not yet having reached puberty, was close to puberty could not be annulled. The authority cited to illustrate this canon uses the case of a girl in her eleventh year: X 4.2.6.
20. Davis, *Fiction in the Archives*, pp. 15–35, 112.
21. Helmholz, *Marriage Litigation*, p. 127.

Chapter 3 Ellen Taliour: Gender and the Remembrance of Times Past

1. The normal expectation would be for a (former) female servant so closely associated with her mistress by the nature of her employment would ally with her erstwhile employer. On the other hand, as an ex-employee Ellen had little to lose from going against her former mistress. Cf. Bernard Capp, *When Gossips Meet: Women, Family, and Neighbourhood in Early Modern England* (Oxford: Oxford University Press, 2003), pp. 156–8.
2. The Statute of Labourers of 1351 required that, other than for seasonal employees, labor normally be contracted by the year or other usual—implicitly extended—term. We may understand that this was binding on both employees and employers. We may speculate that Ellen had contracted mastitis, a common affliction of nursing mothers that can be

associated with fever. Were this so, being obliged to stop feeding would have damaged her health.

3. The canon law presumed witnesses to be trustworthy unless some "infamy" could be brought against them: X 2.20.1.
4. For a discussion of the role of women as remembrancers of past events see Elisabeth van Houts, *Memory and Gender in Medieval Europe* (Basingstoke: Macmillan, 1999), esp. pp. 84–92.
5. Just such an exception is in fact noted elsewhere in this case. One Simon de Folifayt intervened to revive Maud de Herthill's child at birth. This incident is discussed at greater length below. For the exclusion of men from the birthing chamber see Becky R. Lee, "A Company of Women and Men: Men's Recollection of Childbirth in Medieval England," *Journal of Family History* 27 (2002): 94 [92–100].
6. BI, CP.F.256. Birthing practices, albeit for a slightly later era, are described in Adrian Wilson, "The Ceremony of Childbirth and its Interpretation," in *Women as Mothers in Pre-Industrial England*, ed. Valerie Fildes (London: Routledge, 1990), pp. 68–107. They are implicit in the entry of a priest into the birthing chamber carrying a lantern noted in Lee's analysis of later medieval proof-of-age evidence: Lee, "A Company of Women and Men," p. 94.
7. The ten are Richard Forester, the wife of Robert de Rouclif, Emma Sadeler, Joan de Queldac, Marion del See, Alice Barbour, Alice Marschall, Margaret de Rekeby, Tillota de Corton, and Emma D[. . .]. We can only speculate as to their eventual noninclusion, though it is possible that their depositions have simply been lost. It may be that the proctor for John Marrays decided that the case presented by the other witnesses, including the crucial evidence relating to the spousals and the consummation, was already sufficiently presented and that these additional witnesses could add little. What is more puzzling is that the names of some of the key witnesses, notably the members of the Wascelyne household and Dom. William Marrays are not listed.
8. BI, CP.F.40, 111, 175, 224. A couple of other impotence cases survive, but only a small number of the depositions survive.
9. The court of course assumed that the man would be aroused, if at all, by the opposite sex, but this is also the pertinent issue. So long as the man was incapable of being aroused by the opposite sex, and hence could not consummate a marriage or father children, he would be deemed functionally impotent and his marriage null and void.
10. The description of course relates to the canonical requirement that the examination be conducted "a matronis bonae opinionis, fide dignis ac expertis in opera nuptiali": X 4.15.7. The York juries certainly complied with this last requirement, but departed from the procedure laid down in the Decretals by providing for an examination of the man's genitals rather than the woman's (in order to establish virginity or otherwise). These women can be considered as possessing "bona fama" only within this specific context; within conventional medieval understandings of "fama,"

such witnesses would be held to be "infama": cf. Thomas Kuehn, "*Fama* as a Legal Status in Renaissance Florence," in *Fama: the Politics of Talk and Reputation in Medieval Europe*, ed. Thelma Fenster and Daniel Lord Smail (Ithica, NY: Cornell University Press, 2003), pp. 27–46.

11. BI, CP.E.23.
12. BI, CP.E.76.
13. BI, CP.F.119.
14. Jurors in proof-of-age proceedings tended to be of more humble rank: Rosenthal, *Telling Tales*, p. 2.
15. For discussion of a like observation see Bartlett, *The Hanged Man*, pp. 55–6.
16. The original text reads "pu'ū" for "pu[er]u[m]." I am satisfied that no other material possession is intended.
17. There is of course a tendency for women to be especially vulnerable to poverty: cf. Sharon Farmer, "Down, Out and Female in Thirteenth-Century Paris," *American Historical Review*, 103 (1998): 353–5 [345–72].
18. Visual cues are, and were understood at the time, to be important mnemonic devices. Cf. Mary Carruthers, *The Book of Memory: A Study of Memory in Medieval Culture* (Cambridge: Cambridge University Press, 1990), pp. 27–8.
19. Joel Rosenthal likewise finds evidence for the exchange of "women's news" between women refracted through proofs-of-age evidence, a source that in itself relates only to the testimony of men: Rosenthal, *Telling Tales*, p. 61. For a later analogy see Capp, *When Gossips Meet*, esp. pp. 327–8. Cf. Lee, "A Company Women of and Men," 96–7.
20. The use of such writings to aid delivery was a common practice: cf. Marianne Elsakkers, "In Pain You Shall Bear Children (Gen. 3:16): Medieval Prayers for a Safe Delivery," in *Women and Miracle Stories: A Multidisciplinary Exploration*, ed. Anne-Marie Korte (Leiden: Brill, 2001), pp. 179–209.
21. Becky K. Lee, "Men's Recollections of a Women's Rite: Medieval English Men's Recollections Regarding the Rite of the Purification of Women after Childbirth," *Gender and History* 14 (2002): 229 [224–41]; Paula M. Rieder, "The Implications of Exclusion: The Regulation of Churching in Medieval Northern France," *Essays in Medieval History* 15 (1995): 71–80; John Bedell, "Memory and Proof of Age in England 1272–1327," *Past and Present* 162 (1999): 13–14 [4–27]. The feast was also remembered by Margery de Rouclif, who was likewise present at the churching.
22. Patricia Skinner makes a like observation, writing from a high medieval Italian perspective, that "birth dates and relative ages of children may have been information that mothers were more likely to remember carefully": Patricia Skinner, "Gender and Memory in Medieval Italy," in *Medieval Memories Men, Women and the Past, 700–1300*, ed. Elisabeth van Houts (London: Longman, 2001), p. 47 [36–52]. Cf. also Matthew Innes, "Keeping it in the Family: Women and Aristocratic Memory," in *Medieval Memories*, ed. van Houts, p. 17 [17–35].

23. It is possible that the apparent pathos of this sentence may in fact be the accidental product of the clerk abbreviating Isabel's testimony.
24. Genesis 3: 16.
25. Cf. Dorothy M. Owen, *Church and Society in Medieval Lincolnshire* (Lincoln: Lincolnshire Local History Society, 1971), p. 109.
26. Men, notably clergy, might exceptionally be admitted to the birthing chamber where the life of the mother of the child was deemed to be at risk: Lee, "A Company of Women and Men," p. 94.
27. The Statute of Labourers (1351) required that, other than for specified seasonal tasks including harvest, labor should "be hired to serve for a whole year, or for other usual terms": *The Black Death*, ed. and trans. Rosemary Horrox (Manchester: Manchester Medieval Press, 1994), p. 313.
28. The disparity was much slighter in pastoral than arable regions: P.J.P. Goldberg, *Women, Work and Life Cycle: Women in York and Yorkshire c. 1300–1520* (Oxford: Oxford University Press, 1992), pp. 159–160.
29. Servanthood is briefly noticed as a mnemonic device in Bedell, "Memory and Proof of Age," p. 15 and table 2, p. 17.
30. Robert de Rouclif was clearly an astute master. Late in 1371 he registered an agreement with one Alice de Neuton, then servant to Robert Calcrofte, spurrier of York, that she would serve him from the following Pentecost to Martinmas. If she failed to honor this contract, she was bound to pay him 20d. in compensation: YML, M2(1)c, fol. 4.
31. P.J.P. Goldberg, "What was a Servant?" in *Concepts and Patterns of Service in the Later Middle Ages*, ed. Anne Curry and Elizabeth Matthew (Woodbridge: Boydell, 2000), pp. 11–12 [1–20].
32. YML, Dean and Chapter probate register 1, L2(4), fol. 37.
33. Extended breast feeding was probably the norm. Recent analysis of skeletal remains from the Wolds village of Wharram Percy, a few miles east of York, suggest weaning at around two years: cf. M. Richards, S. Mays, and B. Fuller, "Stable C and N Isotope Values of Bone and Teeth Reflect Weaning and Growth Events at the Mediaeval Wharram Percy Site, Yorkshire, UK," *American Journal of Physical Anthropology* 119 (2002): 205–10. Juliet's nurse (*Romeo and Juliet* I: III) remembered that Juliet was nearly fourteen by the fact she had been weaned nearly eleven years earlier.
34. 1 Timothy 2: 15.
35. Something of Bernard's activities in pursuit of property rights etc. can be glimpsed from the Chancery records for 1356: *CPR*, 1354–58, pp. 454, 494, 496. In the first instance cited, concerning a shipwreck at Scarborough, Bernard acted with one Richard de Rouclif.
36. This will be discussed at slightly greater length in chapter 5 below.
37. YML, Dean and Chapter probate register 1, L2(4), fol. 106v.
38. Later in the century it became common practice for the ages of deponents to be recorded. There is no obvious pattern to the deponents whose ages are recorded and no indication that particular age groups are being singled out.

39. Maud de Herthill's name is not found in the court act book for the Dean and Chapter of York's jurisdiction which runs from 1358: YML, M2(1)c.
40. L.R. Poos, "Sex, Lies, and the Church Courts of Pre-Reformation England," *Journal of Interdisciplinary History* 25 (1995): 586–7, 591–2, 594–607 [585–607]; Laura Gowing, *Domestic Dangers: Women, Words, and Sex in Early Modern London* (Oxford: Oxford University Press, 1996), esp. ch. 3; Trevor Dean, "Gender and Insult in an Italian City: Bologna in the later Middle Ages," *Social History* 29 (2004): 218–21 [217–31].
41. X 2.20.1.
42. Cf. Natalie Zemon Davis, "The Reasons for Misrule: Youth Groups and Charivaris in Sixteenth-Century France," *Past and Present* 50 (1971): 41–75.

Chapter 4 Robert Thewed: The Ties of Tenure and Locality

1. Robert Thewed testified on 18 November 1365, his wife on 27 November.
2. Although it is very possible that Margery was single at the time of Alice's birth, the term servant here may well simply mean employee and hence not life-cycle servant.
3. Cf. R.H. Hilton, "The Peasantry as a Class," in *The English Peasantry in the Later Middle Ages*, ed. Hilton (Oxford: Oxford University Press, 1975), pp. 3–19.
4. Cf. Natalie Zemon Davis, *The Gift in Sixteenth-Century France* (Oxford: Oxford University Press, 2000), pp. 62–72.
5. Orme, *Medieval Children*, pp. 37–8; Dinn, "Baptism, Spiritual Kinship, and Popular Religion," pp. 93–106.
6. Neighborliness is also stressed in proof-of-age evidence: Bedell, "Memory and Proof of Age," p. 21. There is also a resonance of the legal convention found for example in coroners' inquests whereby the "first finder" was to notify the four "nearest neighbors." Neighborliness here is legally constituted in terms of knowledge and trustworthiness.
7. Richard K. Emmerson and P.J.P. Goldberg, "'The Lord Geoffrey had me made': Lordship and Labour in the Luttrell Psalter," in *The Problem of Labour in Fourteenth-Century England*, ed. James Bothwell, P.J.P. Goldberg, and W.M. Ormrod (Woodbridge: York Medieval Press, 2000), pp. 43–63.
8. Christopher Woolgar, *The Great Household in Late Medieval England* (New Haven: Yale University Press, 1999), p. 34.
9. In the previous chapter we suggested that Ellen Taliour may have been made pregnant by her employer and Gervase's friend, William de Huntyngton.
10. Although "woman" can be used to designate females of any age and can include servants, the term "maid" might perhaps have been more obvious

for a young, unmarried servant, but not for a mistress. Another deponent is known as Joan Symkyn [= "little" Simon] Woman.

11. Hemholz, *Marriage Litigation*, pp. 155, 160. The underlying concern was a pertinent one, namely that a serf would testify according to his lord's will. A later thirteenth-century Rawcliffe deed refers to one John Godynogh "nativus" and his "sequela," but another slightly later deed already refers to a Swayn de Rouclif as a manumitted serf: YML, St Mary's Abbey Cartulary, XVI A.1, fol. 319v; A.2, fol. 69. It may well be that by the later fourteenth century most or all serfs had been freed.
12. Cf. L.R. Poos, Zvi Razi, and Richard M. Smith, "The Population History of Medieval Villages: A Debate on the Use of Manor Court Records," in *Medieval Society and the Manor Court*, ed. Razi and Smith (Oxford: Oxford University Press, 1996), pp. 298–368. Nicholas Orme offers a brief discussion of child mortality: Orme, *Medieval Children*, pp. 113–16.
13. Several contemporary chroniclers specifically note that the second pestilence was characterized by high child mortality: Horrox, *The Black Death*, pp. 85–6.
14. These anecdotal figures are in fact probably as bad or worse than would be true of developing countries today. For extended maternal breastfeeding see Richards, Mays, and Fuller. "Stable C and N Isotope Values of Bone and Teeth."
15. *Romeo and Juliet* I: III. Nicholas Orme also notes that extended breastfeeding was commonplace: Orme, *Medieval Children*, p. 66.
16. C.C. Dyer, "Gardens and Orchards in Medieval England," in *Everyday Life in Medieval England*, ed. Dyer (London: Hambledon Press, 1994), pp. 113–31.
17. Hunter-Man, "Mind Your Manors," pp. 3–5; YML, St Mary's Abbey Cartulary, XVI A.2, fols 62v, 66.
18. The importance of peat extraction to the economy of nearby Selby Abbey is documented in surviving account rolls. These indicate the use of boats for transporting turves and the employment of women in the backbreaking and dusty task of stacking turves: *Monastery and Society in the Late Middle Ages: Selected Account Rolls from Selby Abbey, Yorkshire, 1398–1537*, ed. John H. Tillotson (Woodbridge: Boydell and Brrewer, 1988), p. 138.
19. For York as textile city see Goldberg, *Women, Work, and Life Cycle*, ch. 2.
20. YML, Dean and Chapter probate register 1, L2(4), fol. 106v.
21. Cf. BI, Prob. Reg. 3 fols 49v (del Syke), 437 (Crosseby), 567v (Clynt). Thomas del Syke, a weaver, left 10d. each to "Christine and Beatrice, resident in Huntington, working for me in my craft."
22. For discussions of migration to York see Peter McClure, "Patterns of Migration in the Late Middle Ages: The Evidence of English Place-Name Surnames," *Economic History Review*, 2nd ser. 32 (1979): 167–82; Goldberg, *Women, Work, and Life Cycle*, ch. 6.
23. Part of Jubbergate, a now much truncated street, fell within the Liberty of St Peter.

24. By the early modern era it is not uncommon to find details of the pattern of residence (and hence migration) recorded as part of the basic biographical information respecting each deponent, but this was not the norm in this kind of case at this date. Some such biographical data is, however, recorded in an early-fifteenth-century book of depositions generated in respect of a dispute over parochial rights where it was useful to demonstrate that witnesses had been long resident within the parish: YML, M2(3)c.
25. The very limited comparative evidence available for the English later Middle Ages suggests that life-long residence within a particular community was a minority experience for persons achieving adulthood: L.R. Poos, *A Rural Society After the Black Death: Essex 1350–1525* (Cambridge, UK: Cambridge University Press, 1991), pp. 162–4; P.J.P. Goldberg, "Migration, Youth and Gender in Later Medieval England," in *Youth in the Middle Ages*, ed. Goldberg and Felicity Riddy (Woodbridge: York Medieval Press, 2004), p. 88 [85–99].
26. Parts of Rawcliffe, Clifton, and Bootham all fell both within the parish of St Olave and the Liberty of St Mary, so the pattern of intensely local migration just described did not necessarily involve leaving either the parish or the liberty.
27. YML, Dean and Chapter probate register 1, L2(4), fol. 37v.
28. Cf. Goldberg, "Migration, Youth and Gender," p. 88.
29. In addition to property in Petergate, he possessed land in Huntington. He also owned the Bootham house rented by Robert de Rouclif (see chapter 5 below): YML, Dean and Chapter probate register 1, L2(4), fol. 37v.
30. Shipton, six miles from York, fell within the parish of Overton, which itself belonged to St Mary's Abbey. Shipton, however, appears to have come within the Liberty of St Peter. This is the toponymic of Cecily de Shupton, who spent time in the de Rouclif household around the times of the births of the two children. An invaluable description of the extent of the Liberty is printed in Adrian Leake, *The Liberty of St Peter of York 1800–1838*, Borthwick Paper 77 (York, 1990), pp. 31–4.
31. Rees Jones, "Property, Tenure and Rents," 2, tenements 37 and 39.
32. Tollerton is about eight miles northwest of Rawcliffe.
33. It is possible Agnes de Polles hailed from Cawood (within the Liberty of St Peter). An Alice Polles of Cawood is associated with a will dated 1398: YML, Dean and Chapter probate register 1, L2(4), fol. 119v.
34. Each county was divided into a number of administrative districts known generally as hundreds, but in this region as wapentakes.
35. Charles R. Young, *The Royal Forests of Medieval England* (Philadelphia: University of Pennsylvania Press, 1979), graph 1, pp. 118–19.
36. There are some extant records for the late thirteenth century.
37. This record is not referenced by Cox and I have been unable to trace it in The National Archives catalogue: J. Charles Cox, *The Royal Forest of England* (London: Methuen, 1905), p. 129.

38. *CPR*, 1354–58, p. 620. Regarders were local men appointed by the county sheriff. They had responsibility to assist in the periodic inspection ("regard") of the forest for encroachments. See Young, *The Royal Forests of Medieval England*, p. 87.
39. The de Rouclifs stabled their horses at Beatrix's hostelry when visiting York, so the logic is that the inn was along the main entrance road into York. In her testimony, Beatrix refers to her husband being killed in Bootham. Thomas may well have been her son; marshals, who cared for horses, might also run a hostelry: *The Poll Taxes of 1377, 1379 and 1381*, ed. Fenwick, 3:139, 149.
40. YML, Dean and Chapter probate register 1, L2(4), fol. 65.
41. Drake, *Eboracum*, p. 624. Although there is no evidence that Kennythorpe ever belonged to the Liberty of St Peter, it is possible that the Wascelyne family may have associated themselves with the Liberty; William Wascelyne of Kennythorpe, d. 1399 or 1400, possibly Stephen and Anabilla's son, requested burial not in his parish church, but in St Michael le Belfrey: YML, Dean and Chapter probate register 1, L2(4), fol. 122.
42. Becky Lee observes that it was often women who negotiated to find wetnurses: Lee, "A Company of Men and Women," 97.
43. BI, CP.E.248 (1345–46). The case is described in detail in Pedersen, *Marriage Disputes*, ch. 2. See especially p. 48.
44. The treasurer held significant assarts within the Forest of Galtres. One John de Shupton is also named as an alleged wrongdoer: *CPR*, 1350–54, p. 280; TNA, C 143/112/9.
45. YML, Dean and Chapter probate register 1, L2(4), fols 37v, 65, 79.
46. *Yorkshire Sessions of the Peace, 1361–1364*, ed. Bertha H. Putnam, Yorkshire Archaeological Record Series 100 (1939), p. 131.
47. Two comparatively late examples of grants of land at Rawcliffe to the abbey are: William Dugdale, *Monasticon Anglicanum: A History of the Abbies and other Monasteries, Hospitals, Frieries and Cathedral and Collegiate Churches . . .in England and Wales. . .originally published in Latin by Sir William Dugdale*, 6 vols. (London: James Bohn, 1846), III:565–6 (grant of toft and two bovates in 1309); TNA, C 143/230/12 (grant of meadow in 1334). At the time of the dissolution, the abbey enjoyed extensive property rights throughout the locality, but especially in Clifton, Shipton and St Marygate: Dugdale, *Monasticon Anglicanum*, III:570.
48. Cox, *The Royal Forest*, pp. 129–30; TNA, C 1/43/82; *Rotuli Parliamentorum*, 6 vols. (London, 1767–83), IV:558–9.
49. If any deponent had been a tenant of Sir Brian, but failed to note this, it would surely have been picked up by one of the witnesses called to undermine the credibility of Sir Brian's witnesses. John de Alne, for example, stated that Alice Sharpe, who is described as Sir Brian's tenant, was also a servant in his garden.
50. Our understanding of neighborliness as performative is influenced by Judith Butler's treatment of gender in her *Gender Trouble: Feminism and the Subversion of Identity* (New York: Routledge, 1990), esp. pp. 24–5, 136.

51. Margery Bell was a witness for John Marrays, but that is immaterial here. Her distinction between friends and neighbors is in fact a distinction between kin and non-kin since the term "friend" invariably implied kin at this period.
52. *Victoria History of the County of York: The City of York*, ed. P.M. Tillott (London: Oxford University Press, 1961), pp. 311–14.
53. We have some extant evidence for the operation of the liberty court of St Mary's, but the only surviving court material for the Liberty of St Peter long postdates this case: TNA, JUST 2/215, 223, 251; YML, F 1/3/1.
54. Dugdale, *Monasticon Anglicanum*, III:570.
55. Sir Brian had also recently sold some property in Rawcliffe to Lady Margery de Rouclif, her son Guy, and her son-in-law William Fairfax: *Feet of Fines for the County of Yorkshire*, III, ed. William Paley Baildon, Yorkshire Archaeological Society Record Ser. 52 (1915), p. 102.
56. There are numerous examples of more conservative and indeed oppressive lordship exercised by monastic landlords in the post-plague era. For a local and near contemporary example of conflict between a peasant family and Meaux Abbey see M.J.O. Kennedy, "Resourceful Villains: The Cellarer Family of Wawne in Holderness," *Yorkshire Archaeological Journal* 48 (1976): 107–17.
57. Alice de Rouclif was baptized in the church, though her deceased older brother had been baptized in the abbey church. In a case of 1398 the abbey prosecuted three women in the Court of York for burying elsewhere a man whom the abbey claimed should have been buried in the churchyard of St Olave's, requiring that they dig up the body and have reburied at St Olave's with due ceremony: Drake, *Eboracum*, pp. 581–2.
58. In the abbey cartulary St Olave's is described as a church dependent on the abbey: YML, XVI A.2, fol. 4v. I am grateful to Dr. Christopher Norton for discussion of this issue.
59. Angelo Raine, *Mediaeval York: A Topographical Survey based on Original Sources* (London: John Murray, 1955), p. 264; Tillott, *The City of York*, p. 398.
60. Drake, *Eboracum*, p. 581.
61. In fact the substantial rebuilding of the church and the creation of a new north aisle that breached the old precinct wall so as to provide direct access by the parishioners only followed the grant of parish status a century after the de Rouclif case.
62. Royal Commission on Historical Monuments, *City of York*, 6 vols. (London, 1972–81), IV:25. It is possible that numbers of parishioners living in Rawcliffe and Clifton found it more convenient to attend respectively the church of St Giles, Skelton, or the chapel of St Mary Magdalene for worship.
63. YML, Dean and Chapter probate register 1, L2(4), fol. 65. Robert is listed in the 1377 poll tax returns for St Olave's parish with his wife and three servants. In 1381 only his widow Katherine is listed, assessed at the above

average rate of 3s. together with her servant Agnes (4d.): *The Poll Taxes of 1377, 1379 and 1381*, ed. Fenwick, 3:139, 149.

64. Janet Burton and Christopher Wilson, *St Mary's Abbey, York* (York: Yorkshire Museum, 1988), p. 13.

Chapter 5 Anabilla Wascelyne: The Ties of Kinship

1. The literature on later medieval English kin networks is comparatively slight, but pertinent are two urban will-based studies: Jenny Kermode, "Sentiment and Survival: Family and Friends in Late Medieval English Towns," *Journal of Family History* 24 (1999): 5–18; Lynne Bowdon, "Redefining Kinship: Exploring Boundaries of Relatedness in Late Medieval New Romney," *Journal of Family History* 29 (2004): 407–20. Zvi Razi has argued for functionally extended families before the plague using manor court roll evidence: Zvi Razi, "The Myth of the Immutable English Family," *Past and Present* 140 (1993): 3–44.
2. This speculation is, of course, somewhat academic. No relationship is recorded in Dom. William's deposition and it was his deposition alone that would subsequently be used by the presiding officer to determine the case.
3. A "Marras" is recorded in the probate inventory of Thomas Vicars of Strensall dated 1451. No such place is recorded in the 1334 lay subsidy, nor has such a location been identified as a deserted medieval village. A perusal of the first Ordinance Survey map for the area around Strensall likewise draws a blank, but it is quite possible that the name means little more than marsh: *Probate Inventories of the York Diocese*, ed. P.M Stell and Louise Hampson (York, n.d.), p. 180.
4. It will be suggested below that he may have hailed from an area called Marshland.
5. *The Heads of Religious Houses: England and Wales, 1216–1377*, ed. David M. Smith and Vera C.M. London (Cambridge, UK: Cambridge University Press, 2002), p. 88; Dugdale, *Monasticon Anglicanum*, III:539.
6. BI, CP.E.132. The case was an action for breach of promise brought by Master Robert, as former rector, against the current rector claiming that, having agreed to the joint arbitration of the abbot and Master Walter Skyrlaw, he had failed to honor in full the damages subsequently awarded by the arbitrators against the rector. In effect the damages awarded would have given Master Robert control over the glebe at Huggate. We may surmise that the abbot was the arbitrator nominated by his namesake, although we cannot know their actual relationship. The case represents a further example of Marrays family interests located in the western part of the Yorkshire Wolds, Huggate being only a few miles from Kennythorpe. Apparently Master Robert hade previously exchanged Huggate for a living at Uldale in the diocese of Carlisle: David M. Smith, *Ecclesiatical*

Cause Papers at York: The Court of York 1301–1399, Borthwick Texts and Calendars 14 (1988), p. 52. A Robert Marrays was presented for fornication with Agnes Wetby within the Dean and Chapter's jurisdiction in York in 1360: YML, M2(1)f fol. 4v.

7. Helmholz, *Marriage Litigation*, pp. 160–1.
8. For example, BI, CP.E.114, 153, 259.
9. BI, CP.E.112.
10. Another monk of St Mary's is noticed in a cause dated 1432 traveling to the horse fair at Pontefract and eating in lay company at "The Lion" there before going on to spend the night in Doncaster: BI, CP.F.104. Cf. David Knowles, *The Religious Orders in England*, 3 vols. (Cambridge, UK: Cambridge University Press, 1948–59), II:209–12.
11. Dom. William's testimony merely states that the conversation took place "in the fields of Grimston and elsewhere," but, given the social rank of those involved, this does seem to imply that they were out riding.
12. It may well be that, in contrast to our own more sexually anxious age, contact between a religious and an underage girl would not of itself have been a cause of concern or scandal precisely because of the former's vows and the latter's youth.
13. Drake, *Eboracum*, p. 624; Dugdale, *Monasticon Anglicanum*, III:571.
14. Alice de Rolleston is described as the "daughter of Anabilla, her fellow witness" despite the fact that Stephen Wascelyne testified at the same time. This and the difference of name suggest the de Rolleston children were not Stephen's daughters.
15. Alice de Rolleston was fourteen at the time of the case, so her mother would likely have been at least thirty. If Dom. William had fathered her as a young adult, he need not have been more than fifty. This would be compatible with his achieving the abbacy in his forties and dying in his sixties. These observations do not strengthen the suggestion that Dom. William was in fact father to Anabilla and John, but they do show that the suggestion is at least compatible with the evidence.
16. The returns are headed "Bretton," which can be identified with Burton, later Burton Salmon in the parish of Monk Fryston: *The Poll Taxes of 1377, 1379 and 1381*, ed. Fenwick, 3:370; A.H. Smith, *The Place-Names of the West Riding of Yorkshire, part IV* (Cambridge, UK: Cambridge University Press, 1961), p. 40. I am grateful to Colin Hinson for helping clarify the identity of this settlement. The "Monk" of Monk Fryston relates to Selby Abbey, which held lands here, rather than St Mary's, York.
17. Saul, *Knights and Esquires*, pp. 19, 25.
18. *Register of the Freemen of the City of York, 1272–1588*, ed. Francis Collins, Surtees Society 96 (1896), p. 85. The form of the entry would suggest that John Marrays, junior, was admitted by right of patrimony, that is, his father was himself a citizen prior to the birth of his son. The conventional, but essentially unsubstantiated, understanding is that a son could be admitted by right of patrimony on achieving his majority at twenty-one. If this

were the case here, and the John Marrays, senior, is indeed the plaintiff in the case, then Alice would have had to have conceived and given birth within a year of the court's verdict, even though she could hardly have been more than thirteen and may well have been younger. This seems unlikely. If, however, majority was attainable after fifteen, then the circumstances would fit quite well. I am grateful to Sarah Rees Jones for discussion of this last. For a discussion of the franchise at York see: R.B. Dobson, "Admissions to the Freedom of the City of York in the Late Middle Ages," *Economic History Review*, 2nd series 23 (1973): 1–22.

19. Malbys made several bequests to the abbey including a horse and foal grazing at Overton park. He also named a group of persons whose bynames include "de Camera" [chamber], "de Stabulo" [stable], "de Salario" [salt or larder], "del Hall" and "Bakester" [baker]. The name John Marras follows immediately and it would be tempting to conclude that he was also a member of the household staff at Overton: BI, Prob. Reg. 1 fol. 82.
20. YML, St Mary's Abbey Cartulary, XVI A.1, fol. 322.
21. For the social origins of nuns see Marilyn Oliva, "Aristocracy or Meritocracy? Office-Holding Patterns in Late Medieval English Nunneries," *Studies in Church History* 27 (1990): 197–208. Barbara Harvey characterizes the monks of Westminster as predominantly "middle class" in social origin: Barbara Harvey, *Living and Dying in England 1100–1540: The Monastic Experience* (Oxford: Oxford University Press, 1993), pp. 75–7.
22. Chichester, West Sussex Record Office, Cowdray archives, Cowdray/ 5129/6; Drake, *Eboracum*, p. 626.
23. Scott L. Waugh, *The Lordship of England: Royal Wardships and Marriages in English Society and Politics 1217–1327* (Princeton: Princeton University Press, 1988), p. 37.
24. The abbots had another residence at Deighton: Dugdale, *Monasticon Anglicanum*, III:540, 570; Drake, *Eboracum*, pp. 577–8.
25. There is no agreement between witnesses on this last date.
26. Cf. Menuge, *Medieval English Wardship*, p. 97.
27. This clause was inadvertently omitted from my published translation.
28. For an example of this kind of detailed knowledge of household possessions, particularly textiles, see the 1450 will of Joan Buckland of Edgcott: *Lincoln Diocese Documents, 1450–1544*, ed. Andrew Clark, EETS o.s. 149 (1914), pp. 38–44.
29. X 4.2.3.
30. This observation is based on a reading of most extant matrimonial causes for the fourteenth and fifteenth centuries.
31. BI, CP.E.82. The pertinent depositions are translated in Goldberg, *Women in England*, p. 157.
32. Chapter 4 above.
33. BI, CP.E.89/26.
34. YML, Dean and Chapter probate register 1, L2(4), fol. 65.

35. Ellen appears to have owned part of a messuage in York from her first marriage: *Feet of Fines for the County of York*, III, ed. William Paley Baildon, Yorkshire Archaeological Society Record Ser. 52 (1915), pp. 38–9. The record refers to Gervase de Rouclif, Elena his wife and *her* heirs.
36. Bradford, West Yorkshire Archive Service, Spencer Stanhope MSS, SpSt/4/11/66/39.
37. The custom of allowing a widow a year's mourning can be traced back to before the Conquest. It is forcefully articulated by Alice Brathwell of Doncaster to deter a pressing suitor in a matrimonial cause of 1391: BI, CP.E.188. There are a few extant matrimonial causes where widows claim to have been forced into second marriages, for example, BI, CP.F.253, 263. This was probably more common within aristocratic society.
38. It was not uncommon for children to begin service in their very early teens, though evidence from York would suggest that girls may have started a little sooner than boys: Goldberg, *Women, Work, and Life Cycle*, pp. 168–9.
39. Barbara Todd's study of widow remarriage in early modern Abingdon has demonstrated that it was widows with young children to support who were most likely to remarry: Barbara J. Todd, "The Remarrying Widow: A Stereotype Reconsidered," in *Women in English Society 1500–1800*, ed. Mary Prior (London: Methuen, 1985), pp. 54–92.
40. Alice's aunt, Margery de Rouclif, testified in November 1365 that Alice was nine at the time of her father's death four years previous, but this conflicts with her own evidence that she would not be thirteen until the following Easter.
41. Cf. Payling, "The Politics of Family," esp. p. 24.
42. I am indebted to Mark Ormrod for talking me through the technicalities of this procedure. It may be noted that had parliament been in session, Ellen would have been able to present her petition there and this would likely have survived, but parliament only sat in January of 1365 and May of 1366.
43. A Margaret Rouclyf is recorded in the extant 1381 poll tax return for Thornthorpe, a village in the immediate proximity of Kennythorpe, but beyond that coincidence, there seems little to relate this woman to Margery or any other Rouclif in the case: *The Poll Taxes of 1377, 1379 and 1381*, ed. Fenwick, 3:210.
44. Only one name separates the two entries: *The Poll Taxes of 1377, 1379 and 1381*, ed. Fenwick, 3:139.
45. Most married women seem to have been identified with reference to their husbands even where their surnames differed. Widows are also identified by reference to their late husbands, but not all widows were so identified: Lady Margery de Rouclif was not identified as a widow, though it is evident that she was.
46. Robert evidently died without surviving children of his own: YML, Dean and Chapter probate register 1, L2(4), fol. 65.

47. The extant 1381 poll tax returns for Kennythorpe list one Joan "Watelyn"—this is Fenwick's transcription and it may well be that Wacelyn was intended—but no other family members: *The Poll Taxes of 1377, 1379 and 1381*, ed. Fenwick, 3:212.
48. John's will, which was proved in 1384, also suggests that he was connected with Selby Abbey: YML, Dean and Chapter probate register 1, L2(4), fol. 79.
49. *York Memorandum Book*, I, ed. Maud Sellers, Surtees Society 120 (1912), pp. 26–9.
50. BI, Prob. Reg. 1, fol. 73v. The original will is preserved in York, Merchant Adventurers' Archive, D 43/6.
51. William Wascelyne of Kennythorpe died in 1399 or possibly at the very beginning of 1400. His will is unfortunately brief and comparatively uninformative. Beyond naming his wife, Agnes, it provides no clues as to his family ties, but it is plausible that he was a child of the Stephen and Anabilla of the case and perhaps a brother of the Katherine noted in John de Rouclif senior's will: YML, Dean and Chapter probate register, L2(4), fol. 122.
52. BI, Prob. Reg. 1, fol. 53v.
53. Baptismal practice is discussed in Orme, *Medieval Children*, pp. 21–9.
54. In a rather earlier marriage case, John de Draycote testified that he knew the groom's age "from the relation of his godmother who raised him from the holy font": BI, CP.E.23. The testimony is transcribed in Helmholz, *Marriage Litigation*, p. 202.
55. As we shall shortly see, this contrasts with John de Melsay's testimony as a godfather.
56. Rosenthal, *Telling Tales*, p. 60; Bedell, "Memory and Proof of Age," p. 19.
57. *The Poll Taxes of 1377, 1379 and 1381*, ed. Fenwick, 3:194–209, 301–453.
58. One of these daughters is not in fact so described, but she shares the same surname as the immediately preceding married couple. As is conventional in the more detailed Howdenshire returns, both these women are also described as "servant."
59. *CPR*, 1364–67, p. 175.
60. X 6.2.22. The canon reads "testimonium matris est suspectum, ubi filia petit in virum aliquem se maiorem." Ellen de Rouclif's promotion of her daughter's marriage to the son of the abbot of St Mary's could have been understood in these terms.
61. *CPR*,1350–54, p. 425; *Feet of Fines for the County of Yorkshire*, III, ed. Baildon, p. 102. The land purchased in 1364 was to pass in time to Guy de Rouclif's heirs. Guy was a career administrator with strong literary connections. He became a senior administrator in the Privy Seal Office and was at the end of his career the manager of the poet Thomas Hoccleve, referred to in his will as "my clerk" and to whom he bequeathed a book called *The War of Troy*. He was also associated with John Gower, who purchased two manors in East Anglia from Rouclif, and perhaps more

generally as part of a "Langlandian reading circle": J.A. Burrow, *Thomas Hoccleve* (Aldershot: Variorum, 1994), pp. 9–10; Kathryn Kerby-Fulton and Steven Justice, "Langlandian Reading Circles and the Civil Service in London and Dublin, 1380–1427," in *New Medieval Literatures*, 1, ed. Wendy Scase, Rita Copeland, and David Lawton (Oxford: Oxford University Press, 1997), pp. 59–83, esp. pp. 64–5; TNA, Prob/11/1.

62. Sir Brian's daughter, Ellen, married John de Ingleby who was associated with the founding of the Charterhouse of Mount Grace. Sir Brian's wife's identity is not recorded. The genealogical information here is largely derived from William Flower's compilation of nearly two centuries later, but Lady Margery is not named in Flower's genealogy of the Roclyff family: *The Visitation of Yorkshire in the Years 1563 and 1564 made by William Flower, Esquire*, ed. Charles Best Norcliffe, Harleian Society 91 (1881), pp. 265–6.
63. The small York parish of St Wilfred was centered on Blake Street and was located next to St Leonard's hospital. It is possible that by this date Lady Margery held a corrody at St Leonard's. Age and incapacity were both canonically valid reasons for the court to come to the witness rather than vice versa: X 2.20.8.
64. The child was presumably given an emergency baptism by the midwife and a subsequent conditional baptism in church. From a theological perspective, the first event constituted the actual baptism, the second ceremonial event serving primarily a social function.
65. Cf. Rowena E. Archer, "'How Ladies ... Who Live on their Manors ought to Manage their Households and Estates': Women as Landholders and Administrators in the Later Middle Ages," in *Woman is a Worthy Wight: Women in English Society c. 1200–1500*, ed. P.J.P. Goldberg (Stroud: Alan Sutton, 1992), pp. 149–81.
66. Scott L. Waugh, *England in the Reign of Edward III* (Cambridge, UK: Cambridge University Press, 1991), pp. 108–9.
67. Carole Rawcliffe, "The Great Lord as Peacekeeper: Arbitration by English Noblemen and their Councils in the Later Middle Ages," in *Law and Social Change in British History*, ed. John A. Guy and H.G. Beale (London: Royal Historical Society, 1984), pp. 34–54.
68. Charles Clay, "The Family of Meaux," *Yorkshire Archaeological Journal* 43 (1971): 99–111.
69. Houghton is located near Market Weighton and remains to this day the location of Houghton Hall.
70. See note 33 above.
71. Implicit in this observation is that St Mary's, like a number of other monastic churches, also functioned to some degree parochially. In fact this case presents the only evidence so far discovered that St Mary's possessed a font and indeed maintained any kind of parochial function. I am grateful to Dr. Christopher Norton for discussing this point.
72. By adding how old John would have been when he moved to Houghton (just under two) to the time he had been resident in Houghton (just under

twelve years), he adduces that John would have been nearly fourteen had he lived.

73. Clay, "The Family of Meaux," p. 106. The couple apparently moved within weeks of William de Houghton's death.

Chapter 6 Dom. William Marrays: Stories and Readers

1. See, *Fama: the Politics of Talk and Reputation in Medieval Europe*, ed. Thelma Fenster and Daniel Lord Smail (Ithica, NY: Cornell University Press, 2003), pp. 1–11 for a discussion of the related concept of "*fama*."
2. Adrian Wilson, "The Ceremony of Childbirth and its Interpretation," in *Women as Mothers in Pre-Industrial England*, ed. Valerie Fildes (London: Routledge, 1990), pp. 68–107.
3. Three are of similar date to the present case: BI, CP.E.33 (1337), CP.E.70 (1356), E.105 (1370), E.126 (1382). Visual testimony for intercourse is not found by the fifteenth century.
4. The canon law laid down that for proof of intercourse testimony of actual sight was preferred, followed by testimony of hearing, and lastly testimony of strong supposition: X 2.20.27.
5. Such observations become much less common by the fifteenth century and may be related to the dissemination of the use of bed curtains and the increasing provision of separate chambers: P.J.P. Goldberg, "John Skathelok's Dick: Voyeurism and 'Pornography' in Late Medieval England," in *Medieval Obscenities*, ed. Nicola McDonald (Woodbridge: York Medieval Press, 2006), pp. 105–23.
6. Account written in 1504 published in *Plumpton Correspondence*, ed. Thomas Stapleton, Camden Society o.s. 4 (1839), p. lxiv.
7. This was true of well-to-do Florentine marriages by the fifteenth century: Christiane Klapisch-Zuber, *Women, Family, and Ritual in Renaissance Italy*, trans. Lydia G. Cochrane (Chicago: University of Chicago Press, 1985), p. 191.
8. For a discussion of this point see Charles J. Reid Jr., *Power over the Body, Equality in the Family: Rights and Domestic Relations in Medieval Canon Law* (Grand Rapids, MI: William B. Eerdmans, 2004), pp. 113–14.
9. Thomas was some thirteen years older than his bride. Karl P. Wentersdorf, "The Clandestine Marriage of the Fair Maid of Kent," *Journal of Medieval History* 5 (1979): 204–5, 220.
10. Thomas Holland went overseas to fight shortly after his contract to Joan Plantagenet. Wentersdorf, "Fair Maid of Kent," 205–7.
11. There is an analogy here with the strategy deployed by John, son of James, a witness in the slightly earlier case of Aunger c. Malecake (BI, CP.E.76). Here William Aunger petitioned for the annulment of his marriage to one Joan Malecake contracted whilst he was under age. Although it was not disputed that William had subsequently achieved his majority, the

case revolved around the issue of whether William had consummated the earlier contract. John, son of James testified that he thought not, both because William had tried to shun Joan, and also because William was not sexually mature, was physically stunted, and looked more like a nine- or ten-year-old.

12. Kathryn Gravdal, *Ravishing Maidens: Writing Rape in French Literature and Law* (Philadelphia: University of Pennsylvania Press, 1991), pp. 135–40.
13. Copies of depositions would have been made for both sets of proctors and for the use of the presiding Official who used them to determine the case.
14. Pedersen, *Marriage Disputes in Medieval England*, pp. 94, 97.
15. P.H. Cullum, "Clergy, Masculinity and Transgression in Late Medieval England," in *Masculinity in Medieval Europe*, ed. Dawn Hadley (London, 1999), pp. 178–96.
16. Here I follow Roger Thompson's usages, namely, "*pornographic*, writing or representation intended to arouse lust, create sexual fantasies or feed auto-erotic desires" and "obscene, intended to shock or disgust, or render the subject of the writing shocking or disgusting": Roger Thompson, *Unfit for Modest Ears: A Study of Pornographic, Obscene and Bawdy Works Written or Published in England in the Second Half of the Seventeenth Century* (London: Macmillan, 1979), p. ix.
17. The use of drapes and of onlookers, who stand as proxy for the observer's own voyeurism, is a motif to be found in late medieval art. This is true, for example, of the Boethius Master's representation of coitus in a manuscript of Bartholomeus Anglicus, Hans Memling's representation of Bathsheba, or various of the erotic drawings of Giulio Romano. For the Boethius Master see Michael Camille, "Manuscript Illumination and the Art of Copulation," *Constructing Medieval Sexuality*, ed. Karma Lochrie, Peggy McCracken, and James A. Schulz, (Minneapolis: University of Minnesota Press, 1997), pp. 78–80.
18. Goldberg, "John Skathelok's Dick," pp. 117–22.
19. It should be noted that clerics and the educated represent likely audiences for the consumption of pornographic discourses. Talvacchia has argued that the earliest patrons of the erotic drawings of Giulio Romano and of his notorious "I modi" engravings were "the elite of Rome's papal curia": Bette Talvacchia, *Taking Positions: On the Erotic in Renaissance Culture* (Princeton: Princeton University Press, 1999), p. 72. Michael Camille has also discussed images of copulation found in medieval learned and clerical texts: Camille, "Manuscript Illumination and the Art of Copulation," pp. 58–90. A parallel observation has been made about the educated and Puritan backgrounds of consumers of pornographic writings, primarily composed in Latin, French or Italian, during the later seventeenth century: Thompson, *Unfit for Modest Ears*, pp. 198–207.
20. X 4.15.7; Jacqueline Murray, "On the Origins and Role of 'Wise Women' in Causes for Annulment on the Grounds of Male Impotence," *Journal of Medieval History* 16 (1990): 235–49; Goldberg, *Women, Work ande Life Cycle*, p. 151.

21. Monks appear normally to have been professed in their very late teens or early twenties: Harvey, *Living and Dying in England 1100–1540*, pp. 118–22.
22. BI, CP.E.89/16, 27. None of the other sets of depositions are annotated.
23. Testimony relating to Alice's spousals was also indicated by two marginal "m"'s placed one above the other.
24. Becky Lee specifically makes this point in citing this case in her analysis of proof-of-age evidence: Lee, "A Company of Women and Men" p. 94, 97n.
25. "They are best thought of as village elders and spokesmen and elders": Rosenthal, *Telling Tales*, p. 2.
26. Rosenthal, *Telling Tales*, pp. 10–12, 19–21.
27. Charles Donahue, Jr., "Proof by Witnesses in the Church Courts of Medieval England: An Imperfect Reception of the Learned Law," in *On the Laws and Customs of England*, ed. Morris S. Arnold, Thomas A. Green, Sally Scully, and Stephen D. White (Chapel Hill: University of North Carolina Press, 1981), pp. 149–51.

Chapter 7 Alice through the Looking Glass

1. T.H. Hollingsworth, "A Demographic Study of British Ducal Families," *Population Studies* 11 (1957): p. 14 [4–26].
2. The ability to control a ward's marriage was recognized as the guardian's right: Waugh, *The Lordship of England*, pp. 146, 207–21.
3. A number of early Canterbury cases are published in *Select Cases from the Ecclesiastical Courts of the Province of Canterbury, c. 1200–1301*, ed. Norma Adams and Charles Donahue, Jr, Selden Society 95 (1981).
4. BI, CP.E.89/26, article 6.
5. BI, CP.E.89/12, especially articles 1–3.
6. Helmholz found only three such actions among the fourteenth-century York cause papers and broadly similar patterns elsewhere: Helmholz, *Marriage Litigation*, p. 68.
7. Helmholz, *Marriage Litigation*, p. 67.
8. J.M.W. Bean, "Henry Percy (c. 1321–68)," in *Dictionary of National Biography*, http://www.oxforddnb.com/ accessed on 17 May 2005.
9. Menuge, *Medieval English Wardship*, pp. 97–9.
10. Menuge, *Medieval English Wardship*, p. 97.
11. BI, CP.E.89/12, article 1; CP.E.89/14.
12. Waugh, *The Lordship of England*, pp. 217–18.
13. Cf. Ruth Mazo Karras, *Sexuality in Medieval Europe: Doing unto Others* (New York: Routledge, 2005), p. 154.
14. "Leman" is a standard Middle English usage for lover or concubine.
15. Similar sentiments with similar objectives can be found in French court material four centuries later. Thus Jeanne James told her suitor, "if he wanted to look upon her as a mistress, he was wrong, and that she would

only listen to him if he intended to marry her." Jeanne, like Alice, was seeking commitment in an essentially unequal power relationship, though Jeanne presumably had not yielded to her suitor's sexual advances: Sarah C. Maza, *Servants and Masters in Eighteenth-Century France: The Uses of Loyalty* (Princeton: University of Princeton Press, 1983), p. 70. I am indebted to Cordelia Beattie for drawing this reference to my attention.

16. Kim M. Phillips, *Medieval Maidens: Young Women and Gender in England 1270–1540* (Manchester: Manchester University Press, 2003), pp. 83–96, 143–76.
17. Anabilla Wascelyne stated she could not remember whether he had said 100 marks or £100, but this does not alter the rhetorical effect of John's statement.
18. Modern legal definitions of rape tend to require that the woman experience penetrative sex without her consent as a consequence of force or threat or because the woman is incapable of giving consent. Sexual intercourse with children below the age of consent is often regarded as statutory rape. The English Sexual Offences Act, 2003, defines rape more simply as any act of sexual intercourse where the woman does not consent. This accords with current feminist thinking and is also the definition used here: The Scottish Parliament, *The Legal Definition of Rape*, Research Note RN 01/46 (Edinburgh, 2001), p. 5. English medieval legal conceptions of rape unsurprisingly stress force or violence, though Kim Phillips has argued that around the mid-thirteenth century, legal rape narratives tended to highlight the loss of virginity rather than violence whereas later medieval rape law tended to conflate rape and abduction: Kim M. Phillips, "Written on the Body: Reading Rape from the Twelfth to Fifteenth Centuries," in *Medieval Women and the Law*, ed. Noël James Menuge (Woodbridge: Boydell, 2000), pp. 125–44. Medieval notions of rape are thus far removed from both the contemporary legal and feminist understandings. Indeed, ironically, medieval law would probably have considered Alice's abduction by Sir Brian de Rouclif more akin to rape than Alice's sexual initiation by John Marrays. Consequently, I do not feel it is either helpful or appropriate to apply later-fourteenth-century legal notions of rape in order to try an understand Alice's experience.
19. E. Schwarz and B.D. Perry, "The Post-Traumatic Response in Children and Adolescents," *Psychiatric Clinics of North America* 17 (1994): 311–26; Nicola Gavey, *Just Sex: The Cultural Scaffolding of Rape* (London: Routledge, 2005), pp. 159–60. In March 2006 Merle Friedman, a clinical psychologist, testified to the Johannesburg High Court in the trial of Jacob Zuma, formerly vice president of South Africa, that freezing was a common response in rape victims, but that it was all the more likely in the case of Zuma's alleged victim since she had looked to him as a father figure.
20. Gavey, *Just Sex*, chs. 5 and 6. Gavey offers a series of case studies of women who felt constrained or coerced to have unwanted sex by reason of their own understanding of prevailing social conventions. Such women may

retrospectively accept that sex was coercive, but will deny that they have been raped.

21. Cf. Helen Cooper, "Good Advice on Leaving Home in the Romances," in *Youth in the Middle Ages*, ed. P.J.P. Goldberg and Felicity Riddy (York: York Medieval Press, 2004), pp. 101–21.
22. Cf. Karen Sullivan, *The Interrogation of Joan of Arc* (Minneapolis: University of Minnesota Press, 1999), pp. 12–15.
23. The spousals are specifically described as occurring within the abbey precinct. If, as is likely, they were conducted in the abbey gatehouse, they would in fact have been hard by the church of St Olave which abutted the gatehouse and could only be entered through the same gateway.
24. Barbara J. Harris, *English Aristocratic Women, 1450–1550: Marriage and Family, Property and Careers* (New York: Oxford University Press, 2002), p. 58.

Chapter 8 Brewing Trouble: The Devout Widow's Tale

1. Unless otherwise stated, all references and quotations in this chapter are derived from this case, which is BI, CP.F.36. The case is briefly, but somewhat inaccurately, discussed in S.M. Butler, "'I will Never Consent to be Wedded with you': Coerced Marriage in the Courts of Medieval England," *Canadian Journal of History* 39 (2004): 247–70.
2. *Probate Inventories of the York Diocese*, ed. P.M. Stell and Louise Hampson (York: privately printed, 1998), pp. 61–8; YML, Dean and Chapter probate register 1, L2(4), fol. 154v. Both, the date of making and of probate fall in March. It is very likely that the William Smyth who testified on Agnes's behalf can be identified with the man of the same name who was paid 5s. 4d. out of Hugh's estate.
3. Agnes's age may be exaggerated as this was part of a strategy to cast doubt on the likelihood of her freely consenting to marry John Dale, described as a young man. We do not know how old she in fact was, but it is likely she was of similar age to her late husband. He was made a freeman of York in 1385, so may have been born in or before c. 1364. This would suggest an age in the mid-forties: *Register of the Freemen*, ed. Collins, p. 82. Sara Butler initially describes Agnes as William Pountfret's servant, but later qualifies this to the suggestion that Pountfret was "seemingly her employer, although in what capacity is unclear": Butler, "'I will Never Consent...,;" p. 258. Neither suggestion is substantiated by the evidence.
4. He was admitted to the franchise in 1368 and was chamberlain in 1381–82. This would suggest that he was in his early sixties by 1411: *Register of the Freemen*, ed. Collins, pp. 63, 78. It is tempting to speculate that his office-holding career, begun in the very year of major civic disturbances in York, was consequently short-lived, though in fact more

ambitious men tended to hold office as chamberlain somewhat sooner. For a discussion of the events in York in 1380–81 see R.B. Dobson, "The Risings in York, Beverley and Scarborough, 1380–1381," in *The English Rising of 1381*, ed. R.H. Hilton and T.H. Aston (Cambridge, UK: Cambridge University Press, 1984), pp. 112–42, esp. pp. 118–24 [112–42].

5. Pountfret's deposition gives his age as sixty years. Pountfret and Thornton are both listed thirty years earlier under All Saints, Pavement in the 1381 poll tax returns for York, though their names are quite widely separated. This could well imply that the two men lived in different parts of the parish at that date. Pountfret was assessed with his wife Avice at 8s. 2d., some four times the mean rate. His two female servants were assessed at 6d. each. Thornton was assessed with his wife Katherine and one female servant, but damage to the roll means that the actual assessment is lost. Both men are described as drapers: *The Poll Taxes of 1377, 1379 and 1381*, ed. Fenwick, 3:142.
6. Helmholz, *Marriage Litigation*, pp. 90–4.
7. D.M. Smith, *The Court of York, 1400–1499: A Handlist of the Cause Papers and an Index to the Archiepiscopal Court Books*, Borthwick Texts and Calendars 29 (2003), pp. 13–14.
8. Butler argues that Agnes Grantham claimed that she was precontracted to John Thornton. In fact her case against John Dale rests solely on force and fear: Butler, "'I will Never Consent…,'" p. 258.
9. Alice de Rouclif's contract, it may be remembered, was allegedly made with a cheerful countenance in the presence of her immediate kin.
10. These articles are dated 26 November 1410.
11. Articles dated 21 February 1411.
12. See note 2 above.
13. These settlements were all within the Liberty of St Peter. It is tempting to conclude that, as discussed in the first part of this book, the Liberty played a role in shaping patterns of migration. In the particular case of Hugh Grantham, it may be that the lure of employment on York Minster, whose eastern parts were being rebuilt from the 1360s, drew the young man to the city and the parish of St Michael le Belfrey: J.H. Harvey, "Architectural History from 1291 to 1558," in *A History of York Minster*, ed. G.E. Aylmer and Reginald Cant (Oxford: Oxford University Press, 1977), p. 163 [149–92].
14. Neither Catton's will nor the associated inventory adds very much to our understanding of the case. He was clearly a weaver of some means possessing net assets, including two looms and various lengths of cloth, valued at some £30. He was a member of both the St Mary's guild of weavers and the fraternity of the Holy Trinity in Fossgate: *Probate Inventories*, ed. Stell and Hampson, pp. 68–72; YML, Dean and Chapter probate register 1, L2(4), fol. 164.
15. *The Book of Margery Kempe*, ed. Lynn Staley (Kalamazoo: The Medieval Institute, 1996), book 1, ll. 204–12.

16. P.H. Cullum, "'And Hir Name was Charite': Charitable Giving by and for Women in Late Medieval Yorkshire," in *Woman is a Worthy Wight: Women in English Society c. 1200–1500*, ed. P.J.P. Goldberg (Stroud: Alan Sutton, 1992), pp. 196–7 [182–211].
17. Sara Butler argues that Agnes was in fact repeatedly raped and cites the phrase "Johannes carnalem copulam extorquisset ab eadem" as evidence of actual rape: Butler, "'I will Never Consent. . .,'" p. 258. This phrase, taken from the deposition of Thomas Catton, is in fact preceded by the words "[Agnes]. . .semper timuit quod idem" [Agnes "the whole time feared that the said John [Dale] would force intercourse with her"]. Article xx of a very full set of 34 articles reads ". . .prefatus Johannes Dale tempore predicto minabatur et conabatur extorquere carnalem copulam de eadem Agnete." Against this has been written the response on behalf of John Dale denying the article and asserting that he had intercourse with her willingly ("voluntate").
18. Cullum, "Vowesses and Female Lay Piety," pp. 21–41.
19. John Watton, who is said to have been twenty-five years at the time of his deposition, can probably be identified with the parochial chaplain of St Crux whose will was proved in 1445: BI, Prob. Reg. 2 fol. 400.
20. The career of William Feryby, a royal clerk and master 1409–15, is somewhat obscure. He had previously been archdeacon of the East Riding 1393–1409 and chancellor to Henry, Prince of Wales in 1403: B. Jones, *Fasti Ecclesiae Anglicanae 1300–1500, vol. VI: Northern Province* (London: The Athlone Press, 1963), p. 22; J.L. Grassi, "Royal Clerks from the Archdiocese of York in the Fourteenth Century," *Northern History* 5 (1970): 26, 30 [12–33]; Patricia Helena Cullum, "Hospitals and Charitable Provision in Medieval Yorkshire, 936–1547" unpublished University of York D.Phil. thesis (1989), pp. 149, 153.
21. *Select Cases in the Court of King's Bench under Edward III*, vol. V, ed. G.O. Sayles, Selden Society 76 (1957), pp. 90–1. In this instance the countess was allegedly taken against her will to the castle of Somerton. Her abductors then raped her and "did their will with her". The jurors, however, ruled that no such abduction or rape had occurred and acquitted the defendants.
22. "et puis la dite Geffrei la prist afforce en counter son gre et la getta de sur un chival drere Iohnan de Causton' et ele chey a terre et rescust si graunt damage de son corps qele ne pout travailler ne aler deuz semeignes apres; et puis le ditz Geffrei et Iohan lamenerunt tanqe a un bois qest apel Boxted' Park' et parceqe ele cria et fist noise ils la treyerunt en bossouns et rounces et estoperunt le bouche la dite Alice dun gaunt et de chaperoun le dite Alice et si vilement la leiderunt tanque ele devynt tut sanglent et prie remedye": *Proceedings before the Justices of the Peace in the Fourteenth and Fifteenth Centuries Edward III to Richard III*, ed. Bertha H. Putnam (London: The Ames Foundation, 1938), no. 68, p. 344. I am grateful to Nicola McDonald for helping me with the French.
23. *CCR*, 1317–21, p. 485; *CCR*, 1358–61, p. 83; *CPR*, 1381–85, pp. 453–4.

24. Woodland is noted in one of the Domesday Book entries relating to Acomb. Thomas Forester, one of the three attackers, is elsewhere identified as the forester of Healaugh Park, which lay further west beyond Acomb Grange.
25. For an invaluable exploration of the cultural significance of forest, see Corinne Saunders, *The Forest of Medieval Romance: Avernus, Broceliande, Arden* (Cambridge, UK: D.S. Brewer, 1993), esp. pp. 133, 135, 184–5 (abduction) and 132, 163 (rape).
26. *Sir Degaré* is found in four late medieval manuscripts of which one is late fourteenth century and two fifteenth century. Corinne Saunders argues that in romance literature it is the threat of rape rather than actual rape that prevails: "Sir Degaré," in *The Middle English Breton Lays*, ed. Anne Laskaya and Eve Salisbury (Kalamazoo: The Medieval Institute, 1995), pp. 89–144; Corinne Saunders, *Rape and Ravishment in the Literature of Medieval England* (Cambridge, UK: D.S. Brewer, 2001), pp. 187, 213–18.
27. The will of William de Ulskelf, who died in September 1391, is extant. He may have been the father of Richard Ulskelf. Both were walkers or fullers and both resided in the parish, though there is tension between the father's provision for his son to be cared for and schooled—the implication being that he was still a child—and the Richard's declared age of forty (in one deposition) and sixty (in a second deposition) some twenty years later. This may only reflect the unreliability of the ages declared by witnesses, but is perhaps evidence that William de Ulskelf was not Richard's father, but some other relative. Unfortunately there appears nothing in William's will to help our analysis beyond the observation that this was evidently an artisanal family of middling rank. The suburban nature of Walmgate is reflected in William de Ulskelf's bequest to his son of two cows: BI, Prob. Reg. 1 fol. 35v.
28. Richard de Ulskelf remembered the date in respect of the feast of St Margaret, no doubt because this was the feast day of his parish church of St Margaret in Walmgate. The feast may also have had symbolic importance in relation to Agnes Grantham for St Margaret famously escaped the belly of the dragon.
29. McSheffrey, *Love and Marriage*, p. 41.
30. Sylvia Landsberg, *The Medieval Garden* (London: British Museum Press, 1996), pp. 49–50. See also Derek Pearsall, "Gardens as Symbol and Setting in Late Medieval Poetry," in *Medieval Gardens*, ed. Elizabeth B. MacDougall (Washington: Dumbarton Oaks Research Library and Collection, 1986), pp. 245, 250 [237–51].
31. Pearsall, "Gardens as Symbol and Setting," pp. 238–45.
32. Cf. Pearsall, "Gardens as Symbol and Setting," p. 241.
33. Sarah Rees Jones, "Historical Introduction," in *Medieval Urbanism in Coppergate: Refining a Townscape*, ed. R.A. Hall and K. Hunter-Mann, , The Archaeology of York, 10, 6 (York: Council for British Archaeology, 2002), pp. 693, 696 [684–98]. The extant property (no. 151) is discussed in Royal Commission on Historical Monuments (England), *An Inventory*

of the Historical Monuments in the City of York: vol. V, The Central Area (London: H.M.S.O., 1981), p. 128. The two bays to the north can only be surmised from the evidence of the numbering of the extant timber framing. The space is currently occupied by the much more recent, but now defunct White Swan hotel and much structural change has occurred, including the curtailment of the eastern part of the parish church, as a consequence of the construction of Piccadilly shortly before the First World War.

34. Many of the properties on Coppergate opposite the church of All Saints were apparently destroyed in a fire in 1694: Drake, *Eboracum*, p. 292.
35. BI, Prob. Reg. 3, fols. 111–12.
36. He was chamberlain in 1379–80, two years before John Thornton: *Register of Freemen*, ed. Collins, pp. 68, 76; note 4 above. Another will, that of William de Pontfract, draper (d. 1390), may well represent the William "senior" implicit in the franchise register entry, but he was apparently not William junior's father since there is no mention of any son in this earlier will: BI, Prob. Reg., 1 fol. 15.
37. Cf. P.H. Cullum, "For Pore People Harberles: What was the Function of the Maisondieu?" in *Trade, Devotion and Governance in Fifteenth Century England*, ed. Dorothy J. Clayton, Richard G. Davies, and Peter McNiven (Stroud: Alan Sutton, 1994), pp. 36–54.
38. Rees Jones, "Historical Introduction," pp. 693, 696. A deed recorded in the cartulary of the Vicars Choral of the Minster records that John de Thornton, citizen and draper, owned the property to the west and that there was reserved to him and his heirs "free supply of all rain water and egress from John's house": *Charters of the Vicars Choral of York Minster, City of York and its Suburbs to 1546*, ed. Nigel Tringham, Yorkshire Archaeological Society Record ser. 148 (1993), no. 577, p. 313.
39. Drake, *Eboracum*, p. 295.
40. *Charters of the Vicars Choral*, ed. Tringham, no. 111, p. 64.
41. Stell and Hampson, *Probate Inventories*, p. 68.
42. Drake, *Eboracum*, p. 295.
43. For a discussion of the notion of the chaste marriage see Diane Elliott, *Spiritual Marriage: Sexual Abstinence in Medieval Wedlock* (Princeton: Princeton University Press, 1993), especially pp. 195–265. See note 3 above.
44. Dorothea of Montau, a native of Danzig, may have been known in York as a consequence of the city's trade links. St Brigit was certainly known. She is depicted in the so-called Bolton Hours owned and probably produced in the city at about this date. The city was also the focus of an abortive attempt to establish a Brigittine house at much the same date. The two may be connected to the legacy of Archbishop Richard Scrope who had spent part of his career in Rome at the time canonization proceedings for Brigit were started and who himself promoted Brigit's interest in the Five Wounds. Scrope's execution in 1405 made him the focus for veneration in York and the city's Corpus Christi guild, founded in

1408, which Pountfret and his vowess kinswoman joined in the first year, seems to have been active in promoting the cult. See chapters by Goldberg and Rees Jones in P.J.P. Goldberg, ed., *Richard Scrope: Archbishop, Rebel, Martyr* (Donington, UK: Shaun Tyas, forthcoming).

Chapter 9 Patriarchy, Civic Identity, and the Widow of Doncaster

1. Unless otherwise stated, all references and quotations in this chapter are derived from this case, which is BI, CP.E.188.
2. It had a recorded tax population of 800 in the 1377 poll tax returns. Using a multiplier of 1.65 to allow for persons below taxation age (fourteen years), clergy (taxed separately), the exempt poor, and the like, this would yield a total population of 1,320. Using like poll tax evidence, and allowing for London, Chester and Durham that are not recorded, it would appear that Doncaster was probably about the fiftieth biggest town in the realm and the fifth largest in the county: *The Poll Taxes of 1377, 1379 and 1381*, ed. Fenwick, 3:269; Alan Dyer, *Decline and Growth in English Towns 1400–1640* (Cambridge, UK: Cambridge University Press, 1995), appendix 1, pp. 56–7.
3. For this and the discussion that follows see P.J.P. Goldberg, "From Conquest to Corporation," in *Doncaster: A Borough and its Charters* ed. B.J. Barber (Doncaster: The Waterdale Press, 1994), pp. 47–65, 116–21.
4. That is to say the burgesses were allowed to collect various revenues from tolls, the mills, the borough court, and so on and from these pay a fixed sum ("fee farm") to the crown, enabling them to keep and spend for their own purposes any surplus.
5. D.A.L. Morgan, "The Individual Style of the English Gentleman," in *Gentry and Lesser Nobility in late Medieval Europe*, ed. M.C.E. Jones (Gloucester: Alan Sutton, 1986), pp. 15–35.
6. BI, Prob. Reg. 1 fol. 9v; Prob. Reg. 2 fol. 9.
7. *The Poll Taxes of 1377, 1379 and 1381*, ed. Fenwick, 3:323–6. I have also found useful the searchable electronic version of the older Yorkshire Archaeological Society edition at http://www.genuki.org.uk/big/eng/YKS/Misc/SubsidyRolls/YKS/SubsidyRolls1379Index.html. Accessed on 7 June 2005.
8. *The Poll Taxes of 1377, 1379 and 1381*, ed. Fenwick, 1:xiv–xvi.
9. BI, Prob. Reg. 1 fol. 9v.
10. BI, Prob. Reg. 2 fol. 9.
11. In the next entry we find "Ricardus Rogerman Magota uxor ejus." The suffix "man" can be read to imply that Richard was Roger's employee, but as a married man he is not specifically described as being in a dependent relationship and it is unclear whether Richard and his spouse coresided with William Roger, a single man, or whether they occupied separate, but adjacent accommodation. We may surmise the former and

posit that Magota (or Margaret) acted as de facto housekeeper for William as well as for her husband. *The Poll Taxes of 1377, 1379 and 1381*, ed. Fenwick, 3:347–51.

12. *The Poll Taxes of 1377, 1379 and 1381*, ed. Fenwick, 3:225 (North Cave).
13. *The Poll Taxes of 1377, 1379 and 1381*, ed. Fenwick, 3:230; BI, Prob. Reg. 1 fol. 80.
14. The depositions appear to record "Grenake." Of the two most likely candidates, namely, Greenoak in Howdenshire (East Riding) and Greenhow in the North Riding, the former seems far the better fit. In the 1334 lay subsidy the hamlet is recorded as "Grenayk" and in the 1379 poll tax as "Greneayk."
15. The number of persons listed in 1379 was 101 suggesting a total population of over 160 persons: *The Poll Taxes of 1377, 1379 and 1381*, ed. Fenwick, 3:169, 199.
16. P.H. Cullum, "Vowesses and Female Lay Piety in the Province of York, 1300–1530," *Northern History* 32 (1996): 21–41.
17. *An Episcopal Court Book for the Diocese of Lincoln 1514–1520*, ed. Margaret Bowker, Lincoln Record Society 61 (1967), p. 53; *The Black Book of Winchester*, ed. W.H.B. Bird (Winchester: The Wikeham Press, 1925), pp. 3–4.
18. BI, Prob. Reg. 2 fol. 633v.
19. Michael Young and Peter Willmott, *Family and Kinship in East London* (London: Routledge and Kegan Paul, 1957); Charlotte Gower Chapman, *Milocca: A Sicilian Village* (Cambridge, MA: Schenkman, 1971).
20. BI, Prob. Reg. 1 fol. 9v.
21. *CPR*, 1361–64, pp. 197–8, 208, 288, 433; *CPR*, 1364–67, p. 146; *CPR*, 1367–70, pp. 60, 144; *CPR*, 1374–77, p. 326; *CPR*, 1381–85, pp. 198, 200; Goldberg, "From Conquest to Corporation," p. 52.
22. *CPR*, 1361–64, p. 150; *CPR*, 1364–67, p. 146; *CPR*, 1374–67, p. 326; *CPR*, 1377–81, p. 128; *CPR*, 1381–85, pp. 198, 200; *CPR*, 1391–96, p. 35; *CPR*, 1399–1401, pp. 258, 274; Goldberg, "From Conquest to Corporation," pp. 52, 58.
23. This is discussed at length in Sarah Rees Jones, "Household, Work and the Problem of Mobile Labour: The Regulation of Labour in Medieval English Towns," in *The Problem of Labour in Fourteenth-Century England*, ed. James Bothwell, P.J.P. Goldberg, and W. M. Ormrod (Woodbridge: York Medieval Press, 2000), pp. 133–153.
24. Philippa Maddern, "Order and Disorder," in *Medieval Norwich*, ed. C. Rawcliffe and R. Wilson (London: Hambledon, 2004), pp. 189–212, esp. pp. 189–91.
25. Chaucer describes a merchant dressed in motley and an account roll dated 1394–95 includes motley "for summer garments for esquires." Well-to-do male dress c. 1400 seems to have been characterized by the brevity of the gown or doublet: *Middle English Dictionary*, see under mōtlē (n.), (a); Margaret Scott, *A Visual History of Costume: The Fourteenth and Fifteenth Centuries* (London: Batsford, 1986), plates 43 and 46, pp. 52–4.

26. Gervase Rosser, "Crafts, Guilds and the Negotiation of Work in Medieval Town," *Past and Present* 154 (1997): 3–31.

Conclusion

1. Elizabeth Robertson, "Public Bodies and Psychic Domains: Rape, Consent, and Female Subjectivity in Geoffrey Chaucer's *Troilus and Criseyde*," in *Representing Rape in Medieval and Early Modern Literature*, ed. Robertson and Christine M. Rose (New York: Palgrave, 2001), p. 283 [281–310].
2. Michael Camille, *Mirror in Parchment: The Luttrell Psalter and the Making of Medieval England* (Chicago: University of Chicago Press, 1998), pp. 95–6.
3. See, for example, Keith Dockray, "Why did Fifteenth-Century English Gentry Marry?: the Pastons, Plumptons, and Stonors Reconsidered," in *Gentry and Lesser Nobility in Later Medieval Europe*, ed. Michael C.E. Jones (Gloucester: Alan Sutton, 1986), pp. 61–80.
4. P.J.P. Goldberg, "Young Women in the *Oxford Dictionary of National Biography*," unpublished paper given at the International Medieval Congress, Leeds, July 2005.
5. Elizabeth Robertson writes: "As Kelly and other have argued, rape, as it appears in various forms of 'rapire' in the fourteenth century, can refer to a wide variety of events including sexual assault, abduction for the purposes of marriage without the consent of the abductee, abduction for the purposes of marriage with the consent of the abductee, and abduction for the purposes of marriage with the later consent of the abductee." See Robertson, "Public Bodies and Psychic Domains," p. 294. The English term "ravished," meaning "abducted," is found in an English petition dated 1437, but the same term, preceded by the phrase "ayenst hir will" is found in another petition of 1439 where actual rape is probably implied. Both terms have been rendered as "raped" in the TNA catalogue: TNA, SC 8/27/1305, 1316.
6. Theobald retrospectively claimed that Elizabeth had consented to this marriage and abduction. He was to die only months later: Frances A. Underhill, *For Her Good Estate: The Life of Elizabeth de Burgh* (New York: St Martin's Press, 1999), pp. 15–16; Waugh, *The Lordship of England*, p. 219; Jennifer Ward, "Elizabeth de Clare," in *The Oxford Dictionary of National Biography*.
7. *CPR*, 1374–77, p. 223.
8. William Flower's pedigree made nearly two centuries later records Ellen as having married one John Ingleby, so what became of this abduction we cannot tell: Norcliffe, *The Visitation of Yorkshire in the Years 1563 and 1564*, pp. 265–6.
9. Waugh, *The Lordship of England*, p. 219. For two further examples from much the same period see *CPR*, 1367–70, p. 472 (Juliana de Rous); *CPR*, 1385–89, p. 326 (Isabella ate Hall).

10. Frederick Pollock and Frederic William Maitland, *The History of English Law before the time of Edward I*, 2 vols. (Cambridge, UK: Cambridge University Press, 1898), 2:365; Helmholz, *Marriage Litigation*, p. 90.
11. *Sessions of the Peace in the City of Lincoln 1351–1354 and the Borough of Stamford 1351*, ed. Elisabeth G. Kimball, Lincoln Record Society 65 (1971), no. 1, p. 2.
12. *CPR*, 1350–54, p. 489.
13. *CPR*, 1385–89, p. 182.
14. *CPR*, 1354–58, p. 445.
15. *CPR*, 1374–77, p. 365.
16. *CPR*, 1391–96, p. 82.
17. *CPR*, 1361–64, p. 533.
18. Cf. Corinne Saunders, "A Matter of Consent: Middle English Romance and the Law of *Raptus*," in *Medieval Women and the Law*, ed. Noël James Menuge (Woodbridge: Boydell, 2000), pp. 105–11 [105–24].
19. Henry Ansgar Kelly, "Statutes of Rapes and Alleged Ravishers of Wives: A Context for the Charges against Thomas Malory, Knight," *Viator* 28 (1997): 361 [361–419]. Kelly positions himself against Cannon who has argued that by the later fourteenth century "the lines between abduction and forced coitus" were blurred "so substantially that any clear, legal distinction between the two wrongs seems to have been all but impossible to make": Christopher Cannon, "*Raptus* in the Chaumpaigne Release and a Newly Discovered Document Concerning the Life of Geoffrey Chaucer," *Speculum* 68 (1993): 82 [74–94].
20. Sue Sheridan Walker, "Punishing Convicted Ravishers: Statutory Strictures and Actual Practice in Thirteenth and Fourteenth-Century England," *Journal of Medieval History* 13 (1987): 237 [237–50]; Henry Ansgar Kelly, "Meaning and Uses of *Raptus* in Chaucer's Time," *Studies in the Age of Chaucer* 20 (1998): 131 [101–65]; Marie A. Kelleher, "Law and the Maiden: *Inquisitio*, *Fama*, and the Testimony of Children in Medieval Catalonia," *Viator* 37 (2006): 356 [351–67] citing Gratian.
21. *English Historical Documents, III: 1189–1327*, ed. Harry Rothwell (London: Eyre and Spottiswoode, 1975), p. 447 cited in Saunders, "A Matter of Consent," p. 110.
22. J.B. Post, "Ravishment of Women and the Statutes of Westminster," in *Legal Records and the Historian*, ed. J.H. Baker (London: Royal Historical Society, 1978), pp. 150–64. Phillips follows Post's reading in her discussion of the changing meanings of rape during the later medieval era: Phillips, "Written on the Body," pp. 135–8, 141–2.
23. He argues that it is only since Edward Coke (1552–1634) that the Statutes of Westminster have routinely been thought of as concerning rape: Kelly, "Statutes of Rape," 364–70, 382–7, 391–5.
24. *CPR*, 1354–58, p. 418.
25. The record indicates that Elizabeth was in fact leaving her husband as part of divorce proceedings. This sounds like a divorce "a mensa et a thoro," which

could be sought on grounds of adultery or cruelty, rather than an annulment, but the evidence is unclear. From a legal perspective Robert was pardoned not because Elizabeth's voluntarily leaving her husband did not count as abduction—Elizabeth was still taken from her husband—but because as a servant he had a duty to obey his mistress's order: *CPR*, 1358–61, p. 191.

26. *CPR*, 1358–61, p. 394.
27. See Chapter 8 above.
28. *CPR*, 1350–4, p. 440.
29. *Lower Ecclesiastical Jurisdiction in Late-Medieval England: The Courts of the Dean and Chapter of Lincoln, 1336–1349 and the Deanery of Wisbech, 1458–1484*, ed. L.R. Poos, Records of Social and Economic History, new ser. 32 (Oxford: British Academy, 2001), pp. 92–3.
30. *Some Sessions of the Peace in Lincolnshire 1381–1396*, vol. II, ed. Elisabeth G. Kimball, Lincoln Record Society 56 (1962), no. 169, p. 59.
31. *Sessions of the Peace in Lincolnshire*, ed. Kimball, no. 412, pp. 152–3.
32. *Sessions of the Peace in Lincolnshire*, ed. Kimball, no. 736, p. 257.
33. Kim Phillips presents a table analyzing references to five elements—"bleeding," "violence/force," "defloration," "abduction," "consent"—within recorded rape case narratives drawn from a sample of 154 cases dated 1198–1256. The bald nature of most records means that the majority of cases mention none of these elements, but whereas "bleeding," "abduction," and "consent" together are elements noted on a total of only ten occasions, "defloration" is noted fourteen times and "violence / force" nineteen times. Only "defloration" and "violence/force" appear to be noted throughout the period encompassed within Phillips's sample: Phillips, "Written on the Body," p. 131.
34. *Britton*, ed. Francis Morgan Nichols, 2 vols (Oxford: Oxford University Press, 1865), 1:55.
35. *Statutes of the Realm*, I:41. This mirrors the rather earlier account in *Glanvill* that the raped woman must show her injuries in the form of bleeding and of torn clothing to trustworthy men: Phillips, "Written on the Body," p. 129.
36. *Britton*, ed. Nichols, 1:17.
37. Cited in Phillips, "Written on the Body," p. 137.
38. Hanawalt notes how the three versions of this rape narrative were refined over time. It is only the third version that contains all three elements: Barbara A. Hanawalt, "Whose Story Was This? Rape Narratives in Medieval English Courts," in *"Of Good and Ill Repute": Gender and Social Control in Medieval England*, ed. Hanawalt (New York: Oxford University Press, 1998), pp. 127–34.
39. Phillips, "Written on the Body," p. 132.
40. Helmholz, *Marriage Litigation*, pp. 90–4.
41. The words of betrothal spoken by Alice had been in the form of present consent but they had the effect of words of future consent because Alice

was then too young to make an immediately binding marriage by words alone. The subsequent consummation, albeit only a couple of weeks later, changed that.

42. Phillips cited three rape cases from the mid-thirteenth century where the victim was taken to a wood, a park, and to moorland respectively: Phillips, "Written on the Body," pp. 133–4.
43. Kelleher, "Law and the Maiden," 357.
44. TNA, SC 8/27/1316.
45. Articles for John Thornton against John Dale dated 21 February 1411 note Thomas Wakfeld of Wighill, Thomas Chamblayn, John Smyth, John de Whetlay, and Thomas Graunge of Healaugh as deponents supporting Dale's original libel. This was presumably where John Dale outlined his case that he was contracted to Agnes Grantham.
46. *Sessions of the Peace in Lincolnshire*, ed. Kimball, no. 238, p. 82 and no. 585, p. 206.
47. For a discussion of the concept of homosociality see Eve Kosofsky Sedgwick, *Between Men: English Literature and Male Homosocial Desire* (New York: Columbia University Press, 1988), pp. 1–5.
48. This has a parallel with the legal requirement that a raped woman make her complaint before trustworthy men first found in Glanvill: Phillips, "Written on the Body," p. 129.
49. Drake, *Eboracum*, p. 295.
50. Bray discusses two particular examples from the later fourteenth century, namely, Sir John Clanvowe and Sir William Neville (d. 1391) and Master John Bloxham and Dns. John Whytton: Alan Bray, *The Friend* (Chicago: University of Chicago Press, 2003), pp. 13–19, 78–82, 106–8, 135–8.
51. Bray notices this theme in *Amys and Amylion*, *Floris and Blanchefleur*, and *Guy of Warwick*: Bray, *The Friend*, pp. 33, 82. These three romances were all popular and circulated widely in English. See also M.J. Ailes, "The Medieval Male Couple and the Language of Homosexuality," in *Masculinity in Medieval Europe*, ed. Dawn Hadley (London: Longman, 1999), pp. 214–37.
52. *Register of the Guild of Corpus Christi in the City of York*, ed. Robert H. Scaife, Surtees Society 57 (1872), p. 12. It may be that the guild was associated with the memorialization of Archbishop Richard Scrope who had been executed for his part in a rebellion against the king in 1405. Scrope himself appears to have been venerated as a virgin martyr and as such a model of chaste living: see essays in *Richard Scrope*, ed. Goldberg.
53. BI, Prob. Reg. 3 fols. 111–12.
54. For the male-headed household as a civic "norm" see Rees Jones, "Household, Work and the Problem of Mobile Labour," pp. 133–53.
55. P.J.P. Goldberg, "Masters and Men in Later Medieval England," in *Masculinity in Medieval Europe*, ed. Dawn Hadley (London: Longman, 1999), p. 64 [56–70].

56. We know about this case only because Waryngton subsequently contested the marriage on grounds of "force and fear" with his master's support: Goldberg, "Masters and Men," pp. 58–61.
57. The centrality of chastity and devotion to the construction of the household is reflected in a recent discussion of a contemporary York book of hours: Sarah Rees Jones and Felicity Riddy, "The Bolton Hours of York: Female Domestic Piety and the Public Sphere," in *Household, Women, and Christianities in Late Antiquity and the Middle Ages*, ed. Anneke Mulde-Bakker and Jocelyn Wogan-Browne (Turnhout: Brepols, 2005), pp. 215–60.
58. Marjorie Keniston McIntosh, *Controlling Misbehaviour in England, 1370–1600* (Cambridge, UK: Cambridge University Press, 1998).
59. Maddern, "Order and Disorder," p. 189; P.J.P. Goldberg, "Coventry's 'Lollard' Programme of 1492 and the Making of Utopia," in *Pragmatic Utopias: Ideals and Communities 1200–1630*, ed. Rosemary Horrox and Sarah Rees Jones (Cambridge, UK: Cambridge University Press, 2001), pp. 97–116.
60. For aristocratic masculinity, the most recent and wide-ranging discussion is Ruth Mazo Karras, *From Boys to Men: Formations of Masculnity in Late Medieval Europe* (Philadelphia, University of Pennsylvania Press, 2003), pp. 20–66. Karras argues that violence lay at the heart of chivalry and hence the construction of aristocratic masculinity (p. 21) and that aristocratic heterosexual desire served to objectify and commoditize women (pp. 47–57). See also Rachel Dressler, "Steel Corpse: Imagining the Knight in Death," in *Conflicted Identities and Multiple Masculinities: Men in the Medieval West*, ed. Jacqueline Murray (Garland: New York, 1999), pp. 135–67; Andrew Taylor, "Chivalric Conversation and the Denial of Male Fear," in *Conflicted Identities*, ed. Murray, pp. 169–88. For a subtle and nuanced study of royal masculinity see W.M. Ormrod, "Monarchy, Martyrdom and Masculinity: England in the Later Middle Ages," in *Holiness and Masculinity in the Middle Ages*, ed. P. H. Cullum and Katherine J. Lewis (Cardiff: University of Wales Press, 2004), pp. 158–73. For an earlier era see M. Bennett, "Military Masculinity in England and Northern France c.1050–c.1225," in *Masculinity in Medieval Europe*, ed. Hadley, pp. 71–88. The socialization of aristocratic girls is discussed in Phillips, *Medieval Maidens*, especially pp. 61–107; John Carmi Parsons, "'Loved Him—Hated Her": Honor and Shame at the Medieval Court," in *Conflicted Identities*, ed. Murray, pp. 279–98; Sharon D. Michelove, "The Education of Aristocratic Women in Fifteenth-Century England," in *Estrangement, Enterprise and Education in Fifteenth-Century England*, ed. Sharon D. Michelove and A.C. Reeves (1998), pp. 117–39; Harris, *English Aristocratic Women*, especially pp. 27–42. For a somewhat later era see Linda Pollock, "'Teach Her to Live under Obedience': The Making of Women in the Upper Ranks of Early Modern England," *Continuity and Change* 4 (1989): 231–58.
61. For bourgeois masculinity see Goldberg, "Master and Men," pp. 56–70; Shannon McSheffrey, "Men and Masculinity in Late Medieval London

Civic Culture: Governance, Patriarchy and Reputation," in *Conflicted Identities*, ed. Murray, pp. 243–78. For the bourgeois workshop, trust, sociability, and so on, see Rosser, "Crafts, Guilds and the Negotiation of Work," *pp.* 3–31; Rees Jones, "Household, Work and the Problem of Mobile Labour," pp. 133–53; P.J.P. Goldberg, "Household and the Organisation of Labour in Late Medieval Towns: Some English Evidence," in *The Household in Late Medieval Cities: Italy and Mediterranean Europe Compared*, ed. Myriam Carlier and Tim Soens (Leuven: Garant, 2001), pp. 59–70; Felicity Riddy, "Looking Closely: Authority and Intimacy in the Late Medieval Urban Home," in *Gendering the Master Narrative: Women and Power in the Middle Ages*, ed. Mary C. Erler and Maryanne Kowaleski (Ithica: Cornell University Press, 2003), pp. 212–28; Isabel Davis, *Writing Masculinity in the Later Middle Ages* (Cambridge, UK: Cambridge University Press, 2007). There is a very substantial literature on urban and bourgeois women, though only some of it specifically framed in terms of the construction of femininity. Much emphasis has, for example, been placed on women's piety: see for example: P.H. Cullum, "'And Hir Name was Charite': Charitable Giving by and for Women in Later Medieval Yorkshire," in *Woman is a Worthy Wight: Women in English Society, c. 1200–1500*, ed. P.J.P. Goldberg (Stroud: Alan Sutton, 1992), pp. 182–211; Caroline Walker Bynum, "The Female Body and Religious Practice in the Later Middle Ages," in *Fragmentation and Redemption: Essays of Gender and the Human Body in Medieval Religion*, ed. Bynum (New York: Zone Books, 1991), pp. 181–238; Felicity Riddy, "Women Talking about the Things of God: A Late Medieval Subculture," in *Women and Literature in Britain, 1150–1500*, ed. Carol Meale (Cambridge, UK: Cambridge University Press, 1993), pp. 104–27. Poos's study of defamation in the Church courts suggests that women's standing in the community was understood in terms of their sexual honor whereas men's had more to do with honesty: L.R. Poos, "Sex, Lies and the Church Courts," 585–607. For discussions of the socialization of young urban women see note 62 below, also P.J.P. Goldberg, "Girls Growing Up in Later Medieval England," *History Today* 45,6 (1995): 25–32; Caroline M. Barron, "The Education and Training of Girls in Fifteenth-Century London," in *Courts, Counties, and the Capital in the Later Middle Ages* (Stroud: Alan Sutton, 1996), pp. 139–53; Katherine J. Lewis, "Model Girls? Virgin Martyrs and the Training of Young Women in Late Medieval England," in *Young Medieval Women*, ed. Katherine J. Lewis, Noël James Menuge, and Kim M. Phillips (Stroud: Alan Sutton, 1999), pp. 25–46.

62. *The Book of the Knight of Tour-Landry* almost certainly circulated across the Channel in French from the later fourteenth century. A unique mid-fifteenth-century English translation is extant: Geoffroy de La Tour-Landry, *Book of the Knight of La Tour-Landry*, ed. Thomas Wright, EETS o.s. 38 (1906). The text was translated and printed by Caxton in 1484, by which date it was probably of more interest to families below the ranks of the greater aristocracy. "How the Goodwife Taught her Daughter" was

probably first composed around or before the middle of the fourteenth century, but is known in a number of manuscript editions up until the later fifteenth century. The earlier texts are edited in *The Good Wife Taught Her Daughter, The Good Wyfe Wold a Pylgremage, The Thewis of Gud Women*, ed. Tauno F. Mustanoja (Helsinki: Suomalaisen Kirjallisuuden Scuran, 1948). For a discussion of this last and the ideology of femininity constructed within the text see Felicity Riddy, "Mother Knows Best: Reading Social Change in a Courtesy Text," *Speculum* 71 (1996): 66–86. For another useful study of conduct literature addressed at bourgeois women see Kathleen M. Ashley, "Medieval Courtesy Literature and Dramatic Mirrors of Female Conduct" in *The Ideology of Conduct: Studies in Literature and the History of Sexuality*, ed. Nancy Armstrong and Leonard Tennenhouse (London: Methuen, 1987), pp. 25–38. See also Anna Dronzek, "Gendered Theories of Education in Fifteenth-Century Conduct Books," in *Medieval Conduct*, ed. Kathleen Ashley and Robert L.A. Clark (Minneapolis: University of Minnesota Press, 2001), pp. 135–59, a study that privileges gender over considerations of social rank.

63. See Isabel Davis, "Men and Margery: Negotiating Medieval Patriarchy," in *A Companion to the Book of Margery Kempe*, ed. John H. Arnold and Katherine J. Lewis (Cambridge, UK: D.S. Brewer, 2004), pp. 35–54.

BIBLIOGRAPHY

Unpublished Primary Sources

Bradford, West Yorkshire Archive Service
Spencer Stanhope MSS, SpSt/4/11/66/39

Chichester, West Sussex Record Office
Cowdray archives, Cowdray/5129/6

Durham, Durham University Archives
1.3.Archiep.2.

London, The National Archives (formerly the Public Records Office)
ancient petitions, SC 8/27/1305, 1316
Chancery petition, C 1/43/82
coroners' rolls, JUST 2/215, 223, 251
Guy de Rouclif's will, Prob/11/1
inquisition ad quod damnum, C 143/112/9
inquisition ad quod damnum, C 143/230/12
poll tax return, E 179/202/61/7
poll tax return, E 179/211/30/15

York, Borthwick Institute for Archives
cause papers, CP.E., F.
probate registers, Prob. Reg. 1, 3

York, Merchant Adventurers' Archive
D 43/6

York Minster Library, Archive of the Dean and Chapter of York
Dean and Chapter probate register 1, L2(4)
F 1/3/1
M2(1)f
St Mary's Abbey Cartulary, XVI A.1, 2

Published Primary Sources

The Anonimalle Chronicle 1333 to 1381, ed. V.H. Galbraith (Manchester: Manchester University Press, 1927).

The Black Book of Winchester, ed. W.H.B. Bird (Winchester: The Wikeham Press, 1925).

The Black Death, ed. and trans. Rosemary Horrox (Manchester: Manchester University Press, 1994).

The Book of Margery Kempe, ed. Lynn Staley (Kalamazoo: The Medieval Institute, 1996).

Calendar of Close Rolls, 1272–1509, 47 vols. (London: H.M.S.O., 1892–1963).

Calendar of Patent Rolls, 1232–1509, 52 vols. (London: H.M.S.O., 1891–1916).

Charters of the Vicars Choral of York Minster, City of York and its Suburbs to 1546, ed. Nigel Tringham, Yorkshire Archaeological Society Record ser. 148 (1993).

Chronica Monasterii de Melsa, ed. Edward Augustus Bond, 3 vols., Rolls Series 43 (1866–68).

Corpus Iuris Canonici, Pars Secunda: Decretalium Collectiones, ed. Emil Ludwig Richter und Emil Friedberg, 2 vols. (Leipzig: Tauchnitz, 1879–81).

English Historical Documents, III: 1189–1327, ed. Harry Rothwell (London: Eyre and Spottiswoode, 1975).

An Episcopal Court Book for the Diocese of Lincoln 1514–1520, ed. Margaret Bowker, Lincoln Record Society 61 (1967).

Feet of Fines for the County of Yorkshire, III, ed. William Paley Baildon, Yorkshire Archaeological Society Record Ser. 52 (1915).

La Tour-Landry, Geoffroy de. *Book of the Knight of La Tour-Landry*, ed. Thomas Wright, EETS o.s. 38 (1906).

The Good Wife Taught Her Daughter, The Good Wyfe Wold a Pylgremage, The Thewis of Gud Women, ed. Tauno F. Mustanoja (Helsinki: Suomalaisen Kirjallisuuden Scuran, 1948).

The Lay Subsidy of 1334, ed. Robin E. Glasscock, Records of Social and Economic History, New Series 2 (Oxford: British Academy, 1975).

Lincoln Diocese Documents, 1450–1544, ed. Andrew Clark, EETS o.s. 149 (1914).

Lower Ecclesiastical Jurisdiction in Late-Medieval England: The Courts of the Dean and Chapter of Lincoln, 1336–1349 and the Deanery of Wisbech, 1458–1484, ed. L.R. Poos, Records of Social and Economic History, new ser. 32 (Oxford: British Academy, 2001).

The Middle English Breton Lays, ed. Anne Laskaya and Eve Salisbury (Kalamazoo: The Medieval Institute, 1995).

Monastery and Society in the Late Middle Ages: Selected Account Rolls from Selby Abbey, Yorkshire, 1398–1537, ed. John H. Tillotson (Woodbridge: Boydell and Brewer, 1988).

Plumpton Correspondence, ed. Thomas Stapleton, Camden Society o.s. 4 (1839).

The Poll Taxes of 1377, 1379 and 1381, ed. Carolyn C. Fenwick, Records of Social and Economic History 27, 29 and 37 (Oxford: British Academy, 1998–2005).

Probate Inventories of the York Diocese, ed. P.M. Stell and Louise Hampson (York: privately printed, 1998).

Proceedings before the Justices of the Peace in the Fourteenth and Fifteenth Centuries Edward III to Richard III, ed. Bertha H. Putnam (London: The Ames Foundation, 1938).

Register of the Freemen of the City of York, 1272–1588, ed. Francis Collins, Surtees Society 96 (1896).

Register of the Guild of Corpus Christi in the City of York, ed. Robert H. Scaife, Surtees Society 57 (1872).

Rotuli Parliamentorum, 6 vols. (London: Record Commission, 1767–83).

Select Cases in the Court of King's Bench under Edward III, vol. V, ed. G.O. Sayles, Selden Society 76 (1957).

Select Cases from the Ecclesiastical Courts of the Province of Canterbury, c. 1200–1301, ed. Norma Adams and Charles Donahue, Jr, Selden Society 95 (1981).

Sessions of the Peace in the City of Lincoln 1351–1354 and the Borough of Stamford 1351, ed. Elisabeth G. Kimball, Lincoln Record Society 65 (1971).

Some Sessions of the Peace in Lincolnshire 1381–1396, vol. II, ed. Elisabeth G. Kimball, Lincoln Record Society, 56 (1962).

Testamenta Eboracensia, vol. I, ed. James Raine, Surtees Society 4 (1836).

The Visitation of Yorkshire in the Years 1563 and 1564 made by William Flower, Esquire, ed. Charles Best Norcliffe, Harleian Society 91 (1881).

Women in England, c. 1275–1525: Documentary Sources, ed. and trans., P.J.P. Goldberg (Manchester: Manchester University Press, 1995).

York Memorandum Book, I, ed. Maud Sellers, Surtees Society 120 (1912).

Yorkshire Sessions of the Peace, 1361–1364, ed. Bertha H. Putnam, Yorkshire Archaeological Record Series 100 (1939).

Secondary Literature

Ailes, M.J. "The Medieval Male Couple and the Language of Homosexuality," in *Masculinity in Medieval Europe*, ed. Dawn Hadley (London: Longman, 1999), pp. 214–37.

Archer, Rowena E. "'How Ladies...Who Live on their Manors Ought to Manage their Households and Estates': Women as Landholders and Administrators in the Later Middle Ages," in *Woman is a Worthy Wight: Women in English Society c. 1200–1500*, ed. P.J.P. Goldberg (Stroud: Alan Sutton, 1992), pp. 149–81.

Arnold, John H. *Inquisition and Power: Catharism and the Confessing Subject in Medieval Languedoc* (Philadelphia: University of Pennsylvania Press, 2001).

———. "Inquisition, Text and Discourse," in Caterina Bruschi and Peter Biller, eds. *Texts and the Repression of Heresy* (Woodbridge: York Medieval Press, 2003), pp. 63–80.

Ashley, Kathleen M. "Medieval Courtesy Literature and Dramatic Mirrors of Female Conduct" in *The Ideology of Conduct: Studies in Literature and the History of Sexuality*, ed. Nancy Armstrong and Leonard Tennenhouse (London: Methuen, 1987), pp. 25–38.

Barron, Caroline M. "The Education and Training of Girls in Fifteenth-Century London," in *Courts, Counties, and the Capital in the Later Middle Ages*, ed. Diana E.S. Dunn (Stroud: Alan Sutton, 1996), pp. 139–53.

Bartlett, Robert. *The Hanged Man: A Story of Miracle, Memory, and Colonialism in the Middle Ages* (Princeton: Princeton University Press, 2004).

Bedell, John. "Memory and Proof of Age in England 1272–1327," *Past and Present* 162 (1999): 4–27.

Bennett, M. "Military Masculinity in England and Northern France c.1050–c.1225," in *Masculinity in Medieval Europe*, ed. Dawn Hadley (London: Longman, 1999), pp. 71–88.

Bowdon, Lynne. "Redefining Kinship: Exploring Boundaries of Relatedness in Late Medieval New Romney," *Journal of Family History* 29 (2004): 407–20.

Bray, Alan. *The Friend* (Chicago: University of Chicago Press, 2003).

Brucker, Gene. *Giovanni and Lusanna: Love and Marriage in Renaissance Florence* (London: Weidenfeld and Nicholson, 1986).

Burrow, J.A. *Thomas Hoccleve* (Aldershot: Variorum, 1994).

Burton, Janet and Christopher Wilson. *St Mary's Abbey, York* (York: Yorkshire Museum, 1988).

Butler, Judith. *Gender Trouble: Feminism and the Subversion of Identity* (New York: Routledge, 1990).

Butler, Sara M. "'I will Never Consent to be Wedded with You': Coerced Marriage in the Courts of Medieval England," *Canadian Journal of History* 39 (2004): 247–70.

Bynum, Caroline Walker. "The Female Body and Religious Practice in the Later Middle Ages," in *Fragmentation and Redemption: Essays of Gender and the Human Body in Medieval Religion* (New York: Zone Books, 1991), pp. 181–238.

Camille, Michael. "Manuscript Illumination and the Art of Copulation," in *Constructing Medieval Sexuality*, ed. Karma Lochrie, Peggy McCracken, and James A. Schulz (Minneapolis: University of Minnesota Press, 1997), pp. 58–90.

———. *Mirror in Parchment: The Luttrell Psalter and the Making of Medieval England* (Chicago: University of Chicago Press, 1998).

Cannon, Christopher. "*Raptus* in the Chaumpaigne Release and a Newly Discovered Document Concerning the Life of Geoffrey Chaucer," *Speculum* 68 (1993): 74–94.

Capp, Bernard. *When Gossips Meet: Women, Family, and Neighbourhood in Early Modern England* (Oxford: Oxford University Press, 2003).

Carruthers, Mary. *The Book of Memory: A Study of Memory in Medieval Culture* (Cambridge, UK: Cambridge University Press, 1990).

Chapman, Charlotte Gower. *Milocca: A Sicilian Village* (Cambridge, MA: Schenkman, 1971).

Clay, Charles. "The Family of Meaux," *Yorkshire Archaeological Journal* 43 (1971): 99–111.

Cohen, Elizabeth S. "Court Testimony from the Past: Self and Culture in the Making of Text," in *Essays on Life Writing: From Genre to Critical Practice*, ed. Marlene Kadar (Toronto: University of Toronto Press, 1992), pp. 83–93.

Cooper, Helen. "Good Advice on Leaving Home in the Romances," in *Youth in the Middle Ages*, ed. P.J.P. Goldberg and Felicity Riddy (York: York Medieval Press, 2004), pp. 101–21.

Charles Cox, J. *The Royal Forest of England* (London: Methuen, 1905).

Cullum, P.H. "'And Hir Name was Charite': Charitable Giving by and for Women in Late Medieval Yorkshire," in *Woman is a Worthy Wight: Women in English Society c. 1200–1500*, ed. P.J.P. Goldberg (Stroud, 1992), pp. 182–211.

———. "Clergy, Maculinity and Transgression in Late Medieval England," in *Masculinity in Medieval Europe*, ed. Dawn Hadley (London: Longman, 1999), pp. 178–96.

———. "For Pore People Harberles: What was the Function of the Maisondieu?" in *Trade, Devotion and Governance in Fifteenth Century England*, ed. Dorothy J. Clayton, Richard G. Davies, and Peter McNiven (Stroud: Alan Sutton, 1994), pp. 36–54.

———. "Vowesses and Female Lay Piety in the Province of York, 1300–1530," *Northern History* 32 (1996): 21–41.

Daniel, Chris. "The Family Seal," *Interim* 19, 2 (1994): 13–17.

Davis, Isabel. "Men and Margery: Negotiating Medieval Patriarchy," in *A Companion to the Book of Margery Kempe*, ed. John H. Arnold and Katherine J. Lewis (Cambridge, UK: D.S. Brewer, 2004), pp. 35–54.

———. *Writing Masculinity in the Later Middle Ages* (Cambridge, UK: Cambridge University Press, 2007).

Davis, Natalie Zemon. "The Reasons for Misrule: Youth Groups and Charivaris in Sixteenth-Century France," *Past and Present* 50 (1971): 41–75.

———. *The Return of Martin Guerre* (Cambridge, MA: Harvard University Press, 1983).

———. *Fiction in the Archives: Pardon Tales and their Tellers in Sixteenth-Century France* (Cambridge, UK: Cambridge University Press, 1987).

———. *The Gift in Sixteenth-Century France* (Oxford: Oxford University Press, 2000).

Dean, Trevor. "Gender and Insult in an Italian City: Bologna in the later Middle Ages," *Social History* 29 (2004): 217–31.

Dinn, Robert. "Baptism, Spiritual Kinship, and Popular Religion in Late Medieval Bury St Edmunds," *Bulletin of the John Rylands Library*, 72 (1990): 93–106.

Dobson, R.B. "Admissions to the Freedom of the City of York in the Late Middle Ages," *Economic History Review* 2nd ser. 23 (1973): 1–22.

———. "The Risings in York, Beverley and Scarborough, 1380–1381," in *The English Rising of 1381*, ed. R.H. Hilton and T.H. Aston (Cambridge, UK: Cambridge University Press, 1984), pp. 112–42.

Dockray, Keith. "Why did Fifteenth-Century English Gentry Marry?: The Pastons, Plumptons, and Stonors Reconsidered," in *Gentry and Lesser Nobility in Later Medieval Europe*, ed. Michael C.E. Jones (Gloucester: Alan Sutton, 1986), pp. 61–80.

Donahue, Charles, Jr. "Proof by Witnesses in the Church Courts of Medieval England: An Imperfect Reception of the Learned Law," in *On the Laws and Customs of England*, ed. Morris S. Arnold, Thomas A. Green, Sally Scully, and Stephen D. White (Chapel Hill: University of North Carolina Press, 1981), pp. 127–58.

Drake, Francis. *Eboracum: or, The History and Antiquities of the City of York, from its Original to the Present times. Together with the history of the Cathedral Church, and the lives of the Archbishops of the See...Collected from Authentick Manuscripts, Publick Records, Ancient Chronicles, and Modern Historians* (London: William Bowyer, 1736).

Dressler, Rachel. "Steel Corpse: Imagining the Knight in Death," in *Conflicted Identities and Multiple Masculinities: Men in the Medieval West*, ed. Jacqueline Murray (Garland: New York, 1999), pp. 135–67.

Dugdale, William. *Monasticon Anglicanum: A History of the Abbies and other Monasteries, Hospitals, Frieries and Cathedral and Collegiate Churches...in England and Wales...Originally Published in Latin by Sir William Dugdale*, ed. John Caley, Henry Ellis, and Bulkeley Bandinel, 6 vols. (London: James Bohn, 1846).

Dyer, Alan. *Decline and Growth in English Towns 1400–1640* (Cambridge, UK: Cambridge University Press, 1995).

Dyer, C.C. "Gardens and Orchards in Medieval England," in Dyer, *Everyday Life in Medieval England* (London: Hambledon Press, 1994), pp. 113–31.

Elliott, Diane. *Spiritual Marriage: Sexual Abstinence in Medieval Wedlock* (Princeton: Princeton University Press, 1993).

Elsakkers, Marianne. "In Pain You Shall Bear Children (Gen. 3:16): Medieval Prayers for a Safe Delivery," in *Women and Miracle Stories: A Multidisciplinary Exploration*, ed. Anne-Marie Korte (Leiden: Brill, 2001), pp. 179–209.

Emmerson, Richard K. and Goldberg, P.J.P. "'The Lord Geoffrey had me made': Lordship and Labour in the Luttrell Psalter," in *The Problem of Labour in Fourteenth-Century England*, ed. James Bothwell, P.J.P. Goldberg, and W.M. Ormrod (Woodbridge: York Medieval Press, 2000), pp. 43–63.

Farmer, Sharon. "Down, Out and Female in Thirteenth-Century Paris," *American Historical Review* 103 (1998): 345–72.

Fenster, Thelma and Daniel Lord Smail, eds. *Fama: The Politics of Talk and Reputation in Medieval Europe* (Ithica, NY: Cornell University Press, 2003).

Gavey, Nicola. *Just Sex: The Cultural Scaffolding of Rape* (London: Routledge, 2005).

Ginzburg, Carlo. *The Cheese and the Worms: The Cosmos of a Sixteenth-Century Miller*, trans. J. and A. Tedeschi (London: Routledge and Kegan Paul, 1980).

Given-Wilson, Chris. *The English Nobility in the Late Middle Ages* (London: Routledge, 1987).

Goldberg, P.J.P. *Women, Work and Life Cycle: Women in York and Yorkshire c. 1300–1520* (Oxford: Oxford University Press, 1992).

———. "From Conquest to Corporation," in *Doncaster: A Borough and its Charters*, ed. B.J. Barber (Doncaster: The Waterdale Press, 1994), pp. 47–65, 116–21.

———. "Girls Growing Up in Later Medieval England," *History Today* 45,6 (1995): 25–32.

———. "Masters and Men in Later Medieval England," in *Masculinity in Medieval Europe*, ed. Dawn Hadley (London: Longman, 1999), pp. 56–70.

———. "What was a Servant?" in *Concepts and Patterns of Service in the Later Middle Ages*, ed. Anne Curry and Elizabeth Matthew (Woodbridge: Boydell, 2000), pp. 1–20.

———. "Coventry's 'Lollard' Programme of 1492 and the Making of Utopia," in *Pragmatic Utopias: Ideals and Communities 1200–1630*, ed. Rosemary Horrox and Sarah Rees Jones (Cambridge, UK: Cambridge University Press, 2001), pp. 97–116.

———. "Household and the Organisation of Labour in Late Medieval Towns: Some English Evidence," in *The Household in Late Medieval Cities: Italy and Mediterranean Europe Compared* ed. Myriam Cariler and Tim Soens (Leuven: Garant, 2001), pp. 59–70.

———. "Migration, Youth and Gender in Later Medieval England," in *Youth in the Middle Ages*, ed. Goldberg and Felicity Riddy (Woodbridge: York Medieval Press, 2004), pp. 85–99.

———. "John Skathelok's Dick: Voyeurism and 'Pornography' in Late Medieval England," in, *Medieval Obscenities*, ed. Nicola McDonald (Woodbridge: York Medieval Press, 2006), pp. 105–23.

———. ed. *Richard Scrope: Archbishop, Rebel, Martyr* (Donington, UK: Shaun Tyas, forthcoming).

Gowing, Laura. *Domestic Dangers: Women, Words, and Sex in Early Modern London* (Oxford: Oxford University Press, 1996).

Grassi, J.L. "Royal Clerks from the Archdiocese of York in the Fourteenth Century," *Northern History* 5 (1970): 12–33.

Gravdal, Kathryn. *Ravishing Maidens: Writing Rape in French Literature and Law* (Philadelphia: University of Pennsylvania Press, 1991).

Hanawalt, Barbara A. "Whose Story Was This? Rape Narratives in Medieval English Courts," in *"Of Good and Ill Repute": Gender and Social Control in Medieval England*, ed. Hanawalt (New York: Oxford University Press, 1998), pp. 124–41.

Handbook of Dates for Students of English History, ed. C.R. Cheney (London: Royal Historical Society, 1978).

Harris, Barbara J. *English Aristocratic Women, 1450–1550* (New York: Oxford University Press, 2002).

Harvey, Barbara. "Work and *Festa Ferianda* in Medieval England," *Journal of Ecclesiastical History* 23 (1972): 289–308.

———. *Living and Dying in England 1100–1540: The Monastic Experience* (Oxford: Oxford University Press, 1993).

Harvey, John H. "Architectural History from 1291 to 1558," in *A History of York Minster*, ed. G.E. Aylmer and Reginald Cant (Oxford: Oxford University Press, 1977), pp. 149–92.

Hawkes, Emma. "Younger Sons, Illegitimate Sons and the Law: A Study of Three Yorkshire Gentry Families, 1480–1540," *Parergon*, n.s.17 (2000): 125–46.

Helmholz, R.H. *Marriage Litigation in Medieval England* (Cambridge, UK: Cambridge University Press, 1974).

———. *The Oxford History of the Laws of England, I: The Canon Law and Ecclesiastical Jurisdiction from 597 to the 1640s* (Oxford: Oxford University Press, 2004).

Hilton, R.H. "The Peasantry as a Class," in Hilton, *The English Peasantry in the Later Middle Ages* (Oxford: Oxford University Press, 1975), pp. 3–19.

Hollingsworth, T.H. "A Demographic Study of British Ducal Families," *Population Studies* 11 (1957): 4–26.

Hunnisett, R.F. "The Reliability of Inquisitions as Historical Evidence," in *The Study of Medieval Records: Essays in Honour of Kathleen Major*, ed. D.A. Bullough and R.L. Storey (Oxford: Oxford University Press, 1971), pp. 206–35.

Hunter-Man, Kurt. "Rawcliffe the 5th," *Interim* 17, 3 (1992): 2–6.

———. "Rawcliffe: Hall's Well that Ends Well," *Interim* 19, 2 (1994): 4–9.

Hutton, Ronald. *The Rise and Fall of Merry England: the Ritual Year, 1400–1700* (Oxford: Oxford University Press, 1994).

Innes, Matthew. "Keeping it in the Family: Women and Aristocratic Memory," in Elisabeth van Houts, ed. *Medieval Memories Men, Women and the Past, 700–1300* (London: Longman, 2001), pp. 17–35.

Jones, B. *Fasti Ecclesiae Anglicanae 1300–1500, vol. VI: Northern Province* (London: The Athlone Press, 1963).

Karras, Ruth Mazo. *Sexuality in Medieval Europe: Doing unto Others* (New York: Routledge, 2005).

Kelleher, Marie A. "Law and the Maiden: *Inqusitio*, *Fama*, and the Testimony of Children in Medieval Catalonia," *Viator* 37 (2006): 351–67.

Kelly, Henry Ansgar. "Statutes of Rapes and Alleged Ravishers of Wives: A Context for the Charges against Thomas Malory, Knight," *Viator* 28 (1997): 361–419.

———. "Meaning and Uses of *Raptus* in Chaucer's Time," *Studies in the Age of Chaucer* 20 (1998): 101–65.

Kennedy, M.J.O. "Resourceful Villains: The Cellarer Family of Wawne in Holderness," *Yorkshire Archaeological Journal* 48 (1976): 107–17.

Kerby-Fulton, Kathryn and Justice, Steven. "Langlandian Reading Circles and the Civil Service in London and Dublin, 1380–1427," in *New Medieval Literatures*, 1, ed. Wendy Scase, Rita Copeland, and David Lawton (Oxford: Oxford University Press, 1997), pp. 59–83.

Kermode, Jenny. "Sentiment and Survival: Family and Friends in Late Medieval English Towns," *Journal of Family History* 24 (1999): 5–18.

Klapisch-Zuber, Christiane. *Women, Family, and Ritual in Renaissance Italy*, trans. Lydia G. Cochrane (Chicago: University of Chicago Press, 1985).

Knowles, David. *The Religious Orders in England*, 3 vols. (Cambridge: Cambridge University Press, 1948–59).

Kuehn, Thomas. "*Fama* as a Legal Status in Renaissance Florence," in *Fama: The Politics of Talk and Reputation in Medieval Europe*, ed. Thelma Fenster and Daniel Lord Smail (Ithica, NY: Cornell University Press, 2003), pp. 27–46.

Landsberg, Sylvia. *The Medieval Garden* (London: British Museum Press, 1996).

Ladurie, Emmanuel Le Roy. *Montaillou: Village Occitan de 1274 à 1324* (Paris: Editions Gallimard, 1978).

Leake, Adrian. *The Liberty of St Peter of York 1800–1838*, Borthwick Paper 77 (York, 1990).

Lee, Becky R. "The Purification of Women after Childbirth: A Window onto Medieval Perceptions of Women," *Florilegium* 14 (1995–96): 43–55.

———. "Men's Recollections of a Women's Rite: Medieval English Men's Recollections Regarding the Rite of the Purification of Women after Childbirth," *Gender and History* 14 (2002): 224–41.

———. "A Company of Women and Men: Men's Recollection of Childbirth in Medieval England," *Journal of Family History* 27 (2002): 92–100.

Lett, Didier. "Adult Brothers and Juvenile Uncles: Generations and Age Differences in Families at the End of the Middle Ages," *The History of the Family* 6 (2001): 391–400.

Longley, Katherine M. "Towards a History of Archive-Keeping in the Church of York," *Borthwick Institute Bulletin* 1 (1975): 59–74.

Lewis, Katherine J. "Model Girls? Virgin Martyrs and the Training of Young Women in Late Medieval England," in *Young Medieval Women*, ed. Katherine J. Lewis, Noël James Menuge, and Kim M. Phillips (Stroud: Alan Sutton, 1999), pp. 25–46.

Maddern, Philippa. "Order and Disorder," in *Medieval Norwich*, ed. Carole Rawcliffe and Richard Wilson (London: Hambledon, 2004), pp. 189–212.

Marshall, W.A. and Tanner, J.M. "Variations in Patterns of Pubertal Changes in Girls," *Archives of Disease in Childhood* 44 (1969): 291–303.

Mays, Simon. "Wharram Percy: the Skeletons," *Current Archaeology* 17 (2004): 45–9.

Maza, Sarah C. *Servants and Masters in Eighteenth-Century France: The Uses of Loyalty* (Princeton: University of Princeton Press, 1983).

McClure, Peter. "Patterns of Migration in the Late Middle Ages: the Evidence of English Place-Name Surnames," *Economic History Review*, 2nd ser. 32 (1979): 167–82.

McIntosh, Marjorie Keniston. *Controlling Misbehaviour in England, 1370–1600* (Cambridge, UK: Cambridge University Press, 1998).

McSheffrey, Sharron. *Love and Marriage in Late Medieval London* (Kalamazoo: The Medieval Institute, 1995).

———. "Men and Masculinity in Late Medieval London Civic Culture: Governance, Patriarchy and Reputation," in *Conflicted Identities and Multiple Masculinities: Men in the Medieval West*, ed. Jacqueline Murray (Garland: New York, 1999), pp. 243–78.

Menuge, Noël James. *Medieval English Wardship in Romance and Law* (Woodbridge: Boydell, 2001).

Mitchell, Linda E. *Portraits of Medieval Women: Family, Marriage, and Politics in England 1225–1350* (New York: Palgrave, 2003).

Morgan, D.A.L. "The Individual Style of the English Gentleman," in *Gentry and Lesser Nobility in late Medieval Europe*, ed. M.C.E. Jones (Gloucester: Alan Sutton, 1986), pp. 15–35.

Murray, Jacqueline. "On the Origins and Role of 'Wise Women' in Causes for Annulment on the Grounds of Male Impotence," *Journal of Medieval History* 16 (1990): 235–49.

O'Hara, Diana. *Courtship and Constraint: Rethinking the Making of Marriage in Tudor England* (Manchester: Manchester University Press, 2000).

Oliva, Marilyn. "Aristocracy or Meritocracy? Office-Holding Patterns in Late Medieval English Nunneries," *Studies in Church History* 27 (1990): 197–208.

Orme, Nicholas. *Medieval Children* (New Haven: Yale University Press, 2001).

W.M. Ormrod, "Monarchy, Martyrdom and Masculinity: England in the Later Middle Ages," in *Holiness and Masculinity in the Middle Ages*, ed. P.H. Cullum and Katherine J. Lewis (Cardiff: University of Wales Press, 2004), pp. 158–73.

Owen, Dorothy M. *Church and Society in Medieval Lincolnshire*, History of Lincolnshire 5 (Lincoln: Lincolnshire Local History Society, 1971).

———. "White Annays and Others," in *Medieval Women*, ed. Derek Baker, Studies in Church History, subsidia I (Oxford: Basil Blackwell, 1978), pp. 331–46.

Palmer, Robert C. *The Whilton Dispute, 1264–1380: A Social-Legal Study of Dispute Settlement in Medieval England* (Princeton: Princeton University Press, 1984).

Parsons, John Carmi. "'Loved Him—Hated Her': Honor and Shame at the Medieval Court," in *Conflicted Identities and Multiple Masculinities: Men in the Medieval West*, ed. Jacqueline Murray (Garland: New York, 1999), pp. 279–98.

Payling, Simon. "The Politics of Family: Late Medieval Marriage Contracts," in *The McFarlane Legacy: Studies in Late Medieval Politics and Society*, ed. R.H. Britnell and A.J. Pollard (Stroud: Alan Sutton, 1995), pp. 21–47.

Pearsall, Derek. "Gardens as Symbol and Setting in Late Medieval Poetry," in *Medieval Gardens*, ed. Elizabeth B. MacDougall, Dumbarton Oaks Colloquium on the History of Landscape Architecture IX (Washington: Dumbarton Oaks Research Library and Collection, 1986), pp. 237–51.

Pedersen, Frederik. *Marriage Disputes in Medieval England* (London: Hambledon, 2000).

Phillips, Kim M. "Written on the Body: Reading Rape from the Twelfth to Fifteenth Centuries," in *Medieval Women and the Law*, ed. Noël James Menuge (Woodbridge: Boydell, 2000), pp. 125–44.

Pollock, Frederick and Frederic William Maitland. *The History of English Law before the Time of Edward I*, 2 vols. (Cambridge, UK: Cambridge University Press, 1898).

Pollock, Linda. "'Teach Her to Live under Obedience': The Making of Women in the Upper Ranks of Early Modern England," *Continuity and Change* 4 (1989): 231–58.

Poos, L.R. *A Rural Society After the Black Death: Essex 1350–1525* (Cambridge, UK: Cambridge University Press, 1991).

———. "Sex, Lies, and the Church Courts of Pre-reformation England," *Journal of Interdisciplinary History* 25 (1995): 585–607.

Poos, L.R., Zvi Razi, and Richard M. Smith. "The Population History of Medieval Villages: A Debate on the Use of Manor Court Records," in *Medieval Society and the Manor Court*, ed. Razi and Smith (Oxford: Oxford University Press, 1996), pp. 298–368.

Post, J.B. "Ages at Menarche and Menopause: Some Mediaeval Authorities," *Population Studies* 25 (1971): 83–7.

———. "Ravishment of Women and the Statutes of Westminster," in *Legal Records and the Historian*, ed. J.H. Baker (London: Royal Historical Society, 1978), pp. 150–64.

Raine, Angelo. *Mediaeval York: a Topographical Survey based on Original Sources* (London: John Murray, 1955).

Rawcliffe, Carole. "The Great Lord as Peacekeeper: Arbitration by English Noblemen and their Councils in the Later Middle Ages," in *Law and Social Change in British History*, ed. John A. Guy and H.G. Beale (London: Royal Historical Society, 1984), pp. 34–54.

Razi, Zvi. "The Myth of the Immutable English Family," *Past and Present* 140 (1993): 3–44.

Rees Jones, Sarah. "Household, Work and the Problem of Mobile Labour: The Regulation of Labour in Medieval English Towns," in *The Problem of Labour in Fourteenth-Century England*, ed. James Bothwell, P.J.P. Goldberg, and W.M. Ormrod (Woodbridge: York Medieval Press, 2000), pp. 133–53.

———. "Historical Introduction," in *Medieval Urbanism in Coppergate: Refining a Townscape*, ed. Richard A. Hall and Kurt Hunter-Mann, The Archaeology of York, 10, 6 (York: Council for British Archaeology: H.M.S.O., 2002), pp. 684–98.

Rees Jones, Sarah and Felicity Riddy. "The Bolton Hours of York: Female Domestic Piety and the Public Sphere," in *Household, Women, and Christianities in Late Antiquity and the Middle Ages*, ed. Anneke Mulde-Bakker and Jocelyn Wogan-Browne (Turnhout: Brepols, 2005), pp. 215–60.

Reid, Charles J. Jr., *Power over the Body, Equality in the Family: Rights and Domestic Relations in Medieval Canon Law* (Grand Rapids, MI: William B. Eerdmans, 2004).

Richards, M., S. Mays, and B. Fuller. "Stable C and N Isotope Values of Bone and Teeth Reflect Weaning and Growth Events at the Mediaeval Wharram Percy Site, Yorkshire, UK," *American Journal of Physical Anthropology* 119 (2002): 205–10.

Riddy, Felicity. "Women Talking about the Things of God: A Late Medieval Subculture." In *Women and Literature in Britain, 1150–1500*, ed. Carol Meale. (Cambridge, UK: Cambridge University Press, 1993), pp. 104–27.

———. "Mother Knows Best: Reading Social Change in a Courtesy Text," *Speculum* 71 (1996): 66–86.

———. "Looking Closely: Authority and Intimacy in the Late Medieval Urban Home," in *Gendering the Master Narrative: Women and Power in the Middle Ages*, ed. Mary C. Erler and Maryanne Kowaleski (Ithica: Cornell University Press, 2003), pp. 212–28.

Rieder, Paula M. "The Implications of Exclusion: The Regulation of Churching in Medieval Northern France," *Essays in Medieval History* 15 (1995): 71–80.

Robertson, Elizabeth. "Public Bodies and Psychic Domains: Rape, Consent, and Female Subjectivity in Geoffrey Chaucer's *Troilus and Criseyde*," in *Representing Rape in Medieval and Early Modern Literature*, ed. Robertson and Christine M. Rose (New York: Palgrave, 2001), pp. 281–310.

Rogers, Nicky. "Signed, Sealed and Deciphered," *Interim* 19, 2 (1994): 10–12.

Rosenthal, Joel T. *Telling Tales: Sources and Narration in Late Medieval England* (University Park: Penn State Press, 2003).

Rosser, Gervase. "Crafts, Guilds and the Negotiation of Work in Medieval Town," *Past and Present* 154 (1997): 3–31.

Royal Commission on Historical Monuments (England), *An Inventory of the Historical Monuments in the City of York: vol. V, The Central Area* (London, 1981).

Saul, Nigel. *Knights and Esquires: The Gloucestershire Gentry in the Fourteenth Century* (Oxford: Oxford University Press, 1981).

Saunders, Corinne. *The Forest of Medieval Romance: Avernus, Broceliande, Arden* (Cambridge, UK: D.S. Brewer, 1993).

———. "A Matter of Consent: Middle English Romance and the Law of *Raptus*," in *Medieval Women and the Law*, ed. Noël James Menuge (Woodbridge: Boydell, 2000), pp. 105–24.

———. *Rape and Ravishment in the Literature of Medieval England* (Cambridge, UK: D.S. Brewer, 2001).

Schwarz, E. and Perry, B.D. "The Post-Traumatic Response in Children and Adolescents," *Psychiatric Clinics of North America* 17 (1994): 311–26.

Margaret Scott, *A Visual History of Costume: The Fourteenth and Fifteenth Centuries* (London: Batsford, 1986).

The Scottish Parliament, *The Legal Definition of Rape*, Research Note RN 01/46 (Edinburgh, 2001).

Sedgwick, Eve Kosofsky. *Between Men: English Literature and Male Homosocial Desire* (New York: Columbia University Press, 1988).

Sheehan, Michael M. "The Formation and Stability of Marriage in Medieval England: the Evidence of an Ely Register," *Medieval Studies* 33 (1971): 228–63.

Skinner, Patricia. "Gender and Memory in Medieval Italy," in *Medieval Memories Men, Women and the Past, 700–1300*, ed. Elisabeth van Houts (London: Longman, 2001), pp. 36–52.

Smith, A.H. *The Place-Names of the West Riding of Yorkshire, part IV* (Cambridge, UK: Cambridge University Press, 1961).

Smith, David. M. and Vera C.M. London, ed. *The Heads of Religious Houses: England and Wales, 1216–1377* (Cambridge, UK: Cambridge University Press, 2002).

———. *Ecclesiatical Cause Papers at York: The Court of York 1301–1399*, Borthwick Texts and Calendars 14 (1988).

———. *The Court of York, 1400–1499: A Handlist of the Cause Papers and an Index to the Archiepiscopal Court Books*, Borthwick Texts and Calendars 29 (2003).

Sullivan, Karen. *The Interrogation of Joan of Arc* (Minneapolis: University of Minnesota Press, 1999).

Talvacchia, Bette. *Taking Positions: On the Erotic in Renaissance Culture* (Princeton: Princeton University Press, 1999).

Taylor, Andrew. "Chivalric Conversation and the Denial of Male Fear," in *Conflicted Identities and Multiple Masculinities: Men in the Medieval West*, ed. Jacqueline Murray (Garland: New York, 1999), pp. 169–88.

Thompson, Roger. *Unfit for Modest Ears: A Study of Pornographic, Obscene and Bawdy Works Written or Published in England in the Second Half of the Seventeenth Century* (London: Macmillan, 1979).

Tillott, P.M., ed. *Victoria History of the County of York: The City of York* (London: Oxford University Press, 1961).

Todd, Barbara J. "The Remarrying Widow: A Stereotype Reconsidered," in *Women in English Society 1500–1800*, ed. Mary Prior (London: Methuen, 1985), pp. 54–92.

Underhill, Frances A. *For Her Good Estate: The Life of Elizabeth de Burgh* (New York: St Martin's Press, 1999).

Van Houts, Elisabeth. *Memory and Gender in Medieval Europe* (Basingstoke: Macmillan, 1999).

Walker, Sue Sheridan. "Punishing Convicted Ravishers: Statutory Strictures and Actual Practice in Thirteenth and Fourteenth-Century England," *Journal of Medieval History* 13 (1987): 237–50.

Waugh, Scott L. *The Lordship of England: Royal Wardships and Marriages in English Society and Politics 1217–1327* (Princeton: Princeton University Press, 1988).

———. *England in the Reign of Edward III* (Cambridge, UK: Cambridge University Press, 1991).

Wentersdorf, Karl P. "The Clandestine Marriage of the Fair Maid of Kent," *Journal of Medieval History* 5 (1979): 203–31.

Wickham, Chris. "Gossip and Resistance among the Medieval Peasantry," *Past and Present* 160 (1998): 3–24.

Wilson, Adrian. "The Ceremony of Childbirth and its Interpretation," in *Women as Mothers in Pre-Industrial England*, ed. Valerie Fildes (London: Routledge, 1990), pp. 68–107.

Woolgar, Christopher. *The Great Household in Late Medieval England* (New Haven: Yale University Press, 1999).

Wunderli, Richard. *Peasant Fires: The Drummer of Niklashausen* (Bloomington, IN: Indiana University Press, 1992).

Young, Charles R. *The Royal Forests of Medieval England* (Philadelphia: University of Pennsylvania Press, 1979).

Young, Michael and Peter Willmott. *Family and Kinship in East London* (London: Routledge and Kegan Paul, 1957).

Unpublished Secondary Literature

Cullum, Patricia Helena. "Hospitals and Charitable Provision in Medieval Yorkshire, 936–1547" unpublished University of York D.Phil. thesis (1989).

Goldberg, P.J.P. "Women in Late Medieval Society: Some Demographic Evidence from the York Region," unpublished University of York MA dissertation (1982).

———. "Young Women in the *Oxford Dictionary of National Biography*," paper given at the International Medieval Congress, Leeds, July 2005.

Rees Jones, Sarah. "Property, Tenure and Rents: Some Aspects of the Topography and Economy of Medieval York," unpublished University of York D.Phil. thesis, 2 vols. (1987).

Electronic Resources

Access to Archives, http://www.a2a.org.uk/

GENUKI, Yorkshire, Some of the Subsidy Rolls (Poll Tax) for the year 1379,
http://www.genuki.org.uk/big/eng/YKS/Misc/SubsidyRolls/YKS/SubsidyRolls1379Index.html.

The Oxford Dictionary of National Biography, http://www.oxforddnb.com/

INDEX